Women and AIDS

Psychological Perspectives

edited by
Corinne Squire

SAGE Publications
London · Newbury Park · New Delhi

First published 1993

SAGE Publications Ltd
6 Bonhill Street
London EC2A 4PU

SAGE Publications Inc
2455 Teller Road
Newbury Park, California 91320

SAGE Publications India Pvt Ltd
32, M-Block Market
Greater Kailash – I
New Delhi 110 048

British Library Cataloguing in Publication data

Women and AIDS. – (Gender & Psychology Series)
    I. Squire, Corinne II. Series
    616.97

    ISBN 0–8039–8587–8
    ISBN 0–8039–8588–6 (pbk)

Library of Congress catalog card number 93–083774

Typeset by The Word Shop, Bury, Lancashire.
Printed in Great Britain by Biddles Ltd, Guildford, Surrey.

Women and AIDS

Gender and Psychology

Series editor: Sue Wilkinson

This international series provides a forum for the growing body of distinctively psychological research focused on gender issues. While work on the psychology of women, particularly that adopting a feminist perspective, will be central, the series will also reflect other emergent trends in the field of gender. It will encourage contributions which are critical of the mainstream of androcentric or 'gender-neutral' psychology and also innovative in their suggested alternatives.

The books will explore topics where gender is central, such as social and sexual relationships, employment, health and illness, and the development of gender identity. Issues of theory and methodology raised by the study of gender in psychology will also be addressed.

The objective is to present research on gender in the context of its broader implications for psychology. These implications include the need to develop theories and methods appropriate to studying the experience of women as well as men, and working towards a psychology which reflects the experiences and concerns of both sexes.

The series will appeal to students of psychology, women's studies and gender studies and to professionals concerned with gender issues in their practice, as well as to the general reader with an interest in gender and psychology.

Sue Wilkinson is senior lecturer in health studies research, University of Hull.

Also in this series

Subjectivity and Method in Psychology
Wendy Hollway

Feminists and Psychological Practice
edited by Erica Burman

Feminist Groupwork
Sandra Butler and Claire Wintram

Motherhood: Meanings, Practices and Ideologies
edited by Ann Phoenix, Anne Woollett and Eva Lloyd

Emotion and Gender:
Constructing Meaning from Memory
June Crawford, Susan Kippax, Jenny Onyx, Una Gault
and Pam Benton

Contents

Acknowledgements

First, and most importantly, I want to thank the contributors to this book, who produced engaging, thought-provoking chapters, often at very busy times for them, and who responded to my requests for revisions patiently and efficiently. Sue Wilkinson's and Karen Phillips's editorial comments were invaluable in clarifying writing and argument. Helpful comments came from the audiences of talks at which I presented some of my preliminary writing on the area: the British Psychological Society's London Conference December 1988; and the International Society for Theoretical Psychology Conference, Worcester, Mass., July 1991. Students at Fresno State University, Trenton State College and Birmingham Polytechnic also made useful criticisms of the work.

Sandy Batista and Yrlaine St Fort at HS Systems Inc., New York, gave me a lot of valuable advice. Thanks also to Debbie Bingham, Yvonne Jones, Carlene Morrison, and everybody else at HSS.

The volunteers, staff and, above all, the clients of the Hyacinth Foundation AIDS Project, New Jersey, taught me about HIV/ AIDS and gave me the idea to put the book together. Special thanks to Anthony Salandra and Chas White.

Notes on Contributors

Hortensia Amaro, PhD, is an associate professor at Boston University School of Medicine and Public Health. She has published widely on substance abuse, reproductive health, mental health, HIV infection among high-risk pregnant women, and HIV-related knowledge, attitudes and risk behaviour among Hispanics. She is currently principal investigator on several projects, including a community-based prevention model programme to reduce drug use and the risk of HIV infection among inner-city pregnant women and their children. Her research has been funded by the National Institute on Drug Abuse, Centers for Disease Control, Office of Substance Abuse Prevention, William T. Grant Foundation and National Center for Health Statistics. She was a founder and elected Board member of the National Hispanic Psychological Association, Massachusetts Multicultural AIDS Coalition, and Latino Health Network, Inc. In 1988 she was appointed to Governor Dukakis's Task Force on AIDS.

W. Rees Davis earned his PhD in experimental psychology from the New School for Social Research in 1986. After graduation, he worked at New York State Psychiatric Institute on a longitudinal study involving the children of schizophrenics and major depressives. Since 1987 he has been involved in research on drug use and AIDS at both the Lower Eastside Service Center and National Development and Research Institutes, Inc. (NDRI).

Sherry Deren received her PhD in social psychology from Columbia University and has been involved in drug abuse research for almost 20 years. As Chief of Evaluation for the New York State Division of Substance Abuse Services, she was responsible for developing and implementing evaluations of drug treatment and prevention programmes. She has been a co-investigator on research related to marijuana use and vocational rehabilitation services for substance abusers. Since 1988 she has been principal investigator on three AIDS prevention research projects at NDRI (National Development and Research Institutes, Inc.), receiving funding from the National Institute on Drug Abuse and the Centers for Disease Control. She has published papers and made presentations in several areas related to substance abuse: AIDS, vocational rehabilitation, programme evaluation and children of substance abusers. She is currently Director of the Institute for AIDS Research at NDRI.

Mindy Thompson Fullilove, MD, is a graduate of Bryn Mawr College and Columbia University College of Physicians and Surgeons. She did psychiatric residency at New York Hospital–Westchester Division, and Montefiore Hospital. She is now Associate Professor of Clinical Psychiatry and Public Health at Columbia University, New York. Her current research interests include the epidemiology of HIV infection in minority communities and trauma as a co-factor in drug abuse. Previously she served as Co-director of Multicultural Inquiry and Research on AIDS (MIRA), a component of the University of California, San Francisco Center for AIDS Prevention Studies. Her recent publications are on traumatic experiences in the lives of women crack users, and methods of research in minority communities.

Robert Fullilove, EdD, is Director of Community Core, HIV Center for Clinical and Behavioral Studies, New York State Psychiatric Institute, and Associate Dean for Minority Affairs, Columbia School of Public Health, New York City. He was previously Co-director of Multicultural Inquiry and Research on AIDS (MIRA), a component of the University of California, San Francisco Center for AIDS Prevention Studies, and has conducted a variety of studies concerning the epidemiology of AIDS and of AIDS risk behaviours in minority communities. He is currently involved in research examining factors governing the use of crack cocaine, and in developing evaluation studies of the effectiveness of AIDS prevention campaigns in minority communities.

Alexandra Juhasz is an independent videomaker and an Assistant Professor of English and Women's Studies at Swarthmore College. Her video and written work focuses upon the representation of AIDS, especially concerning women. Her book, *Re-mediating AIDS: The Politics of Community Produced Video* (forthcoming from Duke University Press), considers how alternative AIDS media construct AIDS in new and political ways in relation to mainstream media representations. She has made numerous videos about AIDS including *Living with AIDS: Women and AIDS*, and *We Care: A Video for Care Providers of People Affected by AIDS*. Recent writing about her own video work is forthcoming in *Camera Obscura* 28.

E. Anne Lown, MPH, is a research fellow at the Department of Epidemiology and Biostatistics, San Francisco General Hospital, University of California, San Francisco. She is currently studying HIV infection and mental illness in the homeless. She previously worked at the HIV Center for Clinical and Behavioral Studies, New York State Psychiatric Institute, on an NIMH-funded study of women, drug use and trauma in New York City. She has practised as a detoxification acupuncturist with substance abusers.

Halina Maslanka is Assistant Project Director for Evaluation on an NIMH Mental Health Training Grant in the Department of Psychiatry, University of Medicine and Dentistry of New Jersey, Newark, New Jersey. She gained a PhD in social/personality psychology at the Graduate School of the City University of New York. Her dissertation looks at the role of social support in ameliorating stress among AIDS volunteers at Gay Men's Health Crisis (GMHC). She worked for a time at GMHC as Coordinator of Research in the Volunteer Office and later as a consultant. She is also involved in evaluating the Clinton Peer AIDS Education Coalition, an AIDS prevention programme utilizing homeless adolescents to perform outreach among prostitutes, drug users and homeless individuals in New York City.

Cindy Patton is Assistant Professor of Rhetoric and Communication at Temple University. She has been an activist, an ethnographer on a Centers for Disease Control funded study of HIV education at methadone clinics, a consultant to the World Health Organization and local AIDS groups, and has written extensively about the epidemic, including *Sex and Germs: The Politics of AIDS* (1985); *Making It: A Woman's Guide to Sex in the Age of AIDS* (with Janis Kelly, 1987), *Inventing AIDS* (1990), and a forthcoming book on women and the HIV epidemic.

Lorraine Sherr, Dip. Clin. Psych., PhD, is a principal clinical psychologist working at St Mary's Hospital, London. Her clinical and research work covers a wide range of psychological aspects of HIV infection. She was awarded a Winston Churchill Fellowship for AIDS in Obstetrics and Paediatrics and held a research grant examining AIDS in obstetrics. She has written *Death, Dying and Bereavement* (1989) and *HIV and AIDS in Mothers and Babies* (1991). She is joint editor of *AIDS Care*, an international journal on psychosocial aspects of AIDS.

Corinne Squire teaches psychology at Brunel University. She is the author of *Significant Differences*: *Feminism in Psychology* (1989), and co-author of *Representations of Morality in Contemporary Culture* (forthcoming). She has also worked in a video company, and as an HIV antibody test counsellor.

Stephanie Tortu earned her PhD in social psychology from the University of Pittsburgh in 1984. After spending three years as an assistant professor at Cornell University Medical College, she joined the research staff at National Development and Research Institutes, Inc. (NDRI) to direct an AIDS risk reduction project. She is currently a co-investigator on an AIDS-related research project in East Harlem. She has authored scientific publications, presented at national conferences, and conducted various training workshops. She has taught a variety of courses at several colleges and is currently on the faculty of New York University.

Jane M. Ussher, PhD, Dip. Clin. Psych., is a lecturer in psychology at University College, London. Working in the area of sexuality and women's health, her publications include *The Psychology of the Female Body* (1989), *Women's Madness: Misogyny or Illness?* (1991), *Gender Issues in Clinical Psychology* (1992) *The Psychology of Women's Health and Health Care* (1992), and *Psychological Perspectives on Sexual Problems* (1993).

Karen Winkler, MS, RN, is a research scientist at the Substance Abuse Core of the HIV Center for Clinical and Behavioral Studies, New York State Psychiatric Institute, New York City. She is currently involved in feminist research and writing on psychological trauma and gender identity in the lives of women in the crack culture. Previously, she worked as a nurse and educator developing community-based services and outreach programmes for pregnant women and adolescents, and taught courses in sexuality and reproductive health.

Lithograph and Xerox transfer by Kiki Smith, made for the 1992
Day Without Art, an event promoting AIDS awareness.

Introduction

Women and AIDS: Responses

Since the early 1980s, Human Immunodeficiency Virus (HIV) and Acquired Immunodeficiency Syndrome (AIDS) have become the objects of extensive medical and social research and policy-making, and of widespread media and public discussion. During these years, the place of women in the epidemic has often been ignored. Alternatively, women have been presented as transmitters of HIV to men and children, or pictured as the innocent victims of morally degenerate men. None of these approaches addresses women's specific relationship to the epidemic: how they interpret the proliferating words and images that surround it; how they inform and protect themselves and those close to them about HIV and AIDS; how they care for people living with AIDS or HIV; and how they live with the conditions themselves. This neglect is especially problematic at a time when diagnosed AIDS cases among women constitute half the total cases in Africa and are a fast growing proportion of the total in many other parts of the world, including Europe and North America (Chin, 1990).

Psychologists became involved with HIV and AIDS very early, 'more quickly than for any other major health issue' (Backer et al., 1988, p. 835). Today, professional psychology has a powerful place in practice and research around HIV and AIDS. The significance and the growing scale of the conditions mean that it is now almost inevitable that a psychologist will have to address them in her or his work at some time (Cochran and Mays, 1989). Much of the work psychologists do in the field is valuable, and driven by deep commitment, but it encounters a number of practical difficulties and theoretical limitations. Prominent among these are: lack of financial and other resources to give adequate counselling or do long-term research; clients and research participants whose involvement is limited by medical problems and poverty; methods and theories which are hard to adapt to such clients and participants; and a conceptual framework which tends to reduce central aspects of the experience of HIV and AIDS – sexuality, 'race'[1] and gender, for instance – to social modifiers of individual experience (Mays and Cochran, 1988; Rieder and Ruppelt, 1989; Silverman, 1989; Squire, 1993). The psychology of AIDS and HIV infection also tends to replicate psychology's usual shortcomings around gender (Burman,

1990; Squire, 1989), and often reproduces the general failure of discourses of HIV and AIDS to represent women adequately. As a result, AIDS-related psychology sometimes ignores women and at other times treats them very conventionally, as partners of heterosexual men or as mothers: victims or sources of infection, rather than women living with AIDS/HIV.

Western feminists have been slow to see AIDS as a women's issue (Segal, 1989). Perhaps this is partly because the condition disproportionally affects poor women, non-white women[2] and women drug users, and Western feminism still predominantly addresses the interests of middle-class women. Partly too, the neglect stems from some activists' belief that AIDS is not really their issue. A few, for instance, have said that lesbian feminists involved with gay community organizing around AIDS/HIV are being 'wives to the gay men's AIDS movement' (Hall et al., 1992, p. 13).[3] But women are developing feminist strategies around AIDS and HIV, within lesbian and gay organizations, minority communities, networks of ex-drug users and sex workers, and groups of women directly affected by AIDS (ACTUP/NY Women and AIDS Book Group, 1990; Patton and Kelly, 1987; O'Sullivan and Thomson, 1992; Richardson, 1989; Rieder and Ruppelt, 1989; Rudd and Taylor, 1992). Moreover, some women, working in psychology and outside it, have been developing feminist initiatives which specifically address psychological issues related to HIV and AIDS. Such initiatives take issue with psychology's common omissions, pathologizations and victimologies around women, HIV and AIDS, and pay serious attention to women's own understandings of the conditions. This book, by gathering together important examples of feminist work on the psychology of AIDS, tries both to provide an overview of such work, and to give a sense of how productive particular instances of the work can be.

Psychological Issues

The central role of sexual and drug practices in HIV transmission and the possibility of changing individual behaviour linked HIV and AIDS to psychology almost from the start. More generally, AIDS and HIV infection have intense and wide-ranging psychological effects on people who have the conditions, on those who know and care for them, and on many who are not so directly affected by AIDS but have simply heard about it. For the conditions affect, not just people's physiologies, but their sexualities, relationships, work and leisure, their ideas about their bodies and their identities, and their expectations about their life and death.

Women encounter particular psychological issues around AIDS and HIV infection. The book's contributions focus on four areas where these issues are very clear. Part I looks at HIV antibody testing of women, and its relationship to reproductive rights. The effect of the epidemic has been to strengthen the existing heavy social regulation of women's reproduction and sexuality, and to put psychological issues which women commonly encounter around reproduction into new and dramatic contexts.

Part II deals with women's perceptions of and practices around their HIV risk, their sexuality and their drug use, and examines the relationship of these perceptions and practices to HIV education and to women's particular circumstances. Reproductive issues arise here, as in Part I. But additional questions emerge about the relationships between self-perceptions and behaviour, attitudes and behaviour, and reported and actual behaviour. Psychological accounts which focus on these relationships often turn out to be inadequate in describing the place of AIDS in women's lives. A more complicated view of subjectivities as multiple and contradictory, and embroiled in specific personal histories and social circumstances, seems to be required.[4]

Part III echoes this subjective complexity, examining women's experiences of working voluntarily and professionally with people living with HIV and AIDS. Women are becoming the main paid and unpaid carers in this field, as in others. In this section, the notion of a gender-neutral AIDS volunteerism, characterized by empathy and caring but unconcerned with social differences, and the ideal of a gender-neutral professional psychology, come into question.

Part IV looks at representations of women and AIDS in scientific, policy and media discourses. What Paula Treichler (1988) has famously called the 'epidemic of signification' around AIDS has had considerable effects. It is this 'epidemic' that gives the association between women and AIDS its culturally shared meanings, which in turn help us all, women and men, to constitute our subjective understandings of 'women and AIDS'. The structures of meaning in cultural representations of AIDS are complicated and contradictory, but these intricacies have largely been ignored in the psychology of HIV and AIDS. This section aims to bring these intricacies into the psychological field.

The preface to each Part gives more detailed accounts of the issues raised by individual chapters. The rest of this Introduction sets out some of the general issues which emerge across the contributions.

The HIV and AIDS Epidemic

The World Health Organization estimated over a million AIDS cases worldwide in 1991 (Merson, 1991). It believed that about ten million people were then infected with HIV, and that around a third of these were likely to be women. Among the 800,000 AIDS cases and six million HIV infections thought to have occurred in Africa by the beginning of the 1990s, women were estimated to constitute over 50 per cent (Chin, 1990; Mayer and Carpenter, 1992; Merson, 1991). In the US, a million seropositive people had been calculated by 1990, one in eight of them a woman (Centers for Disease Control, 1990; Mayer and Carpenter, 1992); and of the 214,609 AIDS cases registered up to March 1992, 22,607 were women (Centers for Disease Control, 1992b).[5] In Europe, approximately 10 per cent of AIDS cases have occurred among women. The rate is slightly lower in Britain; at the beginning of 1992, there were 5,215 reported AIDS cases in Britain, 341 among women. But of new cases over the previous 12 months, women constituted 10 per cent of the total (Public Health Laboratory Service, 1992). In Britain and the rest of Europe, and in the US, AIDS is increasing more rapidly among women than among men (Centers for Disease Control, 1992a; Public Health Laboratory Service, 1992). Rates among women are much higher in certain areas; for instance, New York City, New Jersey, Washington DC, and Dade County Florida. In New York and New Jersey, AIDS is now the leading cause of death among women between the ages of 15 and 44, and it is the sixth leading cause of death for all US women of reproductive age (Centers for Disease Control, 1991c, 1992a; Chu et al., 1990; Ellerbrock et al., 1991).

The contributors to this book all work in the US or Britain, and their empirical research was carried out in these countries. The geographical duality draws attention to the variable epidemiologies of AIDS and HIV infection among women, even between these two Western countries, to differences in social and health service provision, and to the diverse needs and possibilities for psychological work. Contributors also position their work within the international context, recognizing both the specificity of their own concerns to the Western context, and the links between women's concerns about the epidemic in developing and overdeveloped countries. Lorraine Sherr points out the problems HIV antibody testing raises for pregnant women worldwide, for instance, while Cindy Patton criticizes the common segregation in AIDS discourses of African from Western women (see also Rieder and Ruppelt, 1989; Rudd and Taylor, 1992). For many contributors, even a national focus yields parallels with the international situation. Worldwide, the women most affected by AIDS are African, and poor. But in the overdeveloped world too, especially in the US, women living with AIDS are disproportionately poor and black or of colour. Some 53 per cent of diagnosed female AIDS cases are African American women and 20 per cent are Latinas (Centers for Disease Control, 1992b). As Vicky Mays and Susan Cochran (1988) have noted, women's experiences of AIDS/HIV in the West are therefore often bound up with the psychological issues raised by female poverty and being a black. And so, as Hortensia Amaro says in this volume (Chapter 1), not just sexism, but institutional racism and discrimination on the grounds of socioeconomic class, shape women's relationships to HIV and AIDS. Phrases like 'gender-"race"-class-and-sexuality' often operate as easy get-out clauses. Here though they are necessary to invoke the concrete and inescapable frames within which women live with the conditions.

Categorization of Women in AIDS Discourse

Discourse on AIDS – medical and social policy writing, political rhetoric, media representations and public talk about HIV and AIDS – tends to ignore, sideline or pathologize women. The discourse is both under- and over-gendered. The categories of 'women' often seem like screens onto which other social conflicts – around for instance 'race', sexuality and poverty – are being projected in disguised forms. Frequently, too, the discourse repeats the common cultural erasure of women, treating them as undifferentiated 'people', as if their gender were invisible and unimportant. But AIDS discourse also reproduces cultural definitions of women as incarnations of sexual danger, biological power and victimhood. These categorizations of women in AIDS discourse help construct the realities of HIV and AIDS for women.[6] Of course, such a symbolically powerful condition as AIDS cannot, as Simon Watney (1990) points out, be stripped of metaphors. But some metaphors have worse effects than others.

AIDS discourses' categorizations of women have often been criticized by feminists (see, for example, Rieder and Ruppelt, 1989). The categories have a special significance for a feminist *psychology* of AIDS because they fix culturally the 'identities' of women affected by HIV or AIDS: they prescribe their possible subjectivities. Many women cannot recognize themselves in the categories. Without this recognition, we may find it hard to build an understanding of our relationships to HIV and AIDS. AIDS discourses' categorizations of women are repeatedly scrutinized in the book, and are replaced by more wide-ranging and intricate accounts of women's relationships to HIV and AIDS.

The culturally dominant image of the person living with AIDS (PLWA) is of an impossibly weak, thin, male body. A long-time AIDS service worker in the US used to tell the story of the first woman with AIDS he saw: coming towards him very slowly down the hospital corridor was a figure so emaciated, so debilitated he could not believe she was a woman and kept thinking she was, like the other AIDS patients in the hospital, a gay man.

Writing and talk about HIV and AIDS also frequently collapse women into the ungendered categories now culturally marked in the overdeveloped world as HIV-infected, with varying degrees of attached blame. These are transfusion recipients, haemophiliacs, intravenous drug users (IVDUs) and crack users and their hetero-sexual partners, inmates, black people, the urban poor – frequently a euphemism for the previous category – Haitians and Africans. This book consistently undoes such degendering. E. Anne Lown and her co-writers (Chapter 4), for instance, go beyond stereotypes of crack users to explore the gendering of crack cocaine culture and what crack use means to women living in poor inner-city areas who use crack themselves or are partners of crack users. The women's concerns about crack and sexuality are closely connected in the chapter to concerns felt more generally by women about their sexuality and about men's power to define them through sexuality.

'Lesbians' have intermittently been invoked in media discourse about AIDS as women at 'high risk', a phenomenon which, given self-identified lesbians' low rates of HIV infection, indicates the power social fears of homosexuality and female sexuality have in this epidemic over epidemiological knowledge. More generally, women's femaleness often becomes pathologized in AIDS discourse in categories like 'prostitute' or 'AIDS mother'; categories which position women either as *vectors* transmitting HIV to men, or as *vessels* for its transmission into the next generation, but which do not recognize the women's own condition. This reduction of women to vehicles of transmission is a recurring theme in the book. As Lorraine Sherr says (Chapter 2), women 'are placed in a precarious position where their role is defined in terms of their potential to infect another person rather than in terms of their own needs' (p. 56). This positioning of women as infectors of men and children is ironic in view of women's apparently greater risk of becoming HIV-infected during heterosexual intercourse, and in view of the certainty that an HIV-positive newborn, with about a 30 per cent chance of remaining seropositive, will have a permanently seroposi-tive mother.

Popular media representations offer the least subtle versions of the cultural preoccupation with women as sexual transmitters. A recent example was the response to Magic Johnson's declaration that he had tested positive for the HIV antibody. The announcement was widely interpreted as the second event (the first being Rock Hudson's death) to bring AIDS home to heterosexuals in the US, and much the most powerful for young people, especially young black people. As a number of commentators have pointed out (for example, Schulman, 1991), however, the sympathy and concern characterizing media stories about Johnson's seropositivity would not have been so evident for a well-known woman in the same position. If it is attributed to a female speaker, Johnson's claim to have slept with 20,000 partners (Simmons, 1991) has connotations not of success and power but of promiscuity and worthlessness. Some tabloids did indeed manage to find a woman to blame for Johnson's seropositivity, and ran spreads on the particular woman they claimed had infected him.

At times, though, media representations of AIDS foreground women's innocence. Alexandra Juhasz (Chapter 7) describes how this happens within television documentaries which juxtapose presentations of the 'scientific' facts of AIDS with images of blameless female 'victims'. In this scenario, the woman's body, innocent of knowledge and pleasure, is the passive, mysterious object of the researcher's pleasurable search for knowledge. The corollary of this is that all objects of AIDS research are covertly feminized. Juhasz talks too about the horror of femininity that is the flipside of the idealization of feminine innocence. This horror is also apparent in media presentations of innocent female AIDS 'victims' which put them in the context of an implicitly pathological personal relationship, like 'wife of gay man' or 'girl friend of male IVDU'. Mixed with the pity and horror is a silent judgement: 'if she was stupid enough not to know, she deserves it.'

Patton (Chapter 8) notes that the only non-pathologized position from which women can be associated with AIDS is that of the compassionate observer or helper, an implicitly white and middle-class role; and even this woman is, like the woman who uses condoms, 'queered' by the continuing association in the West between AIDS and homosexuality. The personal and social contradictions in this position get unpacked in Halina Maslanka's account of women volunteers at Gay Men's Health Crisis (GMHC) in New York City (Chapter 5), and Jane Ussher's analysis of women psychologists working in the field of HIV and AIDS (Chapter 6).

Categorizations of Women and AIDS-related Practices

The categorizations of women within HIV and AIDS discourse also appear in the practices around HIV and AIDS: in diagnosis, research, treatment, HIV antibody testing, and education and prevention. AIDS cases in general are thought to be under-reported (Centers for Disease Control, 1991a; Chin, 1990), especially among poor people, blacks and Latinos, drug users – and women. For a long time, the Centers for Disease Control (CDC) counted AIDS cases by single exposure route. Even now, the possible heterosexual exposure of women who report intravenous drug use is not recorded, so heterosexual transmission to women may be underestimated. Moreover, CDC criteria for diagnosing AIDS relied until 1991 on the presence of opportunistic infections first documented in gay men during the first wave of the epidemic. Infections more commonly found in women were absent from the list (Denenberg, 1990), and recent CDC and Social Security revisions do not fully address this gender blindness (Massa, 1991). Even those who argue that the natural history of AIDS is not substantially different in women and men acknowledge the 'confused state of knowledge with regard to HIV infection in women' (Brettle and Lean, 1991, p. 1289).

Around HIV and AIDS research and treatment, the gendering of AIDS is more explicit. Women are dropped from research trials if they become pregnant, many researchers are wary of including women because of the possibility that they will get pregnant, and some exclude women on the general grounds of their hormonal variability. In the few attempts made so far to get pregnant women into treatment trials, mother–fetus transmission rate, and not the health of the woman, has been the object of inquiry. Women with HIV and AIDS also have less access to treatment, get less of it (Hogan et al., 1991), and tend to die sooner than men (Rothenberg et al., 1987).[7] These gender differences are confounded by women seeking help and getting diagnosed later, and by the fact that women with HIV and AIDS are more likely than men with HIV and AIDS to be poor and of colour. Many affected women also do not have citizen or residency status, and a disproportionate number are homeless – all of which make health care and health maintenance difficult. The pattern that emerges is one of women with HIV and AIDS going medically unrecognized, unstudied and uncomprehended, receiving minimal outdated care in poor and overstretched institutions, and getting most of this at the end of their lives (Hogan et al., 1991).

HIV antibody testing is also a highly gendered field. Pregnant women, a group frequently screened to give an indication of HIV infection rates within the general population, can as Amaro describes (Chapter 1) find their rights to have a child, have an abortion, or even not to have the test, pitted against the rights of the fetus, a familiar reproductive rights contest. Testing policies can also frame some women – predominantly poor black and Latina women – as likely to be infected, and exempt other women from this suspicion. This framing is now euphemized by geography. Discussing women's recent use of HIV counselling and testing services, the Centers for Disease Control advise that clinics 'in areas with high prevalence of HIV seropositivity should routinely offer all clients HIV counselling and testing. In areas with low prevalence of HIV seropositivity . . . recommendations for HIV testing can be made based on the results of each [person's risk] assessment' (1991c, p. 203).

HIV and AIDS education and prevention also tend to dichotomize women, setting up some women as at high risk and some as at negligible risk. Abstinence or knowing your partner well is offered as the strategy of the normal, innocent woman; condoms as the resort of the promiscuous and unnatural. Emphasis on the use of condoms for safer sex for women positions them again as infective agents, with the responsibility – historically often given to women in the fields of sexually transmitted disease and general health education – of gatekeeping men's and children's health, though men of course remain at least physically in control of condom use. The emphasis on condoms in HIV education also fixes women's sexuality on heterosexual intercourse. Sexuality which does not include penile–vaginal, anal or oral intercourse gets belated, almost embarrassed, mentions in most HIV education aimed at women, and this can only reinforce many people's, especially young people's, perception that sex without intercourse is not 'real' sex. Moreover, as Sherry Deren and her colleagues suggest in Chapter 3, AIDS prevention initiatives directed at women usually concentrate on training them to implement safer practices or on improving their psychological well-being – and just assume that an increase in one will boost the other. But it is not certain that safer sexual and drug practices performed competently in a training situation will be performed well, or at all, in everyday life, and the belief that subjective well-being and low-risk practices are strongly related turns out to be questionable.

Discourses of gender also powerfully affect how PLWAs/HIV are cared for. Most of those looking after PLWAs are women, and the vast majority of them are not dignified with professional or even volunteer status but simply overlooked, their work seen too much as an intrinsic part of being a woman even to be remarked on, let alone paid for or supported. A woman volunteer, though more socially valued, is in a similar position: for middle-class white women, 'woman' and 'volunteer' have been virtually synonymous, as Maslanka points out (Chapter 5). In AIDS-related psychology, however, women's position as practitioners is rather different. Here women have, as Ussher says, to operate as apparently gender-free but implicitly masculinized professionals if they are to be taken seriously in the field (Chapter 6).

AIDS, Women and Change

It is often said that HIV and AIDS have had good effects on many individuals and communities, provoking transformations in ways of thinking, ways of life and ethics. Writing by women frequently bears this out; the stories in *Matters of Life and Death* (Rieder and Ruppelt, 1989), *Women, AIDS and Activism* (ACTUP/NY Women and AIDS Book Group, 1990), *Positive Women* (Rudd and Taylor, 1992) and *Positively Women* (O'Sullivan and Thomson, 1992) provide examples. This book also documents how women make HIV/AIDS into the starting point for personal and social change.

Among the personal gains, women often describe turning their lives around when they are faced with AIDS. When they find out that they are HIV positive, for instance, they may use drugs less or stop using them, or they may have a child. Amaro (Chapter 1) describes a woman, seropositive, the mother of a child with AIDS Related Complex (ARC), and pregnant, to whom the two-to-one odds of having a healthy child gave great hope. Women also develop strategies to live with the reality or possibility of HIV and AIDS. Within the crack culture that Lown and her co-writers describe (Chapter 4), where women's mere survival as users is a struggle, some women may manage by *not* thinking about HIV and AIDS.

It is often said that HIV and AIDS-related work is rewarding, encouraging and uplifting; and while these aspects of the work can be romanticized, there is some truth in the description. Women gain a lot from their work as volunteers and psychologists with people with HIV and AIDS. But the chapters in Part III underline how much such women also need support from their co-workers, and enjoyment of the work, in order to continue with it.

Men who see themselves as part of gay communities have clearly changed these communities in response to AIDS. The HIV community in general has had significant effects on medical definitions, research and treatment, and its activism, often influenced by feminism, is feeding back into women's health initiatives (Gross, 1991; Solomon, 1990). But 'community' is a problematic term (Weeks, 1989). Men who have sex with men but do not identify as gay are not part of an easily definable sexual community. Women affected by HIV and AIDS are often not recognized as a distinct section of the HIV community. Nor does their gender make them part of a recognized community; there is no 'women's community'. And so the ways in which women have made HIV and AIDS into conditions of community change are less obvious. Often, as contributors to this book note, women are important forces in AIDS service organizations in gay men's communities, and even more so in organizations grounded in African American, Latino, and other ethnically defined communities, and in communities defined by religious or civic commitments. But the women's contributions are not easy to distinguish. This is especially so when organizations' own initiatives are overlooked or undervalued, as is often the case with work by AIDS service organizations within black and ethnic minority communities. Such organizations may also subsume their work around AIDS into a more general 'health' or 'education' category (Patton, 1990; White, 1990); and while this is often a valuable approach, it makes women's pursuit of social changes around AIDS even more likely to be overlooked.

There are, however, many community education and service organizations which declare themselves run by and for women – DiAna's Hair Ego, a South Carolina beauty salon providing AIDS education through plays and tupperware parties and distributing leaflets and safer sex packs is a well-known example (DiAna, 1990). Women-orientated organizations are also common within the HIV community: Women and AIDS Resource Network (WARN) in New York and Positively Women in Britain, for instance. Such organizations run what seem the most effective psychological services for women affected by AIDS or HIV: support groups for seropositive women, for instance, or for women who are carers. Young women have been involved in peer education programmes in schools and local communities (Adler, 1992; Terrence Higgins Trust, 1991). Lesbians have worked independently to respond to the epidemic, within organizations like GMHC, but also in relation to particular communities of women, such as sex workers and poor women of colour. Women who are sex workers have created and run successful HIV community education projects, as have some women who are ex-IVDUs (ACTUP/NY Women and AIDS Book Group, 1990; Rieder and Ruppelt, 1989). This book, centred on psychological issues, has limited space to explore the social changes produced by women around HIV and AIDS, but it consistently points them out.

Psychology, AIDS and Feminism

So far, psychologists working on HIV issues and women have predominantly studied conventional college student samples; they have contributed little to research on less accessible groups such as women inmates (Weisfuse et al., 1991), sex workers, carers, and even the poor women and black women who comprise the largest fraction of women affected. It is by and large anthropologists, sociologists, health educators, or community members turned health educators or service providers themselves who develop, evaluate and describe programmes in these communities. The contributors to this book, psychologists and non-psychologists, all work within community organizations and outreach programmes as well as in health and social service agencies, universities and colleges. This means that, although the book cannot 'represent' all the communities of women affected by the epidemic, it is able to emphasize some significant aspects of the epidemic among women that are often left out of psychological accounts.

The contributors also question conventional psychological profes-sionalism and recognize the need for such professionalism to be 'negotiated and balanced', as Jeffrey Weeks (1989, p. 132) puts it. In the course of the book it becomes plain that a feminist psychology of HIV/AIDS, directed at analysing the position of women in the epidemic and contributing to their personal and social struggles, must go beyond the conventional boundaries of psycho-logy to pay serious attention to the knowledge and skills of the communities it is supposed to be studying and serving, and of the community organizations that have grown up within them. The contributors to this book thus indicate the possibility and necessity of the feminist psychology of HIV and AIDS extending our understanding of women's relationships to HIV and AIDS, and interrogating the conventional discipline and altering its shape.

Notes

Parts of this Introduction and of the Prefaces to Parts I–IV appeared in an earlier version in Squire, 1993.
1 'Race' is placed in inverted commas here and elsewhere in order to point up the constructed nature of racial definitions.
2 While 'black' has currency as a description of a political identity both in the US and Britain, it is only in Britain that it has been used to signify that identity across people of African and Caribbean, and Asian, origin. For this reason the book

includes the US locution 'people of colour' as well as 'black'. On 'race' AIDS and women, see Crawford and co-writers (1991).
3 Tessa Boffin (1991) provides a sampling of a wide variety of opinion on what lesbians' relationships with HIV and AIDS are and should be. See also ACTUP/NY Women and AIDS Book Group (1990), and Rieder and Ruppelt (1989).
4 See Henriques et al. (1984) for a working out of this perspective within psychology, and Riley (1988) for an exploration of its meanings for feminism.
5 For the rationales and problems of the estimates, see Centers for Disease Control (1990) and Chin (1990).
6 They are not, of course, the whole of it: as Douglas Crimp says, 'AIDS exists only in and through these constructions', but they do not 'contest the reality of illness, suffering and death' (1988, p. 3).
7 This finding applied to medical care, especially hospital care, over the last 12 months of patients' lives. Hogan et al. (1991) and Bindels et al. (1991) did not find the differential survival rates between women and men with AIDS that have been found in other studies, however. Ellerbrock and colleagues (1991) point out that, for the US, comparable survival times are found when gay men are excluded from consideration.

References

ACTUP/NY Women and AIDS Book Group (ed.) (1990) *Women, AIDS and Activism*. Boston: South End Press.

Adler, T. (1992) AIDS prevention – at-risk groups, teens, APA program's focus. *Monitor* (American Psychological Association) 23 (2), 35.

Backer, T., Batchelor, W., Jones, M. and Mays, V. (1988) Introduction. *American Psychologist* 43, 835–6.

Bindels, P., Poos, R., Jong, J., Mulder, J., Jager, H. and Coutinho, R. (1991) Trends in mortality among AIDS patients in Amsterdam, 1982–1988. *AIDS* 5, 853–8.

Boffin, T. (1991) Fairy tales, 'facts' and gossip: lesbians and AIDS. In T. Boffin and S. Gupta (eds), *Ecstatic Antibodies: Resisting the AIDS Mythology*. London: Rivers Oram Press.

Brettle, R. and Lean, C. (1991) The natural history of HIV and AIDS in women. *AIDS* 5, 1283–92.

Burman, E. (ed.) (1990) *Feminists and Psychological Practice*. London: Sage.

Centers for Disease Control (1990) HIV infection – United States. *Morbidity and Mortality Weekly Reports* RR-16, 1–31.

Centres for Disease Control (1991a) Mortality attributed to HIV infection/AIDS – United States, 1981–90. *Morbidity and Mortality Weekly Reports* 40 (3), 25 January.

Centers for Disease Control (1991b) Characteristics of and HIV infection among women served by publicly funded HIV counselling and testing services – United States, 1989–90. *Morbidity and Mortality Weekly Reports* 40 (12), 29 March.

Centers for Disease Control (1991c) Acquired Immune Deficiency Syndrome – Dade County, Florida, 1981–1990. *Morbidity and Mortality Weekly Reports* 40 (29), 26 July.

Centers for Disease Control (1992a) The second 100,000 cases of Acquired Immunodeficiency Syndrome – United States, June 1981–December 1991. *Morbidity and Mortality Weekly Reports* 41, 28–9, 17 January.

Centers for Disease Control (1992b) *HIV/AIDS Surveillance*. Atlanta, Georgia: US Department of Health and Human Services.

Chin, J. (1990) Global estimates of AIDS cases and HIV infections: 1990. *AIDS* 4 (supplement 1), S277–83.

Chu, S., Buehler, J. and Berkelman, R. (1990) Impact of the human immunodeficiency virus epidemic on mortality in women of reproductive age – United States. *Journal of the American Medical Association* 264, 225–9.

Cochran, S. and Mays, V. (1989) Women and AIDS-related concerns: roles for psychologists in helping the worried well. *American Psychologist* 44, 529–35.

Crawford, A., Kanuha, V., Long, A., Porter, V., Rodriguez, H. and Smith, B. (1991) *Our Lives in the Balance: US Women of Color and the AIDS Epidemic*. Latham, NY: Kitchen Table: Women of Color Press.

Crimp, D. (1988) AIDS: cultural analysis/cultural activism. In D. Crimp (ed.), *AIDS: Cultural Analysis/Cultural Activism*. Boston: MIT Press.

Denenberg, R. (1990) Unique aspects of HIV infection in women. In ACTUP/NY Women and AIDS Book Group (ed.), *Women, AIDS and Activism*. Boston: South End Press.

DiAna, D. (1990) Talking that talk. In ACTUP/NY Women and AIDS Book Group (ed.), *Women, AIDS and Activism*. Boston: South End Press.

Ellerbrock, T., Bush, T., Chamberland, M. and Oxtoby, M. (1991) Epidemiology of women with AIDS – the United States, 1981 through 1990. *Journal of the American Medical Association* 265, 2971–5.

Gross, J. (1991) Turning disease into political capital: first AIDS, and now breast cancer. *New York Times*, 7 January.

Hall, M., Kitzinger, C., Loulan, J. and Perkins, R. (1992) Lesbian psychology, lesbian politics. *Feminism and Psychology* 2, 7–25.

Henriques, J., Hollway, W., Urwin, C., Venn, C. and Walkerdine, V. (1984) *Changing the Subject: Psychology, Social Regulation and Subjectivity*. London: Methuen.

Hogan, A., Solomon, D., Bouknight, R. and Solomon, S. (1991) Underutilization of medical care services by HIV-infected women? Some preliminary results from the Michigan Medicaid Program. *AIDS* 5, 338–9.

Massa, R. (1991) Danger in numbers. *Village Voice* 36, 5 November.

Mayer, K. and Carpenter, C. (1992) Women and AIDS. *Scientific American* 266 (March), 118.

Mays, V. and Cochran, S. (1988) Issues in the perception of AIDS risk and risk reduction activities by Black and Hispanic/Latina women. *American Psychologist* 43, 949–57.

Merson, M. (1991) Foreword. *AIDS* Supplement 1, *AIDS in Africa* 5, i–ii.

O'Sullivan, S. and Thomson, K. (1992) *Positively Women*. London: Sheba.

Patton, C. (1990) *Inventing AIDS*. New York: Routledge.

Patton, C. and Kelly, J. (1987) *Making It: A Woman's Guide to Sex in the Age of AIDS*. Ithaca, NY: Firebrand Books.

Public Health Laboratory Service (1992) *Communicable Disease Report* 2 (4), February.

Richardson, D. (1989) *Women and the AIDS Crisis*. London: Pandora.

Rieder, I. and Ruppelt, P. (eds) (1989) *Matters of Life and Death: Women Speak about AIDS*. London: Virago.

Riley, D. (1988) *'Am I That Name?' Feminism and the Category of 'Women' in History*. Minneapolis: University of Minnesota Press.

Rothenberg, R., Woelfel, B., Stoneburner, R., Milberg, J., Parker, R. and Truman, B. (1987) Survival with the acquired immune deficiency syndrome: experiences with 5833 cases in New York City. *New England Journal of Medicine* 317, 1297–302.

Rudd, A. and Taylor, D. (1992) *Positive Women*. Toronto: Second Story.

Schulman, S. (1991) Laying the blame. *Guardian*, 19 November.

Segal, L. (1989) Lessons from the past: feminism, sexual politics, and the challenge of AIDS. In E. Carter and S. Watney (eds), *Taking Liberties: AIDS and Cultural Politics*. London: Serpent's Tail.

Silverman, D. (1989) The AIDS 'Crisis' and its Impact on Professional–Client Relations: the Social Origin of Counselling. Paper presented at the Swedish–British Medical Sociology Workshop, May–June, Stockholm.

Simmons, D. (1991) Magic's manhood. *Village Voice* 37, 19 November.

Solomon, A. (1990) Voices for changes. *Village Voice* 36, 9 December.

Squire, C. (1989) *Significant Differences: Feminism in Psychology*. London: Routledge.

Squire, C. (1993) Patterns of meaning and power in AIDS-related psychology. In H. Stan (ed.), *Recent Trends in Theoretical Psychology*, 3, 511–17.

Terrence Higgins Trust (1991) *1+1*. London: Terrence Higgins Trust.

Treichler, P. (1988) AIDS, homophobia, and biomedical discourse: an epidemic of signification. In D. Crimp (ed.), *AIDS: Cultural Analysis/Cultural Activism*. Boston, Mass: MIT Press.

Watney, S. (1990) Representing AIDS. In T. Boffin and S. Gupta (eds), *Ecstatic Antibodies: Resisting the AIDS Mythology*. London: Rivers Oram Press.

Weeks, J. (1989) AIDS, altruism and the New Right. In E. Carter and S. Watney (eds), *Taking Liberties: AIDS and Cultural Politics*. London: Serpent's Tail.

Weisfuse, I., Greenberg, B., Back, S., Makki, H., Thomas, P., Rooney, W. and Routenberg, E. (1991) HIV-1 infection among New York City inmates. *AIDS* 5, 1133–8.

White, E. (ed.) (1990) *The Black Woman's Health Book: Speaking for Ourselves*. Seattle: Seal Press.

PART I
HIV AND WOMEN'S
REPRODUCTIVE RIGHTS

Pregnant women receiving prenatal care are the women most accessible for HIV antibody screening. They are also the focus of intense social concern about the economic and social costs of HIV seropositive babies. Unsurprisingly, then, it is in discourse and practice around pregnant women that the characterization of women as the vessels of HIV infection obtains its greatest force.

Now that prenatal HIV testing is widespread, it is during pregnancy that women are most likely to encounter the difficult psychological issues raised by AIDS and HIV infection. Along with this, they may also experience a denial of their reproductive rights and psychological needs by HIV/AIDS service providers. Women thought to be at high risk because of intravenous drug use, sexual contact with male IVDUs, sex work, poverty, ethnic or 'racial' status, or some combination of these, are especially likely to experience such a denial, as the criminalization of pregnant drug users in many US states indicates (Hoffman, 1990). In addition, the considerable political power of pro-life groups manifests itself around AIDS, especially in the US, in support of the interests of the fetus over those of the mother, notably over the issue of seropositive women having abortions.

The two chapters in this section explore psychological issues around reproduction and AIDS/HIV, the first presenting an overview of the US situation, the second addressing HIV antibody testing of pregnant women worldwide and then focusing down on the issues involved with prenatal HIV testing and counselling in Britain.

Hortensia Amaro begins by sketching her personal history of involvement with the epidemic, describing how work on women and AIDS has concentrated on women's reproductive function, and analysing how it has been shaped by racism, class bias, and a perception of drug use as moral transgression. Amaro goes on to challenge the routine HIV testing of pregnant women, pointing to problems raised by so-called 'confidential' testing, to the conflicts over reproductive rights which HIV and AIDS have engendered, and to the psychological and logistical difficulties of providing adequate HIV-related services for pregnant women. Amaro then explores how HIV education programmes can be integrated with counselling and testing opportunities for women, especially women receiving prenatal care. The chapter suggests that the threats to women's reproductive rights which have arisen in the context of AIDS and HIV infection must be resisted by paying attention to women's own understanding of their psychological and social needs, and by formulating and providing counselling services, as well as a full range of other HIV-related services, which meet these needs.

Lorraine Sherr's concerns are similar, but at times broader, at times more specific. She points out the vast number of methodologically various, epidemiologically questionable and ethically dubious HIV antibody screening studies performed on pregnant women worldwide, and argues that such studies, which are rarely integrated into programmes for education or treatment, are a panicky response to insistent political and popular demands for action. She notes too that, despite the test's potentially traumatic impact, counselling is rarely reported in the studies. She then focuses on the neglect of counselling in her more specific account of prenatal testing in Britain, where epidemiological monitoring, rather than education, pregnancy 'option' counselling and early treatment for seropositive women and their children, as in the US, is the primary justification offered. Sherr questions the epidemiological justification, and explores the role of pre- and post-test counselling and the psychological impact of the test. The chapter questions the possibility of meeting pregnant women's HIV-related needs within standard HIV antibody screening programmes, and within the existing health care system.

Both chapters emphasize that, though many policy-makers and health workers themselves see termination as the only post-test option for seropositive pregnant women, most such women do not terminate. It may not be a medical or emotional or, in the US, even a legal option for them. Amaro and Sherr argue for making abortion an explicit and available option for seropositive women, but both also recognize the particular meanings a child may have for a seropositive woman: how she may have strong religious objections to abortion; how pregnancy can be a 'window of opportunity' for a woman trying to stop using drugs; how for women of colour in particular a child can have strong personal and social significance, and can act as what Mays and Cochran (1988) have called in the African American context the start of a family legacy. Concerns about children may spur many women to take steps to improve their own health, and while some Western feminists might see this as a traditional abnegation of women's own needs, the specific and indeed the general cultural value of this communitarian concern can also be read as feminist (Durand, 1990). As Sherr and Amaro suggest, women's power to make decisions around HIV antibody testing and to deal with it psychologically depends on policies and practices that take such aspects of women's lives into account, and that aim to enfranchise all women.

References

Durand, Y. (1990) Cultural sensitivity in practice. In ACTUP/NY Women and AIDS Book Group (ed.), *Women, AIDS and Activism*. Boston: South End Press.

Hoffman, J. (1990) Pregnant, addicted – and guilty? *New York Times Magazine*, 19 August.

Mays, V. and Cochran, S. (1988) Issues in the perception of AIDS risk and risk reduction activities by Black and Hispanic/Latina women. *American Psychologist* 43, 949–57.

1

Reproductive Choice in the Age of AIDS: Policy and Counselling Issues

Hortensia Amaro

Introduction

My first encounter with the specific issues that affect women with the Human Immunodeficiency Virus (HIV) infection and AIDS came during an interview with a woman who was a participant in a study that I and other colleagues were conducting between 1984 and 1988 in Boston. The woman, whom I'll call Mary, was concerned about the health of her newborn child because she was infected with HIV. Two years before, Mary had given birth to a child now diagnosed with AIDS-related complex (ARC). Mary had received little education about HIV infection, and no psychological support to help her cope with her own infection or make behaviour changes to reduce additional risk of exposure to herself or to reduce the possibility of having another pregnancy.

Since that time I have heard the stories of many women with HIV, and those at high risk of becoming infected, through the MOM's Project, a prevention research demonstration project on which I am principal investigator (Amaro, 1990a). The MOM's Project is a community-based demonstration project for the prevention of HIV infection and early intervention with pregnant women who are chemically dependent. The major aim of the programme is to improve women's access to and successful utilization of drug abuse treatment services.

The programme comprises six major components: (a) community outreach; (b) advocacy, case management and referral services; (c) counselling; (d) education/support groups; (e) parenting skills support; and (f) general support services. In addition, the project's affiliation with Boston City Hospital facilitates women's access to prenatal care, substance abuse treatment, pediatric services and general medical care. The programme was previously funded by the National Institute on Drug Abuse and is currently funded by the Centre for Substance Abuse Prevention.

The obstacles to HIV prevention and HIV services that women experience are evidenced every day in the help they seek from the

MOM's Project staff. Experiences such as these have produced in me a profound sense of frustration with the inadequacies of policy, research and services directed at the prevention of spread of HIV infection, and with the inadequacy of the services available for those most directly affected, especially for the women most at risk of HIV infection. Elsewhere I have discussed the barriers to care found by women with HIV and AIDS (Amaro, 1990b). I am aware that it is not only women who experience the frustration of our government's lack of response to this epidemic. The struggle of my brother, Armando, with AIDS only a few years ago brought me personally in touch with this. In this chapter, I will focus on some critical policy and counselling issues that specifically pertain to women in the AIDS epidemic and that bear directly on women's reproductive choices.

Framework of Current Response to HIV Infection and AIDS Among Women

In the United States, nearly all policy issues related to HIV infection and AIDS, such as those related to health care delivery, prevention programmes, HIV antibody testing, discrimination based on antibody status, treatment and a host of others, impact on all individuals with HIV infection and AIDS, including women. But specific issues pertain uniquely to the over 21,858 women who have been diagnosed with AIDS over the past 10 years (Centers for Disease Control, 1991a), and the women – perhaps five times that number (United States Public Health Service, 1988) – estimated to be infected with HIV. Considering the international trend towards the increasing representation of women among those infected suggests that the future effects of this epidemic on women are potentially even greater. And yet women have been among the groups most ignored in research, service delivery and policy considerations related to HIV.

The simple and obvious way in which women differ from men – in their ability to bear children – has in large part been the lens through which public health issues of women and AIDS has been focused. For the most part, when women are discussed in scientific or policy debates about AIDS, they are characterized as 'vessels of infections' or 'vectors of perinatal transmission'. (Cindy Patton and Lorraine Sherr discuss this characterization further in their respective chapters.) As a result of this characterization, much of the attention to issues of women and AIDS has been limited to the role of sex workers in the spread of HIV, to the infection of children during pregnancy and to pediatric AIDS (Anderson et al., 1991;

Wofsy, 1987). Although many more women than children are infected, there is, as Sherr documents in Chapter 2, a disproportionate amount of policy and scientific literature on pediatric AIDS compared to that on the problems women face as infected adults. In part, the exclusion of women from HIV-related policy and research is based on the persistent misperception that AIDS does not affect women. It is also affected by the systematic exclusion of women from HIV research due to regulations governing human subjects and the Food and Drug Administration's guidelines that largely exclude women of childbearing age from participation in clinical studies to evaluate the effectiveness of drug therapies (Levine, 1990).

The view of women as vessels and vectors of transmission fits well into a historical context where women have been defined through their reproductive function. We see this in public health and in medicine, where women's health is almost exclusively seen as 'maternal and child health' that is, those aspects of health related to reproduction, childbearing and childrearing. In fact, 'maternal and child health' often refers exclusively to maternal behaviour that may adversely affect neonatal growth, infant development or child health, rather than to the mother's (woman's) health. Issues related to neonatal growth and infant and child development are valid and important; it is also true that in may circumstances the health and well-being of the child is closely linked to the health and well-being of the mother. Women's health, however, is not encompassed solely by this limited definition of 'maternal' health. The consequence of this myopic vision of women is that many women's health issues are never addressed, and women's experiences related to health and health care are rendered invisible. The invisibility of women in scientific and clinical papers addressing persons infected with HIV was the topic of an open letter presented to the planners of the Third International Conference on AIDS in 1987 by women participants (Thomas, 1987). Although there has been some improvement in addressing the HIV/AIDS-related research and service needs of women, recent AIDS conferences and government funding for research continue to focus primarily on women as vectors of heterosexual or perinatal transmission or as vessels of pediatric AIDS.

The prevailing view, which is concerned with women primarily in relation to their reproductive function and their role in the transmission of HIV, is an example of institutional sexism, the factor that has most powerfully framed the United States' response to HIV infection and AIDS in women. However, this factor is linked with others which play a major role in the way in which research, policy and prevention related to women are framed. The second factor framing the country's response is institutional racism. The fact that the majority of women who are diagnosed with AIDS and who are infected with HIV are black and Latina is not insignificant. This society's devaluation and oppression of people of colour is central to how issues of AIDS and HIV infection among women are being considered. A third factor is socioeconomic class. It is poor women who are most affected by AIDS and HIV infection. But poor women have little say in determining the priority given to their problems, which so brutally shape and, in this case, end their lives.

Finally, social values and norms that place drug addiction within the realm of morality rather than illness have also contributed to the way in which society has responded or not responded to issues of HIV infection and AIDS among women. Entry into drug treatment is jeopardized by multiple obstacles presented to the addicted person, and these are especially onerous for women, including women with children or women who are pregnant. While this is now changing, until recently only a handful of drug treatment programmes nationally accepted pregnant women. Even now treatment programmes rarely provide child care or allow children to stay with mothers in residential treatment (Brown, 1991; Chavkin, 1990; Pollitt, 1990). Models for the treatment of alcohol and drug addiction, especially among women, have also received insufficient funding and research (Amaro, 1990b; Brown, 1991; Sutker, 1981; Vannicelli, 1984).

The AIDS epidemic has presented psychologists, health professionals, as well as society, with challenges that require us to overcome inherent biases towards the populations thus far most affected by HIV in the United States. At the same time, the response to AIDS as a public health problem in the US has been thwarted by a climate of societal, political and judicial conservatism, as well as by a period of economic crisis, budget cutbacks, and reduction of social programmes. It is this social and political context that has framed our national response, or lack of response, to the AIDS epidemic overall, and to the specific concerns of women in this epidemic.

HIV infection and AIDS are fertile soil for encroachment on the reproductive rights of women in general. This curtailment of women's rights has been facilitated by the public's fear of AIDS, the stigma associated with this illness, and by the fact that, to date, AIDS has primarily affected women who are disenfranchised not only because of their sex but also because of their social class, ethnicity and addiction.

Epidemiology of AIDS: The Most Disenfranchised at Risk

Even the most cursory review of the epidemiology of AIDS shows that HIV infection and AIDS cases are growing among women. The proportion of women among persons diagnosed with AIDS has been growing since the beginning of the epidemic (Ellerbrock et al., 1991). The majority (72 per cent) of AIDS cases in women are reported within eight states in the Atlantic coast, Washington DC and Puerto Rico (Ellerbrock et al., 1991). The highest cumulative incidence rates (per 100,000 women) of AIDS cases in women are found in Puerto Rico (71.3), New Jersey (62.9), New York (61.0) and Washington, DC (59.8) (Ellerbrock et al., 1991). As of November 1991, women made up over 10 per cent of the 196,034 AIDS cases reported to date among adults and adolescents in the United States.

The cumulative incidence of AIDS cases among women can, however, be misleading because of the overwhelming predominance of male cases during the first wave of the epidemic. A more accurate picture of the growing impact of AIDS among women emerges from the yearly incidence rates of diagnosed AIDS cases among women. In 1981, women comprised 3 per cent of individuals diagnosed with AIDS, compared to: 6.6 per cent in 1985, 11.5 per cent in 1990, and 12.5 per cent from November 1990 to October 1991 (Centers for Disease Control, 1991a; Guinan and Hardy, 1987).

In some areas, such as New York, New Jersey, Washington DC, Florida and Puerto Rico, women comprise a much larger proportion of people diagnosed with AIDS (Ellerbrock et al., 1991; Guinan and Hardy, 1987). In New York State and New Jersey, AIDS is now the leading cause of death among black women aged 15 to 44 (Centers for Disease Control, 1991b). Based on current trends, AIDS is expected soon to become one of the top five leading causes of death among women of reproductive age (Chu et al., 1990).

A much larger number of women, about 100,000, are estimated to be infected with HIV, but the number of women at *risk* of infection is much greater. Baldwin and Campbell (1987) used data from the National Survey of Family Growth to estimate the number of women in the US at various levels of risk for HIV infection. Their estimates, which are based on data of women's sexual behaviour, contraceptive practices and health care utilization, indicate that 11.4 million women fall into the two highest risk categories, and that the great majority of those at highest risk are poor, young and minority women.

For men diagnosed with AIDS (Centers for Disease Control,

1991a), the primary route of transmission has been sex with another man (65 per cent). Infection through injection drug use (19 per cent), injection drug use and male to male sex combined (7 per cent) and heterosexual contact (3 per cent) represent less common routes of transmission among men diagnosed with AIDS. For women diagnosed with AIDS (Centers for Disease Control, 1991a) the primary route of transmission has been through the use of infected needles and paraphernalia used in injecting drugs intravenously (51 per cent) and through heterosexual contact with an infected partner (34 per cent). Women infected through heterosexual contact have been predominantly (62 per cent) infected through sexual contact with an injection drug user (IDU). Heterosexual contact with a person at risk for AIDS is the only transmission category in which women with AIDS outnumber men with AIDS. AIDS cases among women stemming from heterosexual contact have increased from 12 per cent in 1982 to a current 34 per cent, making this the fastest growing transmission category for women (Centers for Disease Control, 1991a; Guinan and Hardy, 1987; Holmes et al., 1990).

In addition to male–female differences in routes of transmission, women with AIDS and at risk of HIV infection are distinct in key demographic, social, economic and health characteristics from most men diagnosed with AIDS. Women diagnosed with AIDS have been primarily black (52 per cent) and Latina (21 per cent) compared to 85 per cent of men diagnosed with AIDS who have been white (Centers for Disease Control, 1991a). Compared to whites, the cumulative incidence rates are eight times higher among Hispanic women and 13 times higher among black women (Ellerbrock et al., 1991). The majority (85 per cent) of women diagnosed with AIDS are of reproductive age (Ellerbrock et al., 1991).

To date, the AIDS epidemic among women in the US has primarily been concentrated in poor and minority women whose life is affected by their own or their partner's addiction. This picture contrasts strongly with the profile of the majority of men diagnosed with AIDS. And since most of the women diagnosed with AIDS have limited economic and social resources and access to health care, the services that they need and the policy issues that have emerged in relation to their illness are also unique and need to be considered in research, policy and programme development (Amaro, 1990b; Campbell, 1990).

Reproductive Choice in the Age of AIDS

The effects of major social factors that have shaped the US response to HIV and AIDS in women can be clearly observed in the policies and practices that affect the reproductive choices of women infected with HIV (see also Bayer, 1990; Levine and Dubler, 1990). The response to the AIDS epidemic around women is 'turning issues upside down', according to Katherine Franke of the AIDS Antidiscrimination Unit of New York City's Human Rights Commission. In writing about the curtailment of women's rights in the name of 'fetal rights', Franke asserts that the 'epidemic of stigma' surrounding AIDS has unleashed a new wave of racist–classist, sexist, homophobic and xenophobic notions of morality (Franke, 1989a, p. 208). Such notions of moral superiority and their application to AIDS are important not only because they directly infringe on the service needs of women who are infected, but also because they support a new approach to the limitation of women's reproductive choice.

One of the most controversial topics in the HIV epidemic has been HIV antibody testing. Debated issues include which groups of individuals should be tested, under what circumstances testing should be conducted, whether the results of testing should be confidential or anonymous,[1] and whether contacts of individuals who test positive should be traced. Various proposals for mandatory testing have been made and in some cases passed into state and federal law. Those proposals have focused, among others, on individuals requesting a marriage licence, persons entering the military, people in correctional institutions, people admitted to hospitals given out-patient treatments by dentists and doctors, health workers, sex workers, and individuals applying for residency or citizenship. All such proposals for mandatory testing affect women, but the policy that systematically affects the largest group of women at risk is that of routine testing of pregnant women and women seeking family planning services. The Public Health Service guidelines for counselling and antibody testing say:

> All pregnant women at risk for HIV infection should be routinely counseled and tested for HIV antibody. Routine counseling and testing is defined as a policy to provide these services to all clients after informing them that testing will be done . . . Except where testing is required by law, individuals have the right to decline to be tested without being denied health care or services. (United States Public Health Service, 1988, p. 75)

The Public Health Service states the rationale for routine counselling and testing of pregnant women at risk of HIV infection as follows:

> Identifying pregnant women with HIV infection as early in pregnancy as possible is important for ensuring appropriate medical care for these women; for planning medical care for their infants; and for providing counseling on family planning, future pregnancies, and the risk of sexual transmission of HIV to others. (United States Public Health Service, 1988, p. 75)

Prenatal testing for HIV is recommended by many in the field as an important strategy for the prevention of pediatric AIDS. This policy assumes that the logical consequences of an HIV infection and pregnancy is abortion. An important reproductive rights issue introduced by AIDS is the potential coercion of HIV positive women to have abortions (Bayer, 1990). Although no federal agency has to date recommended that HIV positive pregnant women be encouraged to have abortion – a direction which would, of course, be a suspicious philosophical contradiction of federal actions in the realm of abortion in the past decade – statements from federal agencies have pointed in that direction. It is telling to note that, although the use of federal funds has been severely restricted with respect to counselling non-HIV-infected women about pregnancy options, this restriction has not yet been placed on federally funded AIDS projects. In fact, with women at risk for HIV, it is not only acceptable but expected that health care providers will counsel on options to pregnancy, that is, abortion. In some states, for instance New Hampshire, educational materials strongly advise this for infected women. This perspective was reflected in a letter in the *Journal of the American Medical Association*, in which two physicians reported the successful decrease in pediatric AIDS cases through 'early identification of maternal HIV infection, counseling about risks and options, and election of abortion' (Maynard and Indacocchea, 1989).

There is a great potential for the misuse of prenatal HIV antibody test counselling in order to encourage seropositive women to have abortions (Mantell et al., 1988; Wofsy, 1987). As Franke pointed out, the:

> compelling state interest in fetal survival seems to evaporate when the mother and/or fetus have been exposed to HIV. When HIV infections become a factor in the abortion decision, the state's duty to defend potential life shifts to the interest of protecting society from the possibility of another person with AIDS . . . The abandonment of the fight to protect the lives of HIV-positive babies cannot be divorced from the moral judgements passed on anyone who tests positive. (Franke, 1989a, p. 209)

In view of the position of the past two US government administrations on the issue of abortion, the Centers for Disease Control (CDC) and other federal agencies have struggled with the political and philosophical contradictions posed by mention of abortion as a choice in counselling guidelines for HIV-infected women. In 1985, CDC staff presented a draft of perinatal AIDS guidelines that provided for discussion of the option of abortion with seropositive women (Gunn, 1988). But the wording on the draft guidelines changed, from 'HIV-infected women should be appraised of their options for the management of pregnancy', to 'they should be given medical advice to allow them to make informed decisions on reproduction', to 'However, if they bear children these women may require additional medical and social support services due to an enhanced risk of opportunistic infections and psychosocial difficulties during pregnancy.' The final version deleted any reference to choice concerning pregnancy outcome (Grimes, 1988). The objection to including a discussion of the abortion option has been attributed to independent consultants who provided input on the draft regulations. The concern of several consultants was that, on the basis of past practices, 'minority women in public clinic settings would be coerced into having abortions using these guidelines as a basis' (Gunn, 1988).

Involuntary sterilization of infected women and involuntary HIV antibody testing are also proposals likely to receive support from some quarters (Bayer, 1990; Mantell et al., 1988; Newman, 1987). A moment of reflection on the history of population control among women in developing nations, and sterilization among black and Latina women (Levine and Dubler, 1990) in the United States, should suffice to recognize that such coercive practices have been employed before and could be employed again among HIV-infected women. Bayer (1990, p. 183) has noted that experts recognized the potential for coercive policies to promote sterilization among women with HIV.

> The possibility of such massive coercion – despite the array of ethical, legal, constitutional, political, and logistic objections that would be provoked – has also been noted by Norman Frost, chair of the Bioethics Committee of the American Academy of Pediatrics . . . More than 100,000 retarded women were sterilized in the period between 1920 and 1973 on the assumption that they could transmit their condition to their children.

Bayer foresees that, while it is difficult to predict whether drastic coercive measures will receive public support, it is more likely that 'there will be aggressive campaigns to dissuade infected women from bearing children' (1990, p. 183)

Problems with Current Counselling and Testing Practices

Several serious problems exist with current prenatal HIV counselling and testing policies and programmes. These are: (a) the implementation of 'routine counselling and testing' prenatally; (b) threats to women's reproductive choices; and (c) low quality of counselling standards and staff training.

Routine Counselling and Testing Prenatally

There is no question that women have the right to be informed about HIV transmission and the HIV antibody test. There is also no doubt that many women who would benefit from this information do not currently receive it. Knowing whether a woman has been exposed to HIV can be critical in assisting the health care provider better to plan prenatal and postpartum care for both the woman and her infant. Yet, serious potential dangers also accompany the implementation of routine counselling and testing programmes. First, the routine approach to testing is one that encourages confidential rather than anonymous testing for HIV antibody. With confidential testing, a woman's HIV antibody status will most likely be part of her medical record and the information will become available to the many health and social service staff who have access to the record. In contrast with anonymous testing, where a client's name is never identified or connected to test results and the results do not become part of the medical record, the practice of confidential testing places the woman at risk of inappropriate disclosures of the information and of possible discrimination based on knowledge of her antibody status. With anonymous testing, on the other hand, test results are provided only to the individual being tested. The individual can then use her discretion in sharing this information with health care providers and others.

In the United States, there is a growing movement towards promoting confidential rather than anonymous testing, and it is likely that confidential testing will become more common for HIV antibody testing. Anonymous testing, conducted in specially designated anonymous test sites, has been largely supported by federal dollars, whereas testing done in conjunction with a health care facility can be covered by third-party payers. Considering the growth of HIV infection among women, the increasing health-related costs of HIV and AIDS and the relative shortage of dollars for the care of people with HIV and AIDS, it is likely that we will see an increasing move to reduce federal support for the funding of anonymous test sites. While others, such as the American Civil Liberties Union Foundation, have asserted that mandatory testing of pregnant women will deter women at most risk of HIV from seeking prenatal care, a trend towards confidential testing covered by Medicaid or private insurance could also further reduce women's willingness to be tested and/or seek medical services.

The extent of the misuse of results from confidential testing among high-risk women will depend greatly on the political climate. Recent court cases in which women have been charged, convicted and sentenced for child abuse and neglect resulting from their use of illegal substances during pregnancy (Pollitt, 1990; Mariner et al., 1990; Moss, 1990) and the enactment of laws in several states and pending bills in 14 other states criminalizing wilful transmissions of HIV (Franke, 1989a, p. 211) indicate that, in a conservative political climate, women who test positive for the HIV antibody and who become pregnant could be charged by the state, on behalf of the fetus, with intentional homicide or child abuse.

Although this scenario may seem unlikely, there is evidence that arguments about the 'rights of the fetus' have been successfully employed to place judicial restrictions on women's physical activities and to force women to undergo caesarean sections and other procedures. A study of court-ordered obstetrical procedures in cases in which women had refused therapy revealed that the women most likely to be subjected to court-ordered interventions such as caesarean section, intra-uterine transfusions and hospital detentions, were women who were receiving care in teaching hospital clinics or were receiving public assistance, women who were black or Latina, and women who were non-English speaking (Kolder et al., 1987). A survey by Kolder and colleagues of heads of fellowship programmes in maternal–fetal medicine revealed that nearly half (46 per cent) thought that mothers who refused medical advice, and thereby endangered the life of the fetus, should be detained in hospitals or other facilities to ensure compliance. These influential health professionals also believed that the precedent set by the courts in cases requiring emergency caesarean sections for the sake of the fetus should be extended to other procedures that are potentially life-saving for the fetus.

One is left to wonder whether, as medical knowledge about the perinatal transmission of HIV infection increases women might be ordered by courts to submit to medically indicated treatments during pregnancy. The policy of routine testing of pregnant women, instituted to ensure that HIV-infected women receive appropriate medical care, may eventually render women vulnerable to judicial battles over what the state regards as the 'rights of the fetus'.

If pregnant women know or suspect that a positive HIV antibody test could be used against them, as in current practice results of positive toxicology tests to social service workers (Moss, 1990), women will fear the loss of custody through a child abuse or neglect charge or loss of job. Women at most risk of HIV infection may choose not to seek prenatal care or family planning services. If the inappropriate use of HIV antibody tests served to discourage women from seeking services, the effect on women's health could be serious. Participation in prenatal care is already low in the United States, especially among poor and minority women (Brown, 1989). For example, in Massachusetts, where there are fewer financial barriers to prenatal care than in many other states, more than 40 per cent of black and Latina women receive inadequate prenatal care (Cohen et al., 1989). Women who are most at risk of HIV infection, users of illegal drugs, are the most likely not to receive any prenatal care. At Boston City Hospital, 80 per cent of women who delivered after receiving no prenatal care were users of cocaine and intravenous drugs (Keith, 1989). Testing policies and practices that do not protect women from discriminatory actions and legal liabilities will most likely work to deter further the women at highest risk from seeking prenatal care. Current policies and laws that seek to protect HIV-infected people from discrimination need to be extended to protect the specific circumstances of pregnant women.

Other stated reasons for the recommendation that routine counselling and testing be conducted for all women at risk who seek prenatal and family planning services include the following: that women will systematically receive counselling or testing; that prevention of HIV infection among non-infected women can be facilitated through counselling before and after testing; and that counselling can result in risk reduction among infected women so as to reduce infection to others (Centers for Disease Control, 1985; Minkoff and Landesman, 1988). Because of constraints on staff time and clinic resources, however, there is a danger that in the implementation of routine counselling and testing, the counselling component of the programme will be shortchanged.

The risk of testing without adequate counselling is that women will be tested without genuine informed consent. On the other hand, many women who would benefit from being treated may not be tested because they receive inadequate information and counselling. In both cases, a woman's right to make a proper and self-determined decision about testing is being jeopardized.

Threats to Women's Reproductive Choice
Counselling as currently practised is unlikely to meet the mental health needs of clients undergoing a crisis, and may undermine a

woman's right to exercise the choice to continue or terminate the pregnancy. The passage of the Hyde Amendment in 1977 and the restrictions on the use of Medicaid funds for abortions present a very real obstacle for poor women who are infected and who wish to terminate their pregnancies. In addition, the recent decision by the Supreme Court in the 1989 Webster case makes it constitutional for states to prohibit abortions in public facilities, and has added a further barrier to abortion for women in some states.

Even when abortion is legally available and there are no economic barriers to obtaining it, HIV positive women may still find it difficult to obtain abortion services. A study of 30 clinics and private doctors in New York who advertised that they performed abortions showed widespread discrimination against women who identified themselves as seropositive. An investigator from the AIDS Antidiscrimination Unit of the New York City Commission on Human Rights made an appointment with each facility for an abortion, and then disclosed that she had tested HIV antibody positive. Two-thirds of the providers would not keep the appointment after this disclosure. The rationales given and comments made by providers indicated not only a lack of knowledge about HIV infection, but also deeply held animosity and hostility towards women who are infected (Franke, 1989b). Thus, women who are HIV positive and seek to terminate their pregnancy face not only possible legal and economic barriers but also discrimination by health care providers.

Quality of Counselling and Staff Training
For most people, and for women especially, the decision to be tested is very difficult and stressful (Worth, 1990b). It typically involves not one conversation but a series of conversations with a health care professional or counsellor before a person can make a decision. This process requires that the health care professionals providing the information be well informed and trained in counselling and that they devote time at several visits to answering client questions and concerns. By incorporating intensive pre-test and post-test counselling, the stress associated with receiving positive test results can be significantly reduced (Anderson et al., 1991).

Counselling for women who test seropositive is supposed to include information about the possible alternatives: about whether to continue or terminate the pregnancy, facts about the probability of infection of the infant, the implications of that infection for the health, treatment and care of the infant, and the possible medical effects of pregnancy on the progression of HIV infection and AIDS in the women herself (Minkoff, 1987). The client's ability to care for herself and her child, as well as sources of social and material support, need to be discussed. In practice, post-test counselling often falls short of the needs presented by women clients.

The majority of women at risk of HIV infection, who are poor, black or Hispanic, and live in the inner cities, obtain their prenatal care either at community health clinics or at local public hospitals. Staffing and resources in the health care setting are always extremely stretched; consequently, the implementation of routine counselling and testing programmes in prenatal care poses considerable logistical problems. It seems unrealistic to expect that the clinic staff in areas with a high seroprevalence rate will be able to dedicate the time necessary to facilitate the woman's decision whether to be tested, and then to conduct post-test counselling to assist a woman to cope with the meaning of a positive result or to support risk reduction among women who are not yet infected.

There is reason to believe that prenatal HIV testing is likely to elicit routine substantial anxiety in women, which is not likely to be adequately dealt with in one post-test counselling session. Stevens and associates (1989) explored the response to routine HIV testing among a sample of women attending a prenatal clinic in the United Kingdom. Results show that, although more than 80 per cent of women thought that the test should be available at antenatal clinics, only half would personally have the test if asked. The proportion of respondents saying that the HIV test might make them anxious was significantly greater than for a blood pressure test, other blood tests and an ultrasound scan. While the reasons for anxiety about HIV were not explored in the study, it is clear that the meaning of a positive HIV test is not comparable to getting high readings in a blood pressure test or high glucose or cholesterol levels in other tests. The legal, medical and social consequences of a positive HIV test are much more charged than those arising from a positive serology for syphilis.

AIDS Education and Risk Reduction

In order to ensure that women at risk of HIV infection are not denied the right to information or to make their own decisions, the implementation of HIV education and counselling and testing programmes needs to be carefully designed. Psychologists and clinicians who are knowledgeable about women's mental health have an important role to play in the development of HIV counselling. Counselling to reduce the risk of infection, as well as counselling a woman who has just found out she is seropositive, requires knowledge of human behaviour and counselling skills that are not necessarily acquired after the minimal training typically provided to counsellors and to health professionals who counsel women on these matters. In addition, guidelines for training, certification and supervision of HIV antibody test counsellors need to be reviewed to optimize the quality and potential success of risk reduction counselling. Although counselling related to HIV anti-body testing is currently available through Medicaid and at alternative test sites, the amount of reimbursement generally for this service does not allow for the time required to support a pregnant woman through a decision on testing or the adjustment to having a positive test result. Adequate reimbursement for risk reduction counselling, preferably through alternative test sites, is needed.

There is also a critical need to develop education and counselling strategies that are effective in helping women to reduce the risk of infection. Although policy-makers and providers assume that testing women is an effective means of reducing perinatal transmission because knowledge of seropositivity would discourage women from getting pregnant, recent studies suggest that such is not the case. For example, Selwyn and colleagues (1989), in a follow-up study of female IVDUs in treatment in New York City, found that seropositive women and seronegative women who had been tested and knew their test results had similar pregnancy rates after getting the results. Twenty-four per cent of 70 seropositive women and 22 per cent of 121 seronegative women became pregnant one or more times after finding out their antibody status. Similar results have been reported by Sunderland and her colleagues (1989) in another prospective perinatal HIV transmission study. Simply testing women does not result in behaviour change; continuing education and counselling must also be provided.

In addition, the psychological, social and cultural factors that make pregnancy a rational alternative, even if a woman is HIV positive, need to be understood by counsellors (Levine and Dubler, 1990; Mitchell, 1989). For many HIV positive women, a 70 per cent chance of having a child who is not infected may be the best odds they have ever had. Knowing HIV test results does not seem to be a determining factor in a woman's decision to carry out or terminate a pregnancy. The study by Selwyn and colleagues (1989) found no significant differences between HIV seropositive and seronegative groups in the frequency of elective termination – 44 per cent of the HIV positive and 32 per cent of the HIV negative women – even when women who were seropositive were informed of their HIV antibody status before 24 weeks of gestation.

In one interview with a pregnant HIV positive woman who was a recovering heroin addict, the client told me that even though her two-year-old son had been diagnosed with ARC, she wanted to have the baby because *maybe* it would not be infected. For her, the pregnancy provided hope. Referring to poor minority women, Mitchell (1989, p. 842) noted that: 'The women often see their ability to reproduce as the only link to normality and the "American Dream".' For many women infected with HIV or at risk of being infected, AIDS is low on a long list of immediate concerns that includes: addiction, abuse, violence, lack of housing and food, immediate health problems and threat or actual loss of custody of children (Nyamathi and Vasquez, 1989). AIDS prevention targeted at women at risk must address the social and economic context in which the women live (Amaro, 1988, 1990a; Worth, 1989, 1990a, b).

The implementation of appropriate counselling and testing procedures will require that women are provided with accurate and objective information and the avenues by which to ensure their choice regarding pregnancy. One obstacle that will need to be addressed is attitudinal norms among health care and mental health professionals, which reflect judgemental and biased views of women currently at most risk of HIV infection. While a dearth of research exists on providers' attitudes towards women with HIV and their reproductive choices, there is some evidence to support the observation that provider attitudes may play a critical role in how HIV-infected women at high risk are counselled.

Generally, there is overwhelming support for non-directive counselling for women with a high risk of having children with genetic disorders (Bayer, 1990); however, providers may evaluate counselling women at risk of HIV or at risk of having an infected child quite differently. A study of two pediatric residency programmes in New York City found that 65 per cent of those surveyed believed the statement that 'women should not have babies who will be at risk for AIDS' (cited in Bayer, 1990, p. 193). Only a small proportion of the same respondents agreed with this statement when it referred to women having babies at risk of other diseases such as Tay–Sachs disease, cystic fibrosis or Down's syndrome. Nearly half of respondents (43 per cent) favoured mandated HIV testing for pregnant women. Bayer (1990, p. 194) notes that:

> The study's respondents had clearly indicated a greater willingness to adopt a directive posture with regard to AIDS than with other grave genetic disorders. It is possible that both the class and racial/ethnic background of those at risk of transmitting HIV infection played a critical role. That so many infected women were also intravenous drug users may also have been a significant factor.

If counsellors and health care professionals who counsel women during the course of care reflect the biases suggested by these findings, HIV-infected women and women at risk who seek information to make reproductive decisions will be ill served and their right to make informed reproductive decisions will be undermined. Training of counsellors and health care professionals in non-directive counselling for women at high risk of HIV and for women with HIV infection, must be an integral part of the development of prenatal counselling and testing programmes.

The design and implementation of appropriate HIV education, and counselling and testing programmes into routine prenatal care needs to receive more research and programmatic attention than that given to it to date. In so doing, fiscal and staff training needs must be addressed. Prenatal clinics in major urban teaching hospitals and community health centres, where most women at high risk of HIV are served, rely on limited staff to serve large numbers of women. The integration of an education, counselling and testing programme into prenatal care will minimally require funding for a coordinator and mental health counsellor. Those who have developed prenatal education and counselling programmes have noted that 'considerable staff training and support is necessary to provide impetus and direction for the development of an effective patient program' (Mason et al., 1991, p. 119). In the case of the Mount Sinai Medical Center Program reported by Mason and colleagues, a grant for the Health Resource Service Administration (HRSA) provided funding. Funding needs to be provided for additional staff and staff training in order to enable prenatal clinics to deliver top-quality prenatal education, counselling and testing programmes with appropriate informed consent, mental health support services, and staff training to ensure that information presented to women is accurate and non-directive.

The primary purpose of a prenatal education programme should not be to persuade women to be tested upon entering prenatal care. The programme in the Mount Sinai Medical Center found that one session of AIDS education did not have an immediate impact on women's willingness to be tested (Berrier et al., 1991). While prenatal HIV education may not have an *immediate* impact on women's willingness to be tested, as women have time to consider the issues discussed in education sessions, the number of women who choose to be tested may be increased (Mason et al., 1991). However, Berrier and colleagues reported that even after providing the experimental education programme to women entering prenatal care, only half of the women who identified any risk of infection experienced a potential interest in being tested (Berrier et al., 1991) and only 20 per cent of women attending the clinic decided to be tested (Mason et al., 1991). Thus, an HIV education programme with appropriate consent and non-directive counselling will not necessarily result in testing for all or most clinic clients. This is not surprising considering the emotional, social and legal ramifications of a positive HIV test result, especially during pregnancy. The complexity of issues associated with receiving information about testing and the decision to be tested and with receiving positive or negative test results is described in Dooley Worth's (1990b) work based on ethnographic research with women at high risk of infection. She notes that:

> Given the often traumatic, life-changing nature of the experience of undergoing HIV antibody testing for women, suggestions that specific groups of populations of women be 'routinely tested' have serious implications. The experience of the author is that for all women at risk the issue of HIV testing itself raises serious questions about risk taking (theirs and their partners), healthy relationships (including dependency), sexual decision making, reproductive choices, illness, death and dying, regardless of the outcome of testing. (Worth, 1990b, pp. 103–4)

During pregnancy, considering and having an HIV test also brings up issues related to fear and guilt regarding infection of the child and potential loss of custody of the child and/or other children if health care providers discover her drug use during risk assessment. In the case of pregnant women, the model of one pre-test and one post-test counselling session for HIV testing is clearly inadequate and ill matched to the client counselling and support needs associated with the decision to be tested and the consequences of test results. If the goals of counselling women during pregnancy are to support risk reduction and improve access to early treatment, the conceptualization and implementation of counselling programmes prenatally and for women in general will need to be redesigned taking into account the substantial changes that this will require in women's lives and the services needed to support such change.

Conclusion

AIDS prevention targeted at women at risk must not seek to isolate the risk of infection from the social and economic context in which women live. The quality of HIV-related counselling must be professionally upgraded so that it can respond to the critical behavioural and mental health issues raised in testing. Counselling must also incorporate concerns regarding women's life conditions, and assist women in obtaining the services they need in order for them to achieve the stability that will enable them to attend to life changes that promote prevention of infection and reduce the risk of transmission. Moreover, where reproductive issues are fore-grounded in AIDS prevention work with women, policy-makers, clinicians and counsellors have a responsibility to provide non-directive and accurate information, and to ensure that policies about HIC antibody testing and counselling, and their applications, do not undermine women's reproductive rights.

Notes

This contribution was adapted from an invited address to the Division of the Psychology of Women at the 97th Annual Convention of the American Psychological Association, New Orleans, Louisiana, 1989. Other versions have been published in *The Genetic Resource* (1990) 5 (2), 39–44, and in M. Gerber Fried (ed.), *From Abortion to Reproductive Freedom: Transforming a Movement*. Boston: South End Press, 1990.

1   Anonymous testing refers to testing conducted at designated test sites that provide free and anonymous HIV counselling and testing. Confidential testing refers to HIV counselling and testing conducted by a health care provider and typically paid by the patient's normal source of health coverage. Confidential testing is supposed to guard patient confidentiality, however, HIV test results are often available to health care providers through notes on the medical record. Policies adopted to protect client confidentiality and how health care providers gain access to clients' HIV test results differ widely across agencies.

References

Amaro, H. (1988) Considerations for prevention of HIV infection among Hispanic women. *Psychology of Women Quarterly* 12, 429–43.

Amaro, H. (1990a) HIV Prevention with Pregnant Women: Preliminary Findings from the Mom's Project. Paper presented at the 98th Annual American Psychological Association Convention, Boston, Mass., 12 August.

Amaro, H. (1990b) Barriers to Care Faced by Women with HIV and AIDS. Paper presented at the National Conference on Women and HIV Infection, Washington, DC, 13–14 January 1991.

Anderson, J.R., Amaro, H., Bailey, W.A., Barret, R.L., Boccellari, A.A., Boude, L., Body-Franklin, N., Coates, T.J., Franks, P.E., Gornemann, I., Landry, C.P., Lo, B., McKusick, L., Shore, M.D., Steiner, G.L. and Tafoya, T.N. (1991) Review of recent literature on the behavioral and psycho-social aspects of HIV disease. In J.R. Anderson, C.P. Landry and J.L. Kerby (eds), *AIDS: Abstracts of the Psychological and Behavioral Literature 1983–1991* (pp. 1–60). Washington, DC: American Psychological Association.

Baldwin, W. and Campbell, A. (1987) Reproductive Behavior and Women's Risk of AIDS. Paper presented at the NIMH/NIDA Workshop on 'Women and AIDS: Promoting Healthy Behaviors', Bethesda, Maryland.

Bayer, R. (1990) AIDS in the future of reproductive freedom. *The Milbank Quarterly* 68 (2), 179–204.

Berrier, J., Sperling, R., Preisinger, J., Evans, V., Mason, J. and Walther, V. (1991) HIV/AIDS education in a prenatal clinic. An assessment. *AIDS Education Quarterly* 3 (2), 100–17.
Brown, S. (1989) Drawing women into prenatal care. *Family Planning Perspectives* 21 (2), 73–80.
Brown, S.S. (1991) *Children and Parental Illicit Drug Use: Research, Clinical and Policy Issues. Summary of a Workshop.* Washington DC: National Academy Press.
Campbell, C.A. (1990) Women and AIDS. *Social Sciences in Medicine* 30 (4), 407–15.
Centers for Disease Control (1985) Recommendations for assisting in the prevention of the perinatal transmission of human T-Lymphotropic Virus Type III/ Lymphadenopathy-Associated Virus and Acquired Immunodeficiency Syndrome. *Morbidity and Mortality Weekly Reports* 34, 721–32.
Centers for Disease Control (1991a) *HIV/AIDS Surveillance* (November). National Center for Infectious Diseases, Division of HIV/AIDS.
Centers for Disease Control (1991b) Mortality attributable to HIV infection/AIDS – United States, 1981–90. *Morbidity and Mortality Weekly Reports* 40 (3), 41–4.
Chavkin, W. (1990) Drug addiction and pregnancy: policy crossroads. *American Journal of Public Health* 80 (4), 483–6.
Chu, S.Y., Buehler, J.W. and Berkelman, R.L. (1990) Impact of the human immunodeficiency virus epidemic on mortality in women of reproductive age, United States. *Journal of the American Medical Association* 264, 225–9.
Cohen, B., Morison-Aguiar, M., Amaro, H. and Liderman, R.I. (1989) Hispanic births in Massachusetts: 1986–1987. In R.M. Loew and D.J. Lerner (eds), *Mothers, Infants and Children at Risk*, pp. 9–17. Boston, Mass.: Massachusetts Health Data Consortium.
Ellerbrock, T., Bush, T.J., Chamberland, M.E. and Oxtoby, M.J. (1991) Epidemiology of women with AIDS in the United States, 1981 through 1990. *Journal of the American Medical Association* 265 (2), 2971–5.
Franke, K. (1989a) Turning issues upside down. In I. Rieder and P. Ruppelt (eds), *Matters of Life and Death: Women Speak about AIDS*. London: Virago.
Franke, K. (1989b) HIV-related Discrimination in Abortion Clinics in New York City. A report by the AIDS Discrimination Division of the Law Enforcement Bureau of the New York City Commission on Human Rights.
Grimes, D. (1988) The CDC and abortion in HIV-positive women. Letter to the Editor in reply to Gunn (1988). *Journal of the American Medical Association* 259, 217–18.
Guinan, M. and Hardy, A. (1987) Epidemiology of AIDS in women in the United States. *Journal of the American Medical Association* 257, 2039–42.
Gunn, A. (1988) The CDC and abortion in HIV-positive women. Letter to the Editor. *Journal of the American Medical Association* 259, 217–18.
Holmes, K., Karon, J. and Kreiss, J. (1990) The increasing frequency of heterosexually acquired AIDS in the United States, 1983–88. *American Journal of Public Health* 80 (7), 858–63.
Keith, A. (1989) Personal communication on results of a study of urine toxicology screens conducted on all women admitted for delivery at Boston City Hospital without previous prenatal care.
Kolder, V., Gallagher, J. and Parsons, M. (1987) Court ordered obstetrical interventions. *New England Journal of Medicine* 316 (9), 1192–6.

40 *Women and AIDS*

Levine, C. (1990) Women and HIV/AIDS research. The barriers to equity. *Evaluation Review* 3 (2), 50–2.
Levine, C. and Dubler, N.N. (1990) Uncertainty risks and better realities: the reproductive choices of HIV infected women. *The Milbank Quarterly* 68 (3), 321–51.
Mantell, J., Schinke, S. and Akabas, S. (1988) Women and AIDS prevention. *Journal of Primary Prevention* 9 (1&2), 18–40.
Mariner, W.K., Glantz, L.H. and Annas, G.J. (1990) Pregnancy, drugs, and the perils of prosecution. *Criminal Justice Ethics* (Winter/Spring), 30–41.
Mason, J., Preisinger, J., Sperling, R., Walther, V., Berrier, J. and Evans, V. (1991) Incorporating HIV education and counselling into routine prenatal care: A model program. *AIDS Education and Prevention* 3 (2), 118–23.
Maynard, E. and Indacocchea, F. (1989) HIV infection in pregnant women in Rhode Island, 1985 to 1988. Letter to the Editor. *New England Journal of Medicine* 320, 1626.
Minkoff, H. (1987) Care of pregnant women infected with human immunodeficiency virus. *Journal of the American Medical Association* 258 (19), 2714–17.
Minkoff, H. and Landesman, S. (1988) The case for routinely offering prenatal testing for human immunodeficiency virus. *American Journal of Obstetrics and Gynaecology* 159, 793–6.
Mitchell, J. (1988) Women, AIDS, and public policy. *AIDS and Public Policy* 3 (2), 50–2.
Mitchell, J.L. (1989) Drug abuse and AIDS in women and their affected offspring. *Journal of the National Medical Association* 81 (8), 841–2.
Moss, K. (1990) Substance abuse during pregnancy. *Harvard Women's Law Journal* 13, 278–99.
Newman, A. (1987) Patterns in AIDS spread elicits proposal to tighten precautions for involuntary sterilization? *Obstetrics and Gynecology* 22 (1), 36–7.
Nyamathi, M.A. and Vasquez, R. (1989) Impact of poverty, homelessness and drugs in Hispanic women at risk for HIV Infection. *Hispanic Journal of Behavioral Sciences* 11 (4), 299–314.
Pollitt, K. (1990) Fetal rights: a new assault on feminism. *The Nation*, 26 March, 409–17.
Selwyn, P., Schoenbaum, E., Davenny, K., et al. (1989) Prospective study on human immunodeficiency virus infection and pregnancy outcomes in intravenous drug users. *Journal of the American Medical Association* 261, 1289–94.
Stevens, A., Victor, C., Sherr, L. and Beard, R. (1989) HIV testing in antenatal clinics: the impact on women. *AIDS Care*, 1, 165–71.
Sunderland, A., Moroso, G., Human, S., Medez, H., Berthand, J. and Landesman, S. (1989) Influence of HIV Infection on Pregnancy Decision. Paper presented at the Fifth International AIDS Conference, Montreal, Canada.
Sutker, P. (1981) Drug dependent women: an overview of the literature. In G. Beschner, B.G. Reed and J. Mondanaro (eds), *Treatment Services for Drug Dependent Women*, vol. I, pp. 25–51, DHHS Publication NO. (ADM) 87–1177. Alcohol, Drug Abuse and Mental Health Administration.
Thomas, P. (1987) AIDS agenda slights women. *Medical World News*, 27 July, 12–13.
United States Public Health Service (1988) Public Health Service guidelines for counselling and antibody testing to prevent HIV infection and AIDS. *New York State Journal of Medicine* 88, 74–6.

Vannicelli, M. (1984) Treatment outcome of alcoholic women: the state of the art in relation to sex bias and expectancy effects. In S.C. Wilsnack and L.J. Beckman (eds), *Alcohol Problems in Women*, pp. 369–412. New York: Guilford Publications.

Wofsy, C. (1987) Human immunodeficiency virus in women. *Journal of the American Medical Association* 257, 2074–6.

Worth, D. (1989) Sexual decision making and AIDS: why condom promotion among vulnerable women is likely to fail. *Studies in Family Planning* 20 (6), 297–307.

Worth, D. (1990a) Minority women and AIDS: culture, race and gender. In D. Feldman (ed.), *Cultural Aspects of AIDS in the Global Pandemic*. New York: Praeger.

Worth, D. (1990b) Women at high risk of HIV infection: behavioral, prevention ad intervention aspects. In D. Ostrow (ed.), *Behavioral Aspects of AIDS and other STDs*. New York: Plenum Press.

2
HIV Testing in Pregnancy

Lorraine Sherr

Despite the fact that for every three males infected with the Human Immunodeficiency Virus there is one female (WHO, 1990), HIV infection and AIDS are still perceived by many as diseases of gay men.

Heterosexual cases of AIDS in the UK have increased by 98 per cent for the year 1990–1991 and cases in women have increased by 72 per cent over the same period. In the USA the number of AIDS cases increased over the past year by 29 per cent for women compared to 18 per cent for men. Yet attention has not been focused on women during the short history of this devastating epidemic.

HIV is the virus associated with AIDS. It has produced a pandemic which is sweeping across many countries (163 countries are reporting cases to the WHO to date). AIDS is essentially a terminal illness and 50 per cent of individuals diagnosed with the condition have already died (Adler, 1989). It is transmitted sexually in blood and other body fluids, and through needle-sharing and transfusions. It can also cross the placenta and infect the newborn. Societal taboo and ignorance have often meant that those who are affected are abandoned, isolated, shunned by society, deprived of their human rights, expelled from work, denied insurance at the very moment when they are faced with a life-threatening and devastating condition (Green and Miller, 1986).

On exposure to HIV the body reacts by producing an antibody. This antibody can be detected in a test. The test itself has limitations in that it can take anything up to 12 weeks for the body to produce sufficient antibody to record a positive test. In this interim (or window) period, an individual may test negative, yet still be infected and able to transmit the virus to others. Until the test is improved upon it has specific limitations: it cannot tell how one became infected, how long one has been infected, the source of infection, or whether, much less when, one will go on to develop AIDS. Furthermore, it cannot differentiate between maternal and infant antibody and thus can for at least the first 18 months be positive with infant blood even if there is only maternal antibody present.

Health workers have spent much time incorporating psychological care into treatment packages for all those faced with HIV infection generally and HIV testing specifically (Green and McCreaner, 1989; Miller et al., 1986). There is no cure currently available for AIDS and it is important that those undergoing HIV testing do so with informed consent and adequate pre- and post-test counselling. This will not only ensure informed decisions but will be an opportunity to address behaviour change, the only effective means of avoiding HIV infection. It will also provide preparation for the psychological trauma of a positive test result if one ensues. This advice has been accepted and endorsed by official agencies worldwide. Indeed, it is rare to read a paper on HIV infection in gay men that does not note the presence of pre- and post-test counselling. But this is not true of another large body of papers: those which report HIV antibody testing of pregnant women.

In the current stage of this epidemic, the heterosexual spread of HIV has become more apparent. As the virus is known to be able to cross the placenta and infect the newborn, there has been an urgent rush to screen pregnant women for HIV (see Table 2.1). A variety of reasons has been advanced to justify this, including monitoring, epidemiological knowledge and, as Hortensia Amaro describes in Chapter 1, prevention and treatment. This paper examines these notions, and draws attention to the particular difficulties women face with HIV testing.

How Widespread is HIV Testing in Pregnancy?

HIV infection in most countries follows typical patterns. It is very clear that HIV is most prevalent in disadvantaged elements of

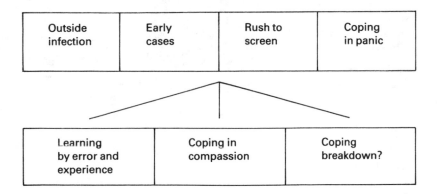

Figure 2.1   *International patterns of reaction phases*

societies. This is not so much a new disease, but a new virus which highlights old problems. International patterns of reaction phases include those shown in Figure 2.1. The initial rush to screen is usually an ill-thought-out reaction by a numbed and frantic organizational system often prompted by fear which is usually the outward manifestation of ignorance. It may stem from the unquestioning belief in a medical science which, with its tests and medicines, has previously delivered cures and understanding. Yet this science now stands by unable to stem the spread of HIV.

HIV testing has been available from the early years of the epidemic. Knowledge of serostatus has often been associated with acute psychological trauma (Marzuk et al., 1988, Miller and Pinching, 1989). Acute psychological distress has been monitored around HIV testing (Cleary et al., 1988; Coates et al., 1988; McCusker et al., 1988; Ostrow et al., 1989; Sherr et al., 1990). Yet no studies have examined the effects of testing on women.

Tables 2.1 and 2.2 set out the numbers of studies worldwide where pregnant women have been subjected to HIV screening either directly or indirectly through their infant. It is interesting to note that no single study has been carried out examining the blood of the partners of pregnant women. Several studies have been reported where seroprevalence has been examined on cord blood or fetal blood samples which would reflect maternal infection (Table 2.2).

Table 2.1   *HIV screening reports worldwide of pregnant women*

Study	n	Place	% (n) HIV positive	Comments
Americas				
Aguero et al. (1987)	860	Lima	0	
Araneta et al. (1987)	3425	New York	1.4 (21)	
Barbacci (1989)	1406	Baltimore	5.3 (49)	
Barton et al. (1989)	585	Chicago	$n=3$	High risk
			$n=0$	Low risk
Berthaud et al. (1987)	301	Brooklyn	5.8	High risk
Boulos (1989)	4336	Haiti, 1986	8.9	
		Haiti, 1988	10.2	
Boulos (1990)	4474	Haiti 86/88	8	Invited
	1720	89/90		participate
Boulos et al. (1987)	799	Haiti	7.1 (57)	
CDC (1990)	1000	Wisconsin	0	
Goedert et al. (1989a)	687		13 (92)	High risk
Halsey et al. (1987)	673	Baltimore 1985	0.74	
	1245	Baltimore 1986	1.3	

Study	n	Place	% (n) HIV positive	Comments
Harrison and More (1987)	532	San Diego	n=10	
Hauer et al. (1987)	All (anon)	San Franscisco		
Hoff et al. (1988)	30708	Massachusettes	0.25	
Holman et al. (1988)	126	Brooklyn	34 (29)	High risk
Holt (1990)	3754	Haiti	4 (160)	
Landesman et al. (1987)	602	Brooklyn	2 (12)	
Lindsay et al. (1989)	3472		0.28 (10)	
Lindsay et al. (1989)	513	Atlanta	5.6	
Maynard (1989)	All attenders	Rhode Island	n=1 n=7 n=9 n=10	(1985) (1986) (1987) (1988)
Mendez et al. (1987)	366	Brooklyn	42 6	IVDU Haitian
MMWR (1987)	2276 973	USA Abidjan	n=77	
Nesheim et al. (1989)	95% all women at clinic	Atlanta	0.6 (102)	All women 1987–89
Novick et al. (1989)	276609	New York	0.66	
Rogers et al. (1990)	21655	Baltimore	0.27	
Schoenbaum et al. (1987)	276	Bronx	38	
Scott et al. (1989)	2061	Florida	3.6 (74)	
Sperling et al. (1989)	224	New York	2.7	
Wenstrom and Zuidema (1989)	349 849	Chicago Chicago	0.6 1.1	Women in labour
Africa				
Barreto et al. (1987)	1000	Maputo 1983	0	
Blanche et al. (1989)	8000	Kinshasa	5.8	
Braddick et al. (1988)	2665	Nairobi	n=62	
Chiphangwi (1989)	200 (85) 85 (87)	Malawi Malawi	2 (4) 8 (7)	
Delaporte (1990)	108	Gabon	17.6 (19)	
Duerr (1990)	951	Rwanda	9.3	
Halsey et al. (1990)	4599	Africa	9.7 (443)	
Hira (1990)	1954	Zambia	12 (227)	
Kanti et al. (1987)	92	Senegal	3 (3)	
Kaptue et al. (1987)	134	Cameroon	–	
Lallemant et al. (1987)	1531	Brazzaville	4 (62)	
Lallemant et al. (1989)	1833	Brazzaville	3.9 (71)	
Makawa et al. (1987)	2000	Congo	10 (203)	
Nsa et al. (1987)	8264	Kinshasa	(n=479)	
Ntabab et al. (1987)	96 (86) 260 (87)	Malawi Malawi	4.2 (4) 6.5 (19)	

Study	n	Place	% (n) HIV positive	Comments
Nzilambi et al. (1988)	7000	Kinshasa	5.6 (135)	
Pruzuck (1990)	2100	Burkina Faso	5.6 (23)	
Ryder et al. (1989)	8108	Kinshasa	$n=466$	
Sangare et al. (1989)	2602	Abidjan	4.23	
Europe				
Bird and Snow (1988)	8000	Stockholm	$(n=20)$	
Brattebo and				
Wiseborg (1988)	24825	Norway	0.012 (3)	
Brossard et al. (1987)	All	Paris	0.27	
	attenders	Paris	0.7	Terminations
Bucherl and				
Frosner (1987)	63	Munich	–	
Ciraru-Vigneron et al.				
(1987)	–	–	1 & 3	
Delaporte et al. (1988)	750	Paris	$n=24$	
De Rossi et al. (1988)	310	Padua	$n=2$	
	210	Padua	$n=7$	High risk
	277	Padua	$n=1$	
Howard et al. (1989)	2800	London	$n=2$	
	982	London	$n=2$	
Ippolito et al. (1989)	39102	Rome	$n=51$	
Jenum et al. (1987)	12511	Oslo	1.008	
Johnston et al. (1989)	436	Edinburgh	8	High risk
Kantanen et al. (1987)	9202	Helsinki	$n=1$	
Kantanen et al. (1988)	9738	Helsinki	$n=1$	
Kozlov (1990)	2229000	Leningrad	$n=50$	
Larsson et al. (1987)	7766	Stockholm	0.04 (3)	
Lindgren et al. (1987)	39500	Sweden	$n=4$	
Medbo and	165000	Norway	0.009 (14)	98% of all
Lindemann (1989)				pregnant
				women tested
Pista et al. (1990)	1519	Portugal	0.7 (10)	
Tovo (1988)	89	Turin	32.6	High risk
Van Lith et al. (1989)	224	Holland	2.7 (6)	
Virnon et al. (1987)	2300	France	0.2	
USSR and Asia				
Pokrovsky (1990)	10565181	USSR	$n=9$	
Vranx et al. (1987)	1918	Badung	$n=37$	
Wang et al. (1987)	583	China	$n=1$	
Zohoun et al. (1987)	83	Benin	0	

Table 2.2 *HIV testing of infants/cord blood*

Study	n	Place	% +VE	Source of sample
Araneta et al. (1987)	3425	USA	1.4	
	1934		1.4	TOP
Ippolito et al. (1989)	23492	Italy	0.119	Children
Ippolito et al. (1990)	39102	Italy	0.0013	Guthrie
Peckham et al. (1989)	115000	London	29	Guthrie
		Inner city	0.049	
		Outer city	0.004	
Wang et al. (1987)	95	Chongqing	n=2	CB

TOP, termination of pregnancy.
CB, cord blood.

The enormous number of studies and the large samples of pregnant women are striking. Pregnant women are often subjected to mass HIV testing. These tests are targeted at various populations, often those noted as 'high-risk groups'. Of the many studies, few even mention the words pre- and post-test counselling. Such an omission would be unacceptable in studies of other groups. In the few studies which mention counselling, it is unclear what the level of intervention was and to what extent women were actively given choice (Sherr, 1991).

Even where a choice is presented, refusal may be difficult for women. In a recent study in Africa (Ndugwa et al., 1990), 53 per cent of women ($n = 783$) who were said to have received counselling, and to have consented, did not return for their results. This is an intriguing finding. It may well be that such women have little understanding or power to refuse, but they can make their personal decision by avoiding test results.

Some studies do not differentiate sufficiently between the notions of informed consent and counselling. Pre-test counselling presumes that the decision to test has not already been made, that women have the option to be tested or not and that no discrimination will be based on the test outcome. If these criteria are not met, then counselling simply has not occurred. Patient education and informed consent, though lofty exercises in their own right, must not be confused with counselling in the true sense of the word. Thus many studies which report on 'counselling for HIV testing' are perpetuating inaccuracies. True choice may be elusive, and there may be elements of coercion or subtle persuasion which affect whether women proceed to HIV testing. It is crucial to understand that counselling implies a process whereby options are examined and a client comes to a decision. Some studies describe counselling during labour. It is difficult to imagine how the women could concentrate at such a time, let alone the physical difficulties of counselling during contractions.

Studies carried out on infant blood can indicate maternal infection. Routine blood samples are collected in the UK for Guthrie tests (these indicate the presence or absence of phenyl-ketonurea which can be treated by dietary adjustments to avoid cognitive deficits). Peckham et al. (1989) tested 115,000 samples discarded after Guthrie testing in inner and outer London. The response rate was high (in excess of 98 per cent of children were screened) and 1 in 2,000 was found to be HIV positive. Yet a few months later the UK government instituted another study to screen pregnant women, thus duplicating data. The latter study did not include funding for pre- and post-test counselling nor did it include funding to train midwives to carry out such counselling. Subsequently, a second seroprevalence study has been carried out on Guthrie blood (Ades et al., 1991; Tappin, 1991) which has tracked a fourfold increase of HIV infection in this London population over the 18-month period. It seems that epidemiological data are now available and duplicate studies serve little end. Funding should now be channelled into counselling, care and prevention.

Were They Pushed or Did They Fall?

As many women attend antenatal clinics anyway, and provide blood samples for other tests, it is easy to include them in seroprevalence studies. Barbacci et al. (1991) compared HIV rates in a group of pregnant women coming forward for HIV testing with a group who declined. The latter had samples of their blood, which were provided for other purposes, tested for HIV antibodies. Despite the fact that these workers reported measures to protect the anonymity of such samples (for example, by removing labels), it is worth noting that Stevens and co-workers (1989) found a high proportion of their sample stated that they "would mind" if their blood was taken and used in such a way. Ethical procedures and the rights of women need much greater examination in this grey area of practice.

Many studies in the USA have shown that high-risk women refuse to participate because they actively choose not to know their sero-status, because they fear that their health care will be wanting if found to be HIV positive, for fear that they will be persuaded to consider termination of pregnancy or for fear that they will be excluded from health care in the first place.

Passive maternal antibody can cross the placenta into the infants' bloodstream. Infants can take up to 2 years to shed such maternal antibody (European Collaborative Study, 1991). The unique situation arises where a woman does not have total control of her own antibodies, some of which now flow in the blood of her infant who may be tested to give results on the mother. When the mother herself is the legal guardian of the child, test permission may be within her right, but when the child is in alternative care the rights of the mother may be limited despite the fact that the test on the infant blood will provide information on her sero-status. This situation may arise when a child is placed in formal care by court proceedings, especially common in the UK where mothers are involved in drug use.

Why Test?

There are invariably advantages and limitations to any testing procedure. These need to be carefully weighed up before any decision to test. The World Health Organization has a well-documented set of guidelines for all screening tests, the major theme of which is associated with the ability to intervene and act upon the outcome result to good effect. With HIV testing, there are a number of factors under current debate.

Epidemiology

The epidemiological argument for antenatal screening raises difficulties. There are those, on the one hand, who argue that data must be made available in order to track the spread of this virus, to plan services and to anticipate demand. Although these arguments are persuasive, they are incomplete. The call for such data needs to address some of the practical implications of this data gathering. For example, how often should seroprevalence surveys be carried out? How long should they be carried out for? Issues of confidentiality, anonymity and informed consent should go without saying.

At some points, community demand and individual rights are at odds. Clearly, policy must endeavour to protect the individual's rights and to have a degree of certainty about the benefits to the community at large if such rights are to be sacrificed (Kirby, 1989). For example, service planning may need an understanding of the nature and location of spread. Vertical transmission rates – that is, the rate of transmission of HIV from mother to child – can be studied only if large samples are gathered prospectively. Such studies may be of little benefit to individual participants, although they may be useful for future populations.

Prevention

Although prevention has been put forward as a reason for antenatal screening, it is important to know that there is no means available at present either to predict or to prevent vertical transmission. Essentially, 'prevention' refers to termination of pregnancy, and may go hand in hand with hidden agendas of the exclusion of HIV positive pregnant women from care, avoidance, isolation and staff concerns for their own health.

In the best interests of the HIV positive pregnant woman, it is important that staff become knowledgeable about the condition and examine their infection control policies for all women. If staff have a set of guidelines for HIV positive women they may overlook possible infection in those they believe not to be infected. The nature of the virus is such that routine infection control is sufficient and necessary for all women. A double standard of care could place both the woman and the staff at unnecessary risk, not only for HIV but for other transmissible infections such as hepatitis B. Essentially, these precautions involve sensible handling of all blood and body fluids, adequate disposal of skin-piercing instruments and blood containers, sterilization of all equipment and avoidance of re-sheathing of used needles. These guidelines, if applied to all, form the soundest protection known to date. This is especially true in the light of the recent UK anonymous survey which showed that 80 per cent of women who were found to be HIV positive, were not otherwise known and thus were passing through the system undetected and possibly unaware of their own status (Ades et al., 1991).

Monitoring Heterosexual Spread

Heterosexual spread has been recorded from the start of the epidemic. It is unclear to what extent any monitoring of the pregnant population can shed light on this spread. Pregnant women are not representative of the heterosexual population at large. The very fact of their pregnancy indicates that they are practising unsafe (unprotected) sex. Pregnant women differ systematically from the adult population generally and adult women specifically. These very differences may limit the extent to which any data from pregnant women can be generalized. To use such data to monitor disease progression and expression in women is to deprive non-pregnant women of appropriate knowledge of the disease.

Limitations of the Test

Any decision to incorporate testing must address the shortcomings of the tests as they currently stand. False-positive results cause unnecessary pain and anguish, especially if irreversible decisions are based on the test results (such as termination of pregnancy). As more tests are carried out, the numbers of false-positives will increase.

Timing and frequency of the test ought to be resolved if the decision to test has been taken. It is unclear when the virus crosses the placenta (early or late pregnancy) or when the infant can become infected (pregnancy, labour or post-partum). Thus testing may need to be repeated. If termination is a realistic option, testing needs to be done early enough in the pregnancy for a safe termination to be possible. Most workers agree that this should be before 16 weeks' gestation. The clarity of decisions are further blurred by the 'window period' where a recently infected woman may test negative despite infection as antibody takes up to 12 weeks to be present in sufficient quantities to allow for detection. Indeed, data suggest that newly infected women who may well be viraemic have a higher incidence of vertical transmission. As most women continue to have sex, rarely protected, during pregnancy, infection during this nine-month period cannot be ruled out. Clearly, HIV testing 12 weeks after each unprotected episode of sex is impractical and unworkable.

Why the Woman?

One interesting question is why should the pregnant woman be tested and not her heterosexual partner? If a man is HIV positive the very act of conception is capable of transmitting HIV. Individuals can become pregnant from a one-off sexual encounter and they can become infected with HIV in a single exposure too. Such a scenario would suggest HIV testing of the father, yet this is not raised as an option in any clinics worldwide.

It is also known that HIV has high affinity for sperm cells but there are no data on the natural history of children born to HIV positive fathers and HIV negative mothers. The absence of paternal screening fails even to identify whether such a group exists.

There are no data on the dual impact of HIV (both parents HIV positive) compared to a single impact (one parent positive and one negative). It seems that the question has not been thoroughly thought through and that during pregnancy women are tested on the basis of the 'sitting duck theory'. Like Mount Everest, they are simply there.

'Testing Testing': The Effects of HIV Screening of Pregnant Women

There is a vociferous literature on the limitations of antenatal screening in general (Chalmers et al., 1989), on the psychological costs of such screening (Farrant, 1980; Garcia, 1982; Marteau, 1989; Reading and Cox, 1982; Sherr, 1989c) and the efficacy of such procedures (Hall and Chng, 1972). This literature is of considerable importance when contemplating HIV testing in pregnancy. Although HIV testing can be viewed as another screening test, women argue that it is like no other test in that it not only reflects on potential life-threatening illness to their baby, but it also marks maternal infection (and possibly paternal infection as well).

Women are often subjected to a battery of antenatal tests which they find difficult to deal with. Great caution should be exercised to ensure that HIV testing is not simply added to this battery. Perhaps it is of greater importance to identify possible risky behaviours and to provide counselling for pregnant women on risk reduction and future protection. Of the few studies which have monitored counselling and testing in pregnant women (Barbacci et al., 1989a, n = 89; Ciraru-Vigneron et al., 1987, n = 60; Irion et al., 1990, n = 47; Johnston et al., 1989, n = 163; Kiragu et al., 1990, n = 108; Selwyn et al., 1989a, n = 64; Selwyn et al., 1989b, n = 191; Sunderland et al., 1988, n = 177; Wiznia et al., 1989, n = 22), the majority examine termination of pregnancy as the outcome measure, while only one (Kiragu et al., 1990) looked at condom use.

A woman attending for antenatal care may be exceedingly vulnerable (Oakley, 1980). She is in a strange environment, she may be subjected to many confusing and humiliating procedures (Cartwright, 1979), she is concerned for the well-being of herself and her baby and may have little say in the process of care (Garcia, 1982). Choice may be difficult. Truly informed choice is dependent on at least full and accurate knowledge, control over her own future and the power to stand up for her decisions. Thus the provision of comprehensive information is a prerequisite if informed consent is to be a reality (Sherr, 1991).

Few women are questioned as to what they would desire. Some studies have reported high acceptability of HIV testing generally (Larsson et al., 1990; Moatti et al., 1990). However, when surveys question women about their personal preferences, rather than the acceptability of testing generally, they find a greater reticence with regard to HIV testing (Stevens et al., 1989).

Problems with Implementing HIV Screening

All testing should be preceded by training of staff who are involved in the testing procedure. Often staff are not skilled in counselling techniques, or even conversant with the basic knowledge and facts about AIDS and HIV infection. Sherr (1987) showed areas of ignorance, overestimations of vertical transmission and confusion about infection control and HIV transmission in obstetric and gynaecology staff.

The sheer size of the pregnant population may render any attempt to provide individual counselling useless. Some attempts have been made to provide alternatives. In London, a series of information pamphlets has been developed. However, these were often problematic in themselves and were seen as an adjunct to counselling rather than a substitute (Sherr and Hedge, 1990). The limitations of written material should be taken into account before such techniques are adopted as the panacea. Readability is often low as material is presented in complex technical language interspersed with jargon. Such material may contain bias, gaps, inaccuracies and fail to address some key elements. Furthermore, written materials, by their nature, preclude interactive dialogue which is often necessary to allay fears, to personalize the messages, to address misunderstandings and inaccuracies and to provide reassurance.

The framing of advice may have profound implications on decision-making (Marteau, 1989). Sherr and colleagues (reported in Sherr, 1991) showed that negative framing of outcome (presenting percentage of infection) was more likely to result in a decision to terminate than positive framing (presenting percentage of non-infection). The provision of information may have little effect on uptake of HIV screening or anxiety about HIV testing. Meadows et al. (1990) showed that the individual health care provider may be a key factor in persuading for or against testing, irrespective of risk levels or hospital policy.

The psychological reactions to HIV testing generally are pro-found (Mansson, 1990). The circumstances of the testing may also play a part in their emotional impact. Tests carried out with no prior consent or knowledge may lead to greater trauma and adjustment than cases where individuals were fully informed and prepared. Pre- and post-test counselling are time-consuming skilled procedures. Indeed, much pre-test counselling is seen as contributing towards behaviour change and risk reduction irrespective of whether the client proceeds to test or not (Higgins et al., 1991; Ostrow, 1990). Counselling has evolved as a part of testing to gain trust, explore risk behaviour, examine behaviour change, address the reasons for undertaking the test, help the client to create coping strategies to deal with all possible outcomes as well as to pace themselves during the agonizing wait for results.

Termination of Pregnancy

Many health workers believe that pregnancy in the presence of HIV should and does lead to termination. This logic is erroneous and shows not only a lack of understanding of women, the societal context in which they live and the nature of childbearing, but also an ignorance of the mass of data which reveals that the majority of pregnant women with HIV go on to deliver. Few terminate (Barbacci, 1989, 1990; Johnston et al., 1989; Selwyn et al., 1989; Wiznia et al., 1989). Those who do terminate are more likely to have had a previous termination, and may well proceed to a subsequent pregnancy (Sunderland et al., 1989).

For those who consider termination, knowledge of the vertical transmission rates is a key element in the decision-making process. The data to hand are mixed and time-limited. It is not only important for carers to be familiar with the data, but also the way they present the data to their clients may have a decided impact on subsequent decisions. Marteau (1989) found that the way information was framed directly affected willingness to consider termination. Alternative frames were provided for pregnant women (Sherr, 1991); for example, 'there is a 25 per cent chance of abnormality' compared to 'there is a 75 per cent chance of normality.' Negative framing with focus on abnormality was more likely to elicit a decision to terminate.

The other option to termination is the avoidance of pregnancy. Yet this carries with it many problems. Women with HIV in the world today tend to be poor, economically and socially disadvantaged and discriminated against. The ethics of imposing birthing limitations on such women fly in the face of the notion that true freedom for women with regard to procreation must be the freedom to bear children with control over the method, circumstances and timing of this act (Katz Rothman, 1986; Wickler, 1986). Counselling can be subtly directive and influence 'choice' if data are presented in biased or distorted ways (Hubbard, 1988).

Vertical Transmission

The chance of vertical transmission of HIV is a key element in any woman's decision to undertake HIV screening or to contemplate

Table 2.3   *Vertical transmission rates of HIV*

Study	Place	n	Vertical transmission rate (%)
Europe			
Blanche et al. (1989)	France	117	27
European Collaborative Study (1991)	Europe	–[1]	12.9
Ippolito et al. (1989)	Italy	660	30
Medbo and Lindemann (1989)	Norway	23	21.7
Mok et al. (1989)	Edinburgh	49	7.1
Tovo (1988)	Italy	89	32.6
Tovo and De Martino (1989)	Italy	231	30
Africa			
Boulos (1990)	Africa	199	23
Delaporte et al. (1988)	Gabon	–	17.6
Hira (1990)	Zambia	227	39
Lallemant et al. (1989)	Congo	–	42
Lepage et al. (1990)	Rwanda	–	33
Pruzuck (1990)	Burkina Faso	23	36–45
Ryder et al. (1989)	Zaire	475	39
South America			
Halsey et al. (1990)	Haiti	–	25
Halsey et al. (1989)	Haiti	154	20–40
Halsey (1990)		443	25
Holt (1990)	Haiti	160	15.4
North America			
Maynard (1989)	Rhode Island	–	31
MMWR (1987)	USA	13	69 (High risk)

[1] Not reported.

pregnancy and its outcome. Improved data are currently available from a number of prospective studies to give some guidance as to the rates of vertical transmission in different settings. Table 2.3 sets out the numerous studies that have provided such data.

From these studies it can be seen that the rates vary for pattern I countries (those where spread was typified early on as between homosexual men as in the USA and Western Europe) and pattern II countries (where spread was typified as heterosexual as in Africa and South America). Vertical transmission in the West is most often reported as 25 per cent or lower, with slightly higher figures, closer to 33 per cent recorded in Africa. Later studies have shown variation which tends to move downwards (for example, the European Collaborative Study (1991) showed a 12.9 per cent vertical transmission rate in its latest report).

The reasons for variation between geographical areas are unclear. It may be length of exposure to the virus, background medical health, nutrition and socioeconomic factors, virus strain or illness progression. The downward trend of vertical transmission rates in studies over time is also difficult to understand. Well children may be lost to follow-up which could inflate the figures. Perhaps over time more comprehensive data will emerge. However, whatever the vertical transmission rate, all studies show that the majority of children will not be infected and that the parents of all children will have an extended period of uncertainty while they wait to know if their child will shed virus or be one of the infected. It is also known that if the infant is infected, progression to AIDS is more rapid than with adults. The mean survival after diagnosis is also shorter than for adults (Peckham et al., 1989). Thus infants fare badly and parents face enormous psychological trauma in the presence of an ill, ailing or dying child.

There is also the problem of competing needs. From the infant's point of view early identification may allow for more efficient management of opportunistic infections and prophylactic treatment. Yet this may be at the cost of maternal trauma. The need to know is complex. As treatment of opportunistic infections improves, decision-making will become more difficult and a balance will be required. The long-term survival impact of prophylactic treatment of opportunistic infections has not been studied.

Vessels and Vectors

All the above data clearly indicate an emerging problem for women. They are viewed as vessels or vectors of HIV. They are placed in a precarious position where their role is defined in terms of their potential to infect another person rather than in the light of their own needs. They are caught in the unique position of having their antibodies open to scrutiny after they leave their own body. The ethics of such procedures are blurred and the rights of pregnant women need to be actively guarded if true protection is to be available.

Counselling for HIV Testing in Pregnancy

It is trite to think that procreation is simply the domain of women (Sherr and Hedge, 1989). Issues surrounding procreation are key

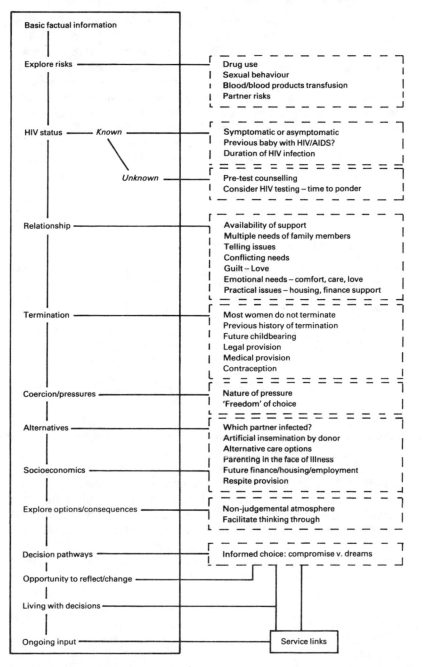

Figure 2.2 *Flow chart showing different decision pathways in counselling for HIV testing in pregnancy.*

elements of HIV antibody test counselling for men and pregnant and non-pregnant women.

Pre-test counselling involves careful exploration of all the issues surrounding the decision to test in a safe, non-judgemental atmosphere. It should allow time for the woman to examine costs and benefits of the test, the availability of management and intervention strategies, and possible outcomes, to understand how she would cope and to explore the mechanisms and support she would require (Sherr, 1991). She needs to weigh up the advantages and hazards of different decision pathways. This process is always supplemented by basic factual information which may have a direct impact on her decisions (Figure 2.2).

Behaviour and Behaviour Change

In addition to the particular issues surrounding the pregnancy, sexual and drug using behaviour and behaviour change can be examined. Much of the counselling time may need to be devoted to an examination of the client's social position and the ease or difficulty with which she can negotiate sex. It is simplistic to think that all women can freely negotiate sex. This is unthinkable for some women and many are torn between their desire to conduct their lives in one way and the reality that faces them, often devoid of options. The notion of choice may be an impossible dream. Other women may well be more in control of their behaviour but may enjoy their lifestyle or have many gains from it which reduce the motivation to alter it.

AIDS and HIV infection do not occur in a vacuum, but are part and parcel of society today. The presence of HIV often changes very little, but serves to enhance or emphasize some of the problems that women face. They are often discriminated against in many strands of their existence – not only sexually, but economically, socially, in employment and in their ability to receive health and welfare services. For women with HIV and AIDS, such issues may surge to the foreground. Women's issues are often ignored in AIDS-related policy and services. For example, it is interesting that all the guidelines in the international press on safe sex make mention of 'unmentionable' items such as condoms, anal sex and even gay sex, yet most omit guidelines specific to women. UK health education material generally does not give women insight into the fact that menstrual blood can transmit HIV. Infected women need specific advice on practical matters such as disposal of sanitary towels and sex during menstruation.

HIV testing in pregnancy may trigger psychological trauma and crisis. Many women experience extreme levels of guilt and anger. They may have agonizing periods of uncertainty which plague their passage through childbirth and early motherhood. This starts with the wait for HIV test results, and proceeds through waiting for symptoms to occur and waiting to see the ultimate HIV status of the baby. Acute anxiety is common and may manifest itself in sudden bursts of panic. Depression can often set in when seropositive women have to contemplate their own future and the fact that their illness may be passed on to their baby or may leave their baby without a parent. Reliance on care providers leaves women out of control. HIV may often be part of other life problems, most notably drugs, relationship trauma, physical or sexual abuse, unemployment, poverty and despair, as E. Anne Lown and her co-writers make clear in Chapter 4.

HIV may mean illness for multiple family members. The illness is often fatal and is compounded by stigma and secrecy. Mok et al. (1989) found that all their subjects kept AIDS a well-guarded secret which limited the emotional and practical support that could be gained from family and peer sources. This leads to reliance on a small number of health care providers.

Conclusion

As the epidemic moves forward, more and more women will be affected by HIV. The speed with which this move can take place should not be underestimated. For example, in Brazil there were no female infections in 1982. By 1984 the ratio of men to women was 120 : 1 and by 1989 this had reached 9 : 1.

HIV in pregnancy may present a situation where the rights of the infant compete with the rights of the mother. Sadly, HIV not only brings with it unique challenges, but also brings out many of the old skeletons in the cupboard. In the face of the limitations of HIV testing, workers need to examine the psychological cost of screening for HIV in pregnancy and to consider if the benefits outweigh the pitfalls. The test in itself is not an end point, but part of total policy. Testing for epidemiological and surveillance purposes has limitations and needs careful implementation to protect the participating individuals. Testing in order to control HIV spread is unproven; it is unclear whether it changes behaviour and it is often carried out at a high psychological cost. Medical treatment and intervention is progressing but still elusive and definitive studies are not yet available.

References

Ades, A., Parker, S., Berry, T., Holland, F., Davison, C., Cubitt, D., Hjelm, M., Wilcox, A., Hudson, C., Briggs, M., Tedder, R. and Peckham, C. (1991) Prevalence of maternal HIV-1 infection in Thames regions: results from anonymous unlinked neonatal testing. *The Lancet* 337, 1562–5.

Adler, M. (1989) *British Medical Journal ABC of AIDS*. London: BMJ.

Aguero, G., Wignall, F.S., Alexander, W. et al. (1987) HIV Infections in Peru. Paper presented at the Third International Conference on AIDS, Washington.

Araneta, M.R., Thomas, P.A., Cedeno, S. et al. (1987) Seroprevalence of HIV I Among Pregnant Women at Time of Birth and Abortion in NYC–87. Paper presented at the Third International Conference on AIDS, Washington.

Barbacci, M. (1989) Identification of HIV Seropositivity during Pregnancy and its Effect on Future Pregnancy Decisions. WHO Conference, Paris.

Barbacci, M. (1990) Paper presented at the Sixth International Conference on AIDS, San Francisco.

Barbacci, M., Chaisson, R., Anderson, J. et al. (1989a) Knowledge of HIV Serostatus and Pregnancy Decisions. Paper presented at the Fifth International Conference on AIDS, Montreal.

Barbacci, M., Quinn, T., Kline, R. et al. (1989b) Failure of Targetted Screening to Identify HIV+ve Pregnant Women. Paper presented at the Fifth International Conference on AIDS, Montreal.

Barbacci, M., Repke, F. and Chaisson, R.E. (1991) Routine prenatal screening for HIV infection. *The Lancet* 337, 709–11.

Barreto, J., Araujo, T., Bergstrom, S. et al. (1987) Comparative study on HIV in pregnant women, Maputo Mozambique 82/83 and 88. Paper presented at the Third International Conference on AIDS, Washington.

Barton, J., O'Connor, T., Cannon, M.J. and Weldon Linne, C.M. (1989) Prevalence of human immunodeficiency virus in a general prenatal population. *American Journal of Obstetrics and Gynecology* 160 (6), 1316–24.

Bayer, R. (1991) AIDS and reproductive freedom. In D. Nelkin, D.P. Willis and S.V. Parris (eds), *A Disease of Society*. Cambridge: Cambridge University Press.

Beck, E., Donegan, C., Cohen, C., Kenny, C., Moss, V., Underhill, G., Terry, P., Jeffries, D., Pinching, A., Miller, D., Cunningham, D. and Harris, W. (1989) Risk factors for HIV Infection in a British population: lessons from a London STD clinic. *AIDS* 3, 533–8.

Berthaud, M., Marcel, A., Sunderland, A. et al. (1987) HIV Infection in Pregnant Haitian Women. Paper presented at the Third International Conference on AIDS, Washington.

Bird, A.G. and Snow, M.H. (1988) HIV monitoring of pregnant women. *The Lancet*, 26 March, 334, 713.

Blanche, S., Rouzioux, C., Gunhard, A. et al. (1989) A prospective study of infants born to women seropositive for Human Immunodeficiency Virus type 1. *New England Journal of Medicine* 320, 1643–8.

Boulos, R. (1989) Paper presented at the Fifth International Conference on AIDS, Montreal.

Boulos, R. (1990) Paper presented at the Sixth International Conference on AIDS, San Francisco.

Boulos, R., Halsey, N., Brutus, J. et al. (1987) Risk factors for HIV I infection in pregnant Haitian women: Paper presented at the Third International Conference on AIDS, Washington.

Boulos, R., Halsey, N., Holt, E., Brutus, J.R., Quinn, T. et al. (1989) Factors associated with HIV 1 in pregnant Haitian Women. WHO Conference, Paris.

Braddick, M., Datta, P., Embree, J. et al. (1987) Progression of IIIV Following Pregnancy. Paper presented at the Third International Conference on AIDS, Washington.

Braddick, M., Kreiss, J., Quinn, T. et al. (1988) Congenital Transmission of HIV in Nairobi, Kenya. Paper presented at the Fourth International Conference on AIDS, Stockholm.

Brattebo, G. and Wiseborg, T. (1988) HIV monitoring of pregnant women. *The Lancet*, 26 March, 713–14.

Brossard, Y., Goudeau, A., Larsen, M. et al. (1987) A Sero Ep Study of HIV in 15,646 Pregnant Women in Paris Feb–Oct 1987. Paper presented at the Third International Conference on AIDS, Washington.

Bucherl, Heiner and Frosner, C.G. (1987) Low Prevalence of HIV I Infection in a Rural Area of Kenya. Paper presented at the Third International Conference on AIDS, Washington.

Cartwright, A. (1979) *The Dignity of Labour*. London: Tavistock.

Cates, W. and Handsfield, H. (1988) HIV counselling and testing: does it work? *American Journal of Public Health* 78, 1533–4.

CDSC (1989) *Communicable Disease Report 1989*, 89/27, 3–4.

Centers for Disease Control (1989) *CDC Surveillance Supplements MMWR*.

Centers for Disease Control (1990) The New Faces of AIDS: A Maternal and Pediatric Epidemic. US Department of Health and Human Services Report, June 1990.

Chalmers, I., Enkin, M. and Keirse, M.J. (1989) *Effective Care in Pregnancy and Childbirth*. Oxford: Oxford University Press.

Chin, J. (1989a) The Economic and Demographic Aspects of HIV Infection in Women and Children. WHO Conference, Paris.

Chin, J. (1989b) Estimates and Projections of Perinatal Transmission of HIV. Paper presented at the Fifth International Conference on AIDS, Montreal.

Chin, J. (1990) Current and future dimensions of the HIV/AIDS pandemic in women and children. *The Lancet* 336, 221–4.

Chiphangwi, J. (1989) Transmission of HIV Infection from Mother to Child in Developing Countries. WHO Conference, Paris.

Chiphangwi, J., Keller, M., Ndovi, E. et al. (1987) Prevalence of HIV I Infection in Pregnant Women in Malawi. Paper presented at the Third International Conference on AIDS, Washington.

Ciraru-Vigneron, N., Nguyen, R., Tan Ung et al. (1987) Prospective Study for HIV Infection among High Risk Pregnant Women. Paper presented at the Third International Conference on AIDS, Washington.

Cleary, P., Singer, E., Rogers, T., Avorn, J., van Devanter, N., Soumerai, S., Perry, S. and Pindyck, J. (1988) Sociodemographic and behavioural characteristics of HIV antibody positive blood donors. *American Journal of Public Health* 78, 953–7.

Coates, T. Morin, S. and McKusick, L. (1988) Long term consequences of AIDS antibody testing on gay and bisexual men. Paper presented at the Fourth International Conference on AIDS, Stockholm.

Delaporte, E. (1990) Paper presented at the Sixth International Conference on AIDS, San Francisco.

Delaporte, E., Dazza, M.C., Wain Hobson, S. et al. (1988) HIV related viruses in pregnant women in Gabon. Paper presented at the Fourth International

Conference on AIDS, Stockholm.

Denayer, M., Jonckheer, T., Piot, P. and Stroobrant, A. (1990) Antenatal testing for HIV. *The Lancet*, 3 February, 292.

De Rossi, A., Chieco Bianchi, L., Giaquinto, C. and Zacchello, F. (1988) HIV monitoring of pregnant women. *The Lancet*, 26 March, 714.

De Rossi, A., Giaquinto, C., Zacchello, F. et al. (1987) Is HIV Testing of Unselected Pregnant Women High Priority in Italy? Paper presented at the Third International Conference on AIDS, Washington.

Duerr (1990) Paper presented at the Sixth International Conference on AIDS, San Francisco.

European Collaborative Study (1988) Mother to child transmission of HIV infection. *The Lancet* 334, 1039–42.

European Collaborative Study (1991) Children born to women with HIV-1 infection. Natural history and risk of transmission. *The Lancet* 337, 253–60.

Farrant, W. (1979) Amniocentesis procedures and correlated stress experience for mothers. Human Relations in Obstetrics Workshop, Warwick.

Farrant, W. (1980) Stress after amniocentesis for high serum alphafeto-protein concentrations. *British Medical Journal* 2, 452.

Garcia, J. (1982) Women's views of antenatal care. In M. Enkin and I. Chalmers (eds), *Effectiveness and Satisfaction in Antenatal Care*. London: Spastics International Medical Publications/Heinemann Medical Books, pp. 81–92.

Goedert, J.J., Mendez, H. and Drummond, J. (1989a) Mother to infant transmission of HIV type 1. *The Lancet*, 9 December, 1334.

Goedert, J.J., Mendez, H., Drummond, J. et al (1989b) Mother to infant transmission of human immunodeficiency virus type 1: association with prematurity or low anti gp 120. *The Lancet*, 9 December, 1351.

Green, J. and McCreaner, A. (1989) *Counselling in AIDS and HIV Infection*. Oxford: Blackwell Scientific Publications.

Green, J. and Miller, D. (1986) *AIDS: The Story of a Disease*. London: Grafton.

Hall, M. and Chng, P.K. (1982) Antenatal care in practice. In M. Enkin and I. Chalmers (eds), *Effectiveness and Satisfaction in Antenatal Care*. London: Spastics International Medical Publications/Heinemann Medical Books.

Halsey, N.A., Townsend, T., Coberly, J. et al. (1987) Seroprevalence of HIV I infection in an obstetrics population. Paper presented at the Third International Conference on AIDS, Washington.

Halsey, N., Boulos, R., Holt, E. et al. (1989) Maternal Infant HIV 1 Infections in a Haitian Slum Population. Paper presented at the WHO Conference on Mothers and Babies, Paris.

Halsey, N.A. et al. (1990) Paper presented at the Sixth International Conference on AIDS, San Francisco.

Harrison, W.O. and More, T.A.L. (1987) Perinatal HIV Screening in a Low Risk Population. Paper presented at the Third International Conference on AIDS, Washington.

Hauer, L.B., Dattell, B.J. and Sweet, R.L. (1987) HIV in Pregnant Women in San Francisco. Paper presented at the Third International Conference on AIDS, Washington.

Higgins, D., Galavotti, C.O., Reilly, K., Schnell, D., Moore, M., Rugg, D. and Johnson, R. (1991) Evidence for the effects of HIV antibody counselling and testing on risk behaviours. *Journal of the American Medical Association* 266 (17), 2419–30.

Hira, S.K. (1990) Paper presented at the Sixth International Conference on AIDS, San Francisco.

Hira, S.K., Kamanga, J., Bhat, G.J., Mwale, C., Tembo, G., Luo, N. and Perine, P.L. (1989) Perinatal transmission of HIV 1 in Zambia. *British Medical Journal* 299, 1250–2.

Hoff, R., Berardi, V., Weiblen, B.J. et al. (1987) HIV seroprevalence in childbearing women. Paper presented at the Third International Conference on AIDS, Washington.

Hoff, R., Berardi, V.P. and Weiblen, B.J. (1988) Seroprevalence of human immunodeficiency virus among childbearing women. *New England Journal of Medicine* 318, 525.

Holman, S., Minkoff, H., Hoegsberg, B., Beller, E. and Goldstein, G. (1988a) Program of routinely offered HIV testing at a prenatal clinic in an urban hospital. Paper presented at the Fourth International Conference on AIDS, Stockholm.

Holman, S., Minkoff, H., Hoegsberg, B., Beller, E. and Goldstein, G. (1988b) A model program for routinely offered HIV antibody testing in pregnancy. Paper presented at the Fourth International Conference on AIDS, Stockholm.

Holman, S., Sunderland, A., Moroso, G. et al. (1987) Multidisciplinary model for HIV testing of pregnant women in a drug treatment program. Paper presented at the Third International Conference on AIDS, Washington.

Holt, E. (1990) Paper presented at the Sixth International Conference on AIDS, San Francisco.

Howard, L.C., Hawkins, D.A., Marwood, R., Shanson, D.C. and Gazzard, B.G. (1989) Transmission of human immunodeficiency virus by heterosexual contact with reference to antenatal screening. *British Journal of Obstetrics and Gynaecology* 96, 135–9.

Hubbard, R. (1988) A Feminist views prenatal diagnosis. *Newsletter of the National Society of Genetic Counselors* 10 (2), 1.

Hull, H.F., Bettinger, C.X.F., Gallaher, M.M., Keller, N.M., Wilson, J. and Mertz, G.J. (1988) Comparison of HIV antibody prevalence in patients consenting to and declining HIV antibody testing in an STD clinic. *Journal of the American Medical Association* 260, 935–8.

Ippolito, G., Stegagno, M., Costa, F., Angeloni, P. et al (1989) Detection of HIV antibodies in newborns: a blind serosurvey in 92 Italian Hospitals. WHO Conference, Paris.

Ippolito, G., Stegagno, M., Angeloni, P. and Guzzanti, E. (1990) Anonymous HIV testing on newborns. *Journal of the American Medical Association* 263 (1), 36.

Irion, O., Rapin, R., Taban, F. and Beguin, F. (1990) Voluntary screening of HIV infection in all pregnant women. Paper presented at the Sixth Conference on AIDS, San Francisco.

Jenum, P.A., Tjotta, E.A. and Orstavik, I. (1987) Anti HIV Screening of Pregnant Women in South Eastern Norway. Paper presented at the Third International Conference on AIDS, Washington.

Johnson, J.P., Alger, L., Nair, P. et al. (1988) HIV Screening in the High Risk Obstetric Population and Infant Serologic Analysis. Paper presented at the Fourth International Conference on AIDS, Stockholm.

Johnston, F.D., Brettle, R., MacCallum, L., Mok, J., Peutherer, J. and Burns, S. (1989) Women's knowledge of their HIV antibody state: its effect on their decision whether to continue the pregnancy. *British Medical Journal* 300, 23–4.

Johnston, F.D., MacCallum, L.R., Brettle, R.P. et al. (1988) Does infection with

HIV affect the outcome of pregnancy? *British Medical Journal* 296, 467.

Kantanen, M.L., Cantell, K., Aho, K. et al. (1987) Screening for HIV Antibody during Pregnancy in Finland. Paper presented at the Third International Conference on AIDS, Washington.

Kantanen, M.L., Cantell, K., Aho, K., Brink, A. and Ponka, A. (1988) Screening for HIV antibody during pregnancy. *Serodiagnosis and Immunotherapy in Infectious Disease* 2, 113–15.

Kanti, P., Ricard, D., MBoup, S. et al. (1987) Perinatal Transmission of HIV-2. Paper presented at the Third International Conference on AIDS, Washington.

Kaptue, L., Durand, J.P., Zekeng, L. et al. (1987) HIV Serosurvey in Cameroon. Paper presented at the Third International Conference on AIDS, Washington.

Katz Rothman, B. (1986) *The Tentative Pregnancy*. New York: Viking Press.

Kiragu, D., Temmerman, M., Wamola, I., Plummer, F. and Piot, P. (1990) Counseling of women with HIV infection. Paper presented at the Sixth International Conference on AIDS, San Francisco.

Kirby, M. (1989) Paper presented at the Fifth International Conference on AIDS, Montreal.

Kozlov, A. (1990) First cases of HIV 1 in Leningrad, USSR. Paper presented at the Sixth International Conference on AIDS, San Francisco.

Lallemant, M. (1989) Étude prospective de la transmission mère enfant d'HIV à Brazzaville, Congo. WHO Conference, Paris.

Lallemant, M., Lallemant, S., Cheyneir, D. et al. (1987) HIV 1 infection in an urban population of Congolese pregnant women. Paper presented at the Third International Conference on AIDS, Washington.

Lallemant, M., Lallemant, S., Cheyneir, D. et al. (1989) Mother–child transmission of HIV 1 and infant survival in Brazzaville, Congo. *AIDS* 3, 643–6.

Landesman, S., Holman, S., McCalla, S. et al. (1988) HIV Sero-survey of Post-partum Women at a Municipal Hospital in NYC. Paper presented at the Fourth International Conference on AIDS, Stockholm.

Landesman, S., Minkoff, H., Holman, S. et al. (1987) Serosurvey of human immunodeficiency virus infection in parturients. *Journal of the American Medical Association*, 258, 2701.

Larsson, G., Bohlin, A.B., Forsgren, M. et al. (1987) Experiences of screening for HIV in pregnant women. Paper presented at the Third International Conference on AIDS, Washington.

Larsson, G., Spangberg, L., Lindgren, S. and Bohlin, A.B. (1990) Screening for HIV in pregnant women: a study of maternal opinion. *AIDS Care* 2 (3), 223–8.

Lepage, P. (1990) Paper presented at the VI Int. AIDS Conference, San Francisco. Abstract no. THC 659.

Lindgren, S., Anzen, B., Bohlin, A.B. et al. (1987) HIV Infection in Pregnant Women and their Children in Sweden. Paper presented at the Third International Conference on AIDS, Washington.

Lindsay, M.K., Peterson, H.B., Feng, T.I., Slade, B.A. et al. (1989) Routine antepartum human immunodeficiency virus infection screening in an inner city population. *Obstetrics and Gynecology* 3 (1), 289–94.

Lo, B., Steinbrook, R.L., Cooke, M., Coates, T.J., Walters, E.J., Hulley, S.B. (1989) Voluntary screening for HIV infection: weighing the benefits and harms. *Annals of Internal Medicine*, 110, 727–33.

Makawa, M., Miehakanda, J., Silou, I. et al. (1987) Seroepidemiology of HIV 1 and HIV 2 Infections in Pregnant Women. Paper presented at the Third International Conference on AIDS, Washington.

Mansson, S.A. (1990) Psychosocial aspects of HIV testing: the Swedish case. *AIDS Care* 2 (1), 5–17.

Marteau, T.M. (1989) Psychological costs of screening. *British Medical Journal* 299, 527.

Marzuk, P.M., Tierney, N., Tardiff, K. et al. (1988) Increased risk of suicide in persons with AIDS. *Journal of the American Medical Association* 259, 1333–7.

Maynard, E.C. (1989) HIV infection in pregnant women in Rhode Island. *New England Journal of Medicine* 320 (24), 1626.

McCusker, J., Stoddard, A., Mayer, K., Zapka, J., Morrison, C. and Saltzman, S. (1988) Effects of HIV antibody test knowledge on subsequent sexual behaviour in a cohort of homosexually active men. *American Journal of Public Health* 78, 462–7.

Meadows, J., Jenkinson, S., Catalan, J. and Gazzard, B. (1990) Voluntary HIV testing in the antenatal clinic: differing uptake rates for individual counselling midwives. *AIDS Care* 2 (3), 229–33.

Medbo, S. and Lindemann, R. (1989) Infants born of HIV Positive Women in Norway. Paper presented at WHO Conference, Paris.

Mendez, H. (1989) Natural history of infants born to HIV 1 seropositive mothers and their seronegative controls. WHO Conference, Paris.

Mendez, H., Willoughby, A., Hittleman, J. et al. (1987) Infants of HIV seropositive women and their seronegative controls. Paper presented at the Third International Conference on AIDS, Washington.

Miller, D. (1987) Paper presented at the International AIDS Conference, Washington USA.

Miller, D., Jeffries, D.J., Green, J., Harris, J.R.W. and Pinching, A.J. (1986) HTLV-III: should testing ever be routine? *British Medical Journal* 292, 941–3.

Miller, D. and Pinching, A.J. (1989) HIV tests and counselling: current issues. *AIDS* 3 (1), 3187–93.

Miller, D., Weber, J. and Green, J. (1986) *Management of AIDS Patients*. Basingstoke: Macmillan.

Minkoff, H.L. and DeHovitz, J.A. (1991) Care of women infected with the human immunodeficiency virus. *Journal of the American Medical Association* 266 (16), 2253–8.

Moatti, J.P., Gales, C., Seror, V., Papiernik, E. and Henrion, R. (1990) Social acceptability of HIV screening among pregnant women. *AIDS Care* 2 (3), 213–22.

Mok, J., Hague, R.A., Yap, P.L. et al. (1989) Vertical transmission of HIV: A prospective study. *Archives of Disease in Childhood* 64, 1140–5.

Morbidity and Mortality Weekly Reports (1987) 11 September, 36 (35), 593–5.

Ndugwa, C. et al. (1990) Paper presented at the Sixth International Conference on AIDS, San Francisco.

Nesheim, S.R., Jones, D.S., Sawyer, M.K. and Nahmias, A.J. (1989) The natural history of HIV infection in a population based cohort of infants born to HIV positive women: the first two years. WHO Conference, Paris.

Novick, B.E. and Rubinstein, A. (1987) AIDS – the paediatric perspective. *AIDS* 1, 3–7.

Novick, L.F., Berns, D., Stricof, R. et al. (1989) HIV seropravelence in newborns in New York State. *Journal of the American Medical Association* 261, 1745–50.

Nsa, W., Ryder, R., Baende, E. et al. (1987) Mortality from Perinatally Acquired HIV Infections in African Children. Paper presented at the Third International Conference on AIDS, Washington.

Ntabab, H.M., Liomba, C.N., Schmidt, H.J. et al. (1987) HIV I Prevalence in Hospital Patients and Pregnant Women in Malawi. Paper presented at the Third International Conference on AIDS, Washington.

Nzilambi, N., Ryder, R.W., Behets, F. et al. (1987) Perinatal HIV Transmission in Two African Hospitals. Paper presented at the Third International Conference on AIDS, Washington.

Nzilambi, N., Ryder, R., Behets, F. et al. (1988) Perinatal HIV Transmission in Two African Hospitals. Paper presented at the Fourth International Conference on AIDS, Stockholm.

Oakley, A. (1980) *Women Confined: Towards a Sociology of Childbirth.* Oxford: Martin Robertson.

Ostrow, D. (1990) *Behavioural Aspects of AIDS.* London: Plenum Medical Press.

Ostrow, D., Monjan, A. and Joseph, J. (1989) HIV related symptoms and psychological functioning in a cohort of homosexual men. *American Journal of Psychiatry* 146, 737–42.

Peckham, C., Tedder, R.S., Briggs, M., Ades, A., Hjelm, M., Wilcox, A., Parramjejia, N. and O'Connor, C. (1989) Prevalence of maternal HIV infection based on unlinked anonymous testing of newborn babies. *The Lancet,* 335, 516–19.

Pista, A. et al. (1990) Prevalence of HIV 1 and 2: 3 year study. Paper presented at the Fourth International Conference on AIDS, Stockholm.

Pokrovsky, V.V. (1990) Paper presented at the Sixth International Conference on AIDS, San Francisco.

Pruzuck, A. (1990) Paper presented at the Sixth International Conference on AIDS, San Francisco.

Reading, A. and Cox, D. (1982) The effects of ultrasound examination on maternal anxiety levels. *Journal of Behavioural Medicine.*

Rogers, M.F., White, C.R., Sanders, R. et al. (1990) Lack of transmission of human immunodeficiency virus from infected children to their household contacts. *Pediatrics* 85, 210–14.

Ryder, R.W. (1989) Perinatal Transmission of the HIV type 1 to Infants of Seropositive Women in Zaire. WHO Conference, Paris.

Ryder, R.W., Nsa, W., Hassig, S.E. et al. (1989) Perinatal transmission of HIV type 1 to infants of seropositive women in Zaire. *New England Journal of Medicine* 320, 1637–42.

Sangare, L. et al. (1989) Statut sérologique population prostituées au Burkina Fasso THG026. Paper presented at the Fifth International Conference on AIDS, Montreal.

Schoenbaum, E.E., Davenny, K. and Selwyn, P.A. (1988) The impact of pregnancy on HIV related disease. *Royal College of Obstetrics and Gynaecology,* 65–75.

Scott, G. (1989) Natural History of HIV in Children. Paper presented at the Fifth International Conference on AIDS, Montreal.

Scott, G., Fischl, M.A., Klimas, N. et al. (1985) Mothers of infants with the acquired immunodeficiency syndrome. *Journal of the American Medical Association* 253, 363–6.

Scott, G., Hutto, C. et al. (1987) Probability of Perinatal Infections in Infants of HIV 1 Positive Mothers. Paper presented at the Third International Conference on AIDS, Washington, DC.

Scott, G.B., Hutto, C., Makuch, R.W., Mastrucci, M., O'Connor, T., Mitchell, C., Trapido, E. and Parks, W.P. (1989) Survival in children with perinatally acquired human immunodeficiency virus type 1 infection. *New England Journal of Medicine* 321 (26), 1791–6.

Selwyn, P.A., Carter, R.J., Schoenbaum, E.E. et al. (1989) Knowledge of HIV antibody status and decision to continue or terminate pregnancy among intravenous drug users. *Journal of the American Medical Association* 261, 3567–71.

Selwyn, P.A., Schoenbaum, E.E., Davenny, K. et al. (1989) Prospective study of HIV infection and pregnancy outcomes in intravenous drug users. *Journal of the American Medical Association* 261, 1289–94.

Sherr, L. (1987) The impact of AIDS in obstetrics on obstetric staff. *Journal of Reproductive and Infant Psychology* 5, 87–96.

Sherr, L. (1989a) Changes in the impact of AIDS in obstetric staff. WHO Conference, Paris.

Sherr, L. (1989b) The psychosocial cost of HIV screening in antenatal clinics. WHO Conference, Paris.

Sherr, L. (1989c) Anxiety and Communication in Obstetrics. Unpublished PhD thesis, Warwick University.

Sherr, L. (1991) *HIV and AIDS in Mothers and Babies*. Oxford: Blackwell Scientific Publications.

Sherr, L., Davey, T. and Strong, C. (1990) Counselling implications of anxiety and depression in AIDS and HIV infection. *Counselling Psychology Quarterly* 4 (1), 27–35.

Sherr, L. and Hedge, B. (1989) On becoming a mother: counselling implications for mothers and fathers. WHO Conference, Paris.

Sherr, L. and Hedge, B. (1990) The impact and use of written leaflets as a counselling alternative in mass antenatal HIV screening. *AIDS Care* 2 (3), 235–45.

Sherr, L., Jeffries, S., Victor, C. and Chase, A. (in preparation) HIV testing challenges for GP antenatal attenders.

Sperling, R.S., Sacks, H.S., Mayer, L., Joyner, M. and Berkowitz, R.L. (1989) Umbilical cord blood serosurvey for HIV in parturient women in a voluntary hospital in New York City. *Obstetrics and Gynecology* 73 (2), 179–81.

Stevens, A., Victor, C. and Sherr, L. (1990) Antenatal testing for HIV. *The Lancet*, 3 February, 292.

Stevens, A., Victor, C., Sherr, L. and Beard, R. (1989) HIV testing in antenatal clinics: the impact on women. *AIDS Care* 1 (2), 165–71.

Sunderland, A., Moroso, G., Berthaud, M., Holman, S., Landesman, S., Minkoff, H. et al. (1988) Influence of HIV Infection on Pregnancy Decisions. Paper presented at the Fifth International Conference on AIDS, Montreal.

Sunderland, A., Moroso, G., Holman, S. et al. (1989) Influence of HIV Infection on Pregnancy Decisions. Paper presented at the Fifth International Conference on AIDS, Montreal.

Tappin, D., Girdwood, R., Follett, E. et al. (1991) Prevalence of maternal HIV infection in Scotland based on unlinked anonymous testing of newborn babies. *The Lancet* 337, 565–7.

Tovo, P.A. (1988) Epidemiology, clinical features and prognostic factors of paediatric HIV infection. *The Lancet* ii, 1043–6.

Tovo, P.A. and De Martino, M. (1989) The Italian Register for HIV Infection in Children: Epidemiological and Clinical Results. WHO Conference, Paris.

Van Lith, J.M., Tijmstra, T. and Visser, G. (1989) The attitudes of pregnant women to HIV testing. *Nederlands Tijd. Gen* 133 (25), 1273–7.

Virnon, D., Bernard, N., Melchoir, J. et al. (1987) Anti HIV 1 Screening in Pregnant Women: A Prospective Study. Paper presented at the Third International Conference on AIDS, Washington, DC.

Vranx, R., Alisjahbana, A., Deville, W. et al. (1987) Anti HIV Prevalence in Indonesia. Paper presented at the Third International Conference on AIDS, Washington, DC.

Wang, Q., Hardy, W., Chein, N. et al. (1987) A Preliminary Serologic Screening for Retrovirus Infection in Sichuan Province of the People's Republic of China. Paper presented at the Third International Conference on AIDS, Washington, DC.

Wenstrom, K.D. and Zuidema, L.J. (1989) Determination of the seroprevalence of HIV infection in gravidas by non-anonymous versus anonymous testing. *Obstetrics and Gynecology* 74 (4), 558–61.

Wickler, N. (1986) Society's response to the new reproductive technologies: the feminist perspective. *South California Law Review* 59 (5), 1043–57.

Wiznia, A., Bueti, C., Douglas, C. et al. (1989) Factors Influencing Maternal Decision-making Regarding Pregnancy Outcome in HIV Infected Women. Paper presented at the Fifth International Conference on AIDS, Montreal.

World Health Organization (1990) *The Global AIDS Situation Updated*. Information Sheet no 68.

Zohoun, I., Bigot, A., Sankale, J.L. et al. (1987) Prevalence of HIV 1 and HIV 2 in Benin. Paper presented at the Third International Conference on AIDS, Washington, DC.

PART II
HIV TRANSMISSION RISK

Psychologists have instigated a large number of studies to find out what women know about HIV/AIDS, to inform them about sexual and drug use practices which carry a low risk of HIV transmission, to produce in them more positive attitudes to these practices and to encourage implementation of the practices. Programmes designed to change practices often concentrate on imparting knowledge or skills, such as the use of condoms, and how to clean drug injection equipment, or works, with bleach and water. More complex programmes focus on women's psychological states, looking at the relationship between these and behaviour, deploying models of the attitude–behaviour relationship often abstracted from other 'health behaviours', like smoking, and trying to raise levels of, for instance, personal efficacy. From this perspective, women's doubts about themselves and their ability to change their practices are likely to impede behaviour change, but these attitudes are open to change, and the change process and its behavioural effects are measurable. A large set of assumptions is operating here: most important, perhaps, is the assumption that, ultimately, psychological factors determine the safety of sexual practices and drug use.

Psychological programmes for attitude and behaviour change also tend to gloss over women's own knowledge of AIDS/HIV, which is often considerable. 'High-risk' women have good knowledge of transmission risks, for instance (Mandell, 1991), and female sex workers were the first to point out that nonoxynol-9, a spermicide which inhibits HIV growth in the test tube, was also associated with potentially HIV-transmitting vaginal lesions (Bird, 1991).

Psychological interventions in attitudes and behaviour also try to change socially established and intensely felt attitudes about, for instance, the unacceptability of condom use and other safer sex practices, or the positive meaning of 'unsafe' sex or sharing works, at an individual and rational level. Often this is too simple. Condoms have different meanings for different women.[1] Even for the same woman, the meanings may change; studies of gay men have shown that there can be 'slipping' even among those highly committed to condom use. Moreover, the value of more emotionally involving and community-orientated programmes has been well documented: for instance, HIV education through encouraging story-telling within families (Bracho de Carpio et al., 1990), using drama and follow-up discussions with young women and men (Frankham, 1991), constituting community opinion leaders as health educators (Kelly et al., 1991) or making safer sex part of a programme aimed at eventual healthy conception (Wells, 1991).

Psychological interventions may also adopt a standard of 'good' communication about sexuality that pays no attention to the varying sexual vernaculars which women use (Patton, 1991), or to the possibility that women rely more on interpersonal and less on media learning about HIV than men (Centers for Disease Control, 1991). And intervention programmes rarely offer help with all the material factors which may inhibit change, such as the cost of condoms; the cost and availability of new drug works and cleaning agents; the lack of drug treatment facilities, especially for pregnant women;[2] and women's lack of social and economic power in heterosexual relationships and in drug-using communities. Women, like men, are not just gendered subjects. They have a variety of competing social and personal interests, and they have to negotiate between these. This does not make it easy for psychological interventions to have predictable effects – or indeed any effects – on thinking and practices around HIV and AIDS.

In this section, Sherry Deren and her colleagues (Chapter 3) describe an HIV risk reduction project conducted with women who were IVDUs or heterosexual partners of IVDUs which foregrounds some of these problems. The two interventions used, information provision and practical and negotiation skills training, were both associated with reported changes in women's risky practices. These changes were not general enough to cause complacency. Moreover, scoring high on psychological well-being was not correlated with reducing risky practices. Clearly, to pose a psychologically empowering cognitive change like 'increased personal efficacy' as the answer to high HIV risk practices is to neglect the disempowering social constraints with which many women live. Deren and her co-writers also note that behaviour change associated with the interventions cannot easily be separated from changes caused simply by being in the study, by general social concern about AIDS and by new social expectations about responsible drug use and sexual practices, particularly in New York, where the study was done. Feeling good about yourself was not even a *result* of behaviour change; the women reported lower psychological well-being along with their lower-risk practices, and this has to be seen, Deren and her co-writers suggest, in the context of a worsening AIDS problem within the community and among the women themselves, against which the women's changed lifestyle may have counted, subjectively speaking, for little.

Women crack cocaine users are perhaps the women most pathologized as 'infected' with AIDS, but there is very little psychological research about women who use crack. E. Anne Lown and her co-writers (Chapter 4) adopt an ethnographic method of 'social-sexual history' interviewing in order to hear the voices of women crack users. They refuse a pathologized picture of 'crack-heads'. Instead, they analyse the gendering of sexual power in crack culture, and the stigmatized place of women crack users, concentrating especially on the denigration of women who participate in 'tossin'', sex-for-drugs exchanges. Women crack users' neglect of HIV and AIDS issues appears here in the context of the 'traumatization' of poor US inner-city communities. In such circumstances, HIV and AIDS will often have low priority in the lives of women. And for women crack users, whose survival is even more problematic, ignoring the conditions or denying their relevance may be a strategy that allows them to survive.

Lown's and her colleagues' documentation of the intense difficulty of some women's lives indicates the distance which separates the women they studied from the young white college women who have been the main participants in psychological studies of women's AIDS-related attitudes and behaviours. But much of what emerges from detailed and careful psychological research about women thought to be at risk, as from the studies in this section, applies to women generally. The limited usefulness of psychological models of personal efficacy for predicting sexual and drug practices, for instance, should be recognized by all intervention programmes aimed at women, as should women's sexual stigmatization, their lesser sexual, social and economic power, and the effects of these disparities on their ability to have safer sex. The distancing strategies that women crack users deploy around HIV and AIDS issues are called on by many other women. Jo Frankham (1991), for instance, describes young rural British women using distancing, 'it couldn't happen to us' arguments. The AIDS-related problems that women IV and crack users and women partners of male IVDUs face, then, and how they address them, are often similar to the problems and strategies of many other women who have no contact with IV drugs or crack and who are distinguished from them by class, 'race' or geography. It is important to recognize these commonalities at a time when cultural discourse on AIDS persistently asserts the risky nature of being some kinds of women, while gracing other women with absolute freedom from risk.

Notes

1   For many women who identify as lesbians, condoms are irrelevant to their sexual practices. Some young women who have sex with men view condoms primarily in terms of their contraceptive efficiency (Frankham, 1991), while for other young women less concerned about pregnancy their implications for sexuality are more important (Levinson, 1991). Among female sex workers in Seattle, African American women made judgements about condom use on the basis of what sex acts were involved, while white and Latina women looked at the client (Fishbein, 1991).
2   Some of the material factors affecting safer drug use are discussed in Des Jarlais and Friedman (1988) and Brettle (1991).

References

Bird, K. (1991) The uses of spermicide containing nonoxynol-9 in the prevention of HIV infection. *AIDS* 5, 791–6.
Bracho de Carpio, A., Carpio-Cedraro, F. and Anderson, L. (1990) Hispanic families learning and teaching about AIDS. *Hispanic Journal of Behavioural Sciences* 12, 165–76.
Brettle, K. (1991) HIV and harm reduction for injecting drug users. *AIDS* 5, 126–36.
Centers for Disease Control (1991) HIV infection prevention messages for injecting drug users: sources of information and uses of mass media – Baltimore, 1989. *Morbidity and Mortality Weekly Reports* 40 (28), 19 July.
Des Jarlais, D. and Friedman, S. (1988) The psychology of preventing AIDS among intravenous drug users: a social learning conception. *American Psychologist* 43, 865–70.
Fishbein, M. (1991) Commercial Sex Workers' Beliefs about Condom Use. Paper presented at the American Psychological Association Annual Conference, San Francisco, August.
Frankham, J. (1991) 'AIDS – it's like one of those things that you read in the newspapers . . . it doesn't happen to you'. In J. Shostak (ed.), *Youth in Trouble: Educational Responses*. London: Kogan Page.
Kelly, J., St Lawrence, J., Diaz, Y., Stevenson, Y., Hauth, A., Brasfield, T., Kalichman, S., Smith, J. and Andrew, M. (1991) HIV Risk Behaviour Reduction Following Interventions with Key Opinion Leaders of Populations: an Experimental Study. Paper presented at the American Psychological Association Annual Conference, San Francisco, August.
Levinson, R. (1991) Contraceptive Self-efficacy: Implications for Sex Education Interventions. Paper presented at the American Psychological Association Annual Conference, San Francisco, August.
Mandell, W. (1991) Social-environmental Factors that Control Health Behaviour. Paper presented at the American Psychological Association Annual Conference, San Francisco, August.
Patton, C. (1991). Safe sex and the pornographic vernacular. In Bad Object-Choices (ed.), *How Do I Look? Queer Film and Video*. Seattle: Bay Press.
Wells, Y. (1991) Increasing Safer Sex Behaviour among Minority Women. Paper presented at the American Psychological Association Annual Conference, San Francisco, August.

3

An AIDS Risk Reduction Project With Inner-city Women

Sherry Deren, Stephanie Tortu and W. Rees Davis

As of October 1991, there were 20,309 AIDS cases reported for women in the United States, representing approximately 10 per cent of the adult AIDS cases (Centers for Disease Control, 1991). This has increased from a rate of 6–7 per cent of adult cases in the early and mid-1980s (Guinan and Hardy, 1987). The two highest risk categories for women are intravenous drug use (accounting for 51 per cent of the cases for women) and heterosexual contact with an intravenous drug user (21 per cent).

As a result of high rates of intravenous drug use (New York State Division of Substance Abuse Services, 1989), the Harlem community in New York City has one of the highest rates of AIDS in New York. As of December 1991, the AIDS rate per 100,000 adults in Harlem was 1,252 (New York State Department of Health, 1991). The project described in this chapter was undertaken in Harlem as a research/demonstration project to asssess the efficacy of an AIDS risk reduction intervention strategy, targeting intravenous drug users and their sexual partners, and incorporating special efforts to recruit women.

The Harlem Community

The Harlem community is located in upper Manhattan, just above Central Park. It is primarily an African American residential community, though there is also a large number of Puerto Ricans living in East Harlem. A gradual movement of African Americans into Harlem began at the turn of the century when extensive redevelopment in the area west of Herald Square forced them out of their homes. Then, during the 1920s and 1930s, African American migrants from the South and African Caribbeans from the West Indies, facing discrimination in other areas of New York, poured into Harlem. Thus was created a well-known, vibrant community and centre of African American culture often referred to as 'The Capital of Black America'.

Today, Harlem suffers from all the problems that are common to poor inner-city neighbourhoods in the US. Though there is a small middle to upper-class community living in new, private apartments or houses, most of the inhabitants live in either public housing or substandard housing (City of New York, 1990). In 1988, the total population was 350,600, of whom almost 30 per cent received some type of income support. In 1989, more than 20 per cent of the births in Central Harlem were to mothers 20 years and under; many young people fail to complete high school; and, among 16 to 19-year-olds, the unemployment rate is currently over 50 per cent (City of New York, 1990). The age-adjusted rate of mortality among African Americans in Central Harlem is the highest in New York City; it is double that of US whites, and 50 per cent higher than US African Americans (McCord and Freeman, 1990). Crime, drug trafficking and drug use are well-entrenched facts of everyday life, and, though the social service and medical needs of this community are enormous, these services are often poorly delivered (City of New York, 1987)

Goals of the Harlem AIDS Project

In 1987, the National Institute on Drug Abuse, in response to the growing incidence of AIDS among intravenous drug users and their sexual partners, created the National AIDS Demonstration and Research (NADR) Projects. These programmes, established in over 60 locations throughout the United States, collected data regarding both drug- and sex-related AIDS risk behaviour from over 50,000 intravenous drug users and their sexual partners. In addition, the programmes tested the efficacy of a variety of intervention techniques designed to reduce the risk of AIDS among members of these risk groups.

The Harlem AIDS Project (HAP) was funded by NIDA in late 1988 as part of the NADR group of programmes, and it began interviewing and providing risk reduction services in May 1989. The project was designed to test the efficacy of an AIDS intervention strategy based on cognitive-behavioural methods of behaviour change.

Previous research has shown that providing information only to subjects at risk of disease has not been greatly successful in modifying risk behaviours. More successful approaches have emphasized a cognitive social learning model of skill development (Botvin et al., 1990), and are based on the recognition that new behavioural skills are best learned in a social context, and correct practice of risk reduction skills increases self-efficacy, a critical factor in successful AIDS prevention efforts (Bandura, 1987).

Building on a foundation of AIDS information, the intervention emphasized the demonstration, guided practice, and corrective feedback of the behavioural skills needed by intravenous drug users and their sex partners in order to reduce their risk of AIDS (Bandura, 1990). The skills taught included needle cleaning, condom use and negotiation strategies. The psychological goals of the enhanced intervention were: to increase personal awareness of AIDS risk; to assist clients in the development of the skills needed to reduce AIDS risk; to increase self-efficacy regarding the practice of AIDS risk reduction skills; and to help clients learn to apply the skills in high-risk situations. Project participants who received this intervention were compared to those who received AIDS information only, without skill building.

The project recruited both men and women, and made special efforts to work with women by recruiting through street outreach and in the obstetrics and gynaecological clinics of Harlem Hospital, a large community hospital. In this chapter, the project design will be described and preliminary data on the women in the sample will be presented regarding, among other things: demographic characteristics of the women at risk, specific drug- and sex-related risk behaviours compared at baseline and follow-up, and several psychological variables that are hypothesized to have a relationship to AIDS risk behaviours. The public health implications of this work with high-risk women will also be discussed.

Overview of the Research Design

Recruitment
Outreach was conducted both on the streets of Harlem and in the obstetrics and gynaecological clinics of Harlem Hospital. Those eligible for inclusion in the project were either: (a) drug injectors who had used intravenous drugs within the six months before recruitment, but had not been in drug treatment during the previous month; or (b) the sex partners of intravenous drug users, defined as individuals who had sex with IVDUs during the six months before recruitment who themselves had not shot drugs during that time period.

Clients who met these criteria were escorted by an outreach worker to one of three project field offices that were located in Central, West and East Harlem.

Baseline Interview and Intervention Activities
After arriving at the field office, each participant was introduced to an interviewer, and after reviewing and signing the informed

consent, participated in a one-hour baseline interview. Topics covered will be described below. Following the interview, each person received a research stipend of $15, and was introduced to one of the project's health educators. The health educator invited the person to attend the 'Standard' intervention group session, usually held the same day.

The first group session was designed to provide basic information on AIDS transmission and risk reduction. General topics of discussion included modes of transmission and methods of prevention, how to assess one's own level of risk, and an emphasis on the message that AIDS is preventable. The format used in this session was essentially a didactic presentation of facts, along with appropriate discussion questions posed by the health educator. At the end of this session, the clients were randomly assigned to the 'standard' condition (in which case no additional sessions were attended) or the 'enhanced' condition.

Those in the 'enhanced' condition were assigned to attend second and third group sessions. In these sessions, participants learned those specific behaviours which can reduce risk. These behaviours included bleach-based needle cleaning techniques and condom use. In addition, because risk reduction behaviours must usually be introduced into the framework of an existing relationship, instruction in various negotiation techniques was also included. The format used in sessions two and three was one of demonstration of needle cleaning and correct condom use techniques by the health educator. This was followed by practice of these behaviours by the participants. Role plays, with situations suggested by the group members, were used to practise negotiation techniques and to assist clients in learning to apply the skills in high-risk situations.

At the end of the first group session, all clients were told about the availability of a referral service provided by a referral coordinator. Clients who needed assistance with their health or social service needs were encouraged to use the referral service. Clients were also informed that they could meet individually, on a short-term basis, with the health educator for more intensive AIDS risk reduction counselling. A total of 21.5 per cent of the women used the referral services and 5.5 per cent used the risk reduction counselling services, with 3.7 per cent using both services.

Second Interview and 'Booster' Intervention
Approximately six months after the initial interview, clients participated in a second, follow-up interview. Clients were notified by mail when they were due for their second interview. In response to this letter, clients could contact the project by telephone and

make an appointment for their follow-up interview. If the letter produced no response, the outreach team would canvass the neighbourhood and attempt to contact clients through friendship networks, or by visiting known street 'hang outs' and shelters for the homeless.

The follow-up interview included the same topics covered in the baseline interview and focused on assessing whether any changes in risk behaviours had occurred since the initial interview. After the follow-up interview was conducted, clients were invited to participate in 'booster' group sessions to review the material provided in the initial intervention. Those clients who participated in the single 'standard' group were assigned to a standard booster session, which focused on reviewing the information regarding AIDS transmission and prevention. Clients who previously participated in the three 'enhanced' skill-building sessions participated in two 'booster' sessions, which focused on reviewing the behavioural skills previously learned. After the 'booster' session(s), clients were again informed of the availability of the individualized referral and counselling services.

Data Collection

The Baseline Interview The first part of the initial interview consisted of a standard questionnaire used by all NADR projects. It included the following topics:

1 Demographic information.
2 Drug use history and injection drug-related risk behaviours.
3 Drug treatment history and degree of mobility.
4 Sexual practices and sexual risk behaviours.
5 General health status.
6 AIDS knowledge and HIV testing information.

The second part of the interview measured several psychological variables of interest. Selected items were chosen from several scales and adapted for use with the client population. The scales from which the items were derived were: personal efficacy (Paulhus, 1983); general well-being (a measure of psychological well-being; Veit and Ware, 1983); assertiveness (Gambrill and Richey, 1975); and AIDS locus of control (based on the health locus of control scale, developed by Wallston et al., 1976).

Examples of items from the personal efficacy scale include 'Often people get ahead just by being lucky', and 'My major successes are entirely due to my hard work and ability.' Agreement was indicated on a 1–5 scale and scored so that higher scores indicated a greater sense of personal efficacy. The psychological well-being scale included measures of how often clients felt 'relaxed and free of tension' and 'bothered by nervousness'. Frequency was indicated on a 1–5 scale, and higher scores indicated more positive psychological well-being. Examples from the assertiveness scale included measures of how often subjects 'Refuse an unfair demand made by a friend', and 'Say something that your friends do not agree with.' Frequency was measured using a 1–5 scale, scored so that higher scores indicated a greater degree of assertiveness. Examples of items from the AIDS locus of control scale included: 'It is my own behaviour which determines whether I get AIDS', and 'No matter what I do, I'm going to get AIDS.' Agreement was indicated on a 1–5 scale and scored so that higher scores indicated greater internality.

Measures were also taken of the clients' perception of any risk reduction efforts either they or their partners had made before the baseline interview. A similar interview schedule was used for the six-month follow-up interview.

Post-group Questionnaires   A brief questionnaire was completed by all clients after their last group session. Thus, clients in the standard intervention completed the form after the first session, and clients in the enhanced intervention completed the form after the third session. Questionnaire topics included: AIDS information learned in the group(s); self-efficacy regarding the practice of risk reduction efforts; and the intention to practice risk reduction.

Results

Description of Sample
A total of 653 women participated in the Harlem AIDS Project. The women were primarily African American (71 per cent) and Hispanic (25 per cent). Because there were so few women of other racial/ethnic background, only African American and Hispanic women are included in these analyses ($n = 624$).

A summary of the demographic and social characteristics of these women, by ethnic group, appears in Table 3.1. Close to half (46 per cent) reported living in others' homes. Approximately half (46 per cent) of the women were married or living as married. The majority had children, with about half of the children living with their mothers. Almost two-thirds of these women were IVDUs (65 per cent) and 35 per cent were sexual partners of IVDUs. Significant ethnic differences were found in age (African Americans were older, 34.4 *v.* 32.9, $p < 0.01$); housing status (Hispanic women were

Table 3.1   *Demographic and social characteristics*

	African American (*n*=464)	Hispanic (*n*=160)	*p*
Age (mean)	34.4	32.9	< 0.01
Housing status (%)			< 0.05
Own home	36	44	
Living in other's home	48	39	
Shelter/streets	10	13	
Other	6	4	
Marital status (%)			n.s.
Never married	23	15	
Married/living as married	45	50	
Separated/divorced/widowed	17	21	
Boyfriend/not living together	15	14	
Children			
Total number (mean)	1.7	1.8	n.s.
Have one or more (%)	72	77	n.s.
Living with children (%)	30	38	n.s.
Jail experience (%)	53	58	n.s.
Risk category (%)			< 0.05
IVDU	63	72	
Sexual partner of IVDU	37	28	

more likely to be living in their own homes, 44 per cent *v.* 36 per cent, *p*< 0.05); and risk categories (the Hispanic women recruited were more likely to be IVDUs, 72 per cent *v.* 63 per cent, *p*< 0.05).

Table 3.2 presents data on the economic characteristics of this sample. The majority of women were unemployed (79 per cent) and less than half (45 per cent) had a high-school diploma. Primary income sources were welfare (59 per cent) and illegal activities (38 per cent). The African American women were more likely to have a high-school diploma (50 per cent *v.* 32 per cent, *p*< 0.0001) and were significantly more likely to have the income sources of jobs (9 per cent *v.* 4 per cent, *p*< 0.05). Hispanic women were more likely to report receiving income from illegal activities in the past six months (48 per cent *v.* 34 per cent, *p*< 0.01).

Risk Behaviours: Drug- and Sex-related
The drug and sexual risk behaviours of these women are summarized in Tables 3.3 and 3.4. Among IVDU women, Hispanics

Table 3.2   *Economic characteristics*

	African American (*n*=464)	Hispanic (*n*=160)	*p*
Current employment status (%)			n.s.
Full/part-time employment	6	1	
Unemployment	77	87	
Homemaker	7	4	
Other	10	8	
High school graduate (%)	50	32	< 0.0001
Current income sources (%)[1]			
Job	9	4	< 0.05
Unemployment/disability	5	9	n.s.
Welfare	59	61	n.s.
Spouse/sex partner	30	31	n.s.
Other family members	23	20	n.s.
Friends	21	11	< 0.01
Illegal activities	34	48	< 0.01
Other	3	12	< 0.001

[1] Total exceeds 100 per cent due to persons who reported multiple sources of income.

injected heroin and speedball at significantly higher rates than African Americans (61.3 *v.* 39.8 and 55.2 *v.* 36.1, respectively, both *p*< 0.01). There were no significant differences by ethnicity in risk behaviours related to needle hygiene: women reported injecting in shooting galleries about 16 per cent of the time, using a new needle about three-quarters of the time and sharing works (cooker or cotton) about one-third of the time. Reports of non-injected drug use, for the total sample of women, indicated that although African American women reported significantly higher monthly levels of alcohol use (39.3 *v.* 22.2, *p*< 0.001), the two groups were similar on frequency of other substances. For both groups, crack was the most frequently used substance, on the average of about twice a day.

Among the women engaged in sex with a single partner during the previous six months, approximately two-thirds reported never using condoms; among those engaged with multiple partners, about one-third reported never using condoms. There were no significant differences in condom use by ethnicity. Also, there were no significant correlations between condom and drug use. There was a significant difference by ethnicity in the number of sexual partners reported (*p*< 0.05). Hispanic women were more likely to report none in the past six months (9 per cent *v.* 4 per cent) and African Americans were more likely to report two or more (52 per cent *v.* 46

Table 3.3   *Drug risk behaviours*

IVDUs[1]	African American (*n*=290)	Hispanic (*n*=115)	*p*
Injected drug use (mean no. of injections per month)			
Cocaine	40.1 (*n*=242)	45.7 (*n*=98)	n.s.
Heroin	39.8 (*n*=260)	61.3 (*n*=110)	< 0.01
Speedball	36.1 (*n*=229)	55.2 (*n*=98)	< 0.01
Injection behaviours (mean % of time)			
Used shooting galleries	0.16 (*n*=288)	0.16 (*n*=114)	n.s.
Used a new needle	0.77 (*n*=289)	0.73 (*n*=114)	n.s.
Shared cooker or cotton	0.34 (*n*=289)	0.30 (*n*=115)	n.s.

Total[2]	African American (*n*=464)	Hispanic (*n*=160)	*p*
Non-injected drug use (mean no. of uses per month)			
Alcohol	39.3 (*n*=436)	22.2 (*n*=133)	< 0.001
Marijuana	18.4 (*n*=420)	16.1 (*n*=145)	n.s.
Crack	66.2 (*n*=401)	62.9 (*n*=126)	n.s.
Cocaine	22.9 (*n*=378)	15.3 (*n*=122)	n.s.
Heroin	19.5 (*n*=278)	27.7 (*n*=118)	n.s.

[1] Based on intravenous drug users only.
[2] Based on intravenous drug users and sexual partners.

Table 3.4   *Sexual risk behaviour*

	African American (*n*=464)	Hispanic (*n*=160)	*p*
Condom use (% of time never used)			
Single sex partners	71	63	n.s.
Multiple sex partners	33	26	n.s.
Number of sex partners			< 0.05
None	4	9	
One	44	45	
Two	16	11	
Three or more	36	35	
Prostitution[1]			
Exchanged sex for money	37	33	n.s.
Exchanged sex for drugs	21	23	n.s.

[1] Asked only of those with two or more sex partners, assumes no prostitution by those with only one partner.

per cent). Approximately one-third of the women had been involved in the exchange of sex for money, and one-fifth in the exchange of sex for drugs.

Psychological Variables and Post-group Questionnaire
Results of the baseline data on four psychological variables are presented in Table 3.5. African American women obtained significantly higher scores on personal efficacy, AIDS locus of control and general well-being. There was no significant difference on assertiveness. At the last group session, all clients were asked to complete a questionnaire regarding their knowledge of AIDS, their intention to make risk reduction behaviour changes and their confidence (self-efficacy) in being able to make these changes. No significant differences were found for knowledge and confidence. African American women scored significantly higher in their intention to make behaviour changes.

Table 3.5   *Psychological variables*

	African American (n=464)	Hispanic (n=160)	p
Baseline interview			
Assertiveness	3.35	3.31	n.s.
Personal efficacy	3.72	3.59	< 0.001
AIDS locus of control	4.07	3.75	< 0.0001
General well-being	2.91	2.65	< 0.0001
Post-group questionnaire			
Intention	4.63	4.46	< 0.02
Knowledge	3.57	3.48	n.s.
Confidence	4.38	4.30	n.s.

Behaviour Changes before the Study
As part of the baseline instrument, women were asked 'Please think back to when you first heard about AIDS and the time since then. Since you first heard about AIDS, in what ways have you tried to change your behaviour to reduce your chances of getting the AIDS virus?' Subjects were also asked how successful their efforts had been in trying to change their behaviour. The responses were grouped according to drug-related changes and sexual behaviour changes. Table 3.6 indicates that the majority of women had attempted at least one behaviour change. About two-thirds (67 per cent) of African American IVDUs reported trying to make at least

one drug behaviour change compared to 78 per cent of Hispanic IVDUs ($p<$ 0.05). About half (53 per cent) of African American IVDUs tried to make at least one sexual behaviour change, as did 56 per cent of Hispanic IVDUs (not significant). More sexual behaviour changes were attempted by the sexual partners, with 69 per cent and 67 per cent of African American and Hispanic sexual partners, respectively, trying to make at least one behaviour change. Examples of the type of changes reported were increasing needle cleaning (for drug behaviour changes) and increasing condom use (for sexual behaviour changes). Regarding the success at change, clients reported relatively high levels of success (mean scores higher than 4 on scale ranging from 1 to 5). Hispanic IVDUs reported significantly more success at drug-related changes than African American IVDUs (4.6 $v.$ 4.1, $p<$ 0.001). Comparable levels of success at sexual behaviour changes, for both African American and Hispanic women, were reported for IVDUs and sexual partners.

Table 3.6   *Behaviour changes since hearing about AIDS*

	African American ($n=464$)	Hispanic ($n=160$)	p
Reported at least one change (%)			
IVDUs			
Drug behaviour	67	78	< 0.05
Sexual behaviour	53	56	n.s.
Sexual partners			
Sexual behaviour	69	67	n.s.
Success at change (mean)			
IVDUs			
Drug behaviour	4.1	4.6	< 0.001
Sexual behaviour	4.3	4.5	n.s.
Sexual partners			
Sexual behaviour	4.2	4.1	n.s.

Correlational analyses were conducted to assess the relationship between the baseline psychological measures and whether or not women had made any changes before coming to the programme and their success at making these changes. There were no statistically significant t-test results on the comparison of means for those who reported making at least one change and those who did not report making at least one change. In addition, there were no significant correlations between the psychological variables and the clients' reported success at change.

Changes in Risk Behaviours from Baseline to Six-month Follow-up

The follow-up sample for African American and Hispanic women consisted of 380 women or 61 per cent of the women initially interviewed. Nearly every risk-related variable examined was significantly different in the expected direction between baseline and follow-up. The differences were statistically significant at the $p < 0.0001$ level, indicating that the differences are dramatic ones. Since these results were similar for both African Americans and Hispanics, all of the results will be reported for the follow up sample irrespective of ethnic group.

Table 3.7 *IVDU injection risk behaviours: changes from baseline to follow-up*

Variable[1]	Baseline	Follow-up	p
Monthly injection frequency (mean)	43	13	< 0.0001
% time shooting at home	62	78	< 0.0001
% time shooting at shooting galleries	14	4	< 0.0001
% time rented works used	12	2	< 0.0001
% time given works used	15	3	< 0.0001
% time shared cooker/cotton	35	17	< 0.0001
% time shared rinse water	23	8	< 0.0001

[1] Data on the first variable were based on current injection; for all other variables, clients were asked to report on their behaviour during the previous six months.

For IVDUs, Table 3.7 shows significant decreases in overall mean injection rates, from an average of 43 injections per month at baseline to 13 at follow-up ($p < 0.0001$). This is in part due to the IVDU clients who reported no longer shooting up at follow-up, a total of 31 per cent. The overall decline in injection frequency occurred for all drugs taken together and for the specific drugs of cocaine, heroin and speedball. The locations where IVDUs inject drugs also changed significantly, as injections at home increased (62 per cent to 78 per cent, $p < 0.0001$) and injections in shooting gallery settings decreased (14 per cent to 4 per cent, $p < 0.0001$). Sharing of any of the equipment used to inject also decreased. Data in Table 3.7 show that renting works, using works given by others, and sharing cookers, cotton and rinse water occurred much more often

Table 3.8   *Sex risk behaviours: changes from baseline to follow-up*

Variable	Baseline	Follow-up	*p*
Condom use with single partner (%)	18	43	< 0.0001
Condom use with multiple partners (%)	41	64	< 0.0001
No. of sex partners (mean)	31	15	< 0.0001

Table 3.9   *Psychological variables: changes from baseline to follow-up*

Variable	Baseline	Follow-up	*p*
AIDS locus of control	4.0	2.8	< 0.0001
General well-being	2.9	2.6	< 0.0001
Personal efficacy	3.7	2.5	< 0.0001
Assertiveness	3.3	3.4	n.s.

at baseline than at follow-up (all significant at $p < 0.0001$).

IVDUs and sexual partners increased the percentage of times condoms were used in having sex between baseline and follow-up (see Table 3.8). This increase occurred for those engaged in sex with a single partner (from 18 per cent to 43 per cent, $p < 0.0001$) and those engaged in sex with multiple partners during the six months before interview (41 per cent and 64 per cent, $p < 0.0001$). Clients also significantly reduced the number of sexual partners between baseline and follow-up (mean of 31 at baseline to 15 at follow-up, $p < 0.0001$). It appears that between baseline and follow-up the respondents dramatically reduced their risk of contracting HIV through injection paraphernalia and sexual contacts.

Changes in Psychological Variables between Baseline and Follow-up
At the same time that considerable risk reduction occurred with the sample of high-risk respondents, a number of counter-intuitive results developed from analyses of the psychological variables. Table 3.9 shows that the mean at baseline for AIDS locus of control scale variable was considerably *higher* than the follow-up mean, indicating that feelings of control over contracting HIV moved from an internal to an external locus during the time between baseline and follow-up ($p < 0.0001$). Since substantial risk reduction was

reported, it would be logical to assume that AIDS locus of control would be more internal, but the opposite occurred. The personal efficacy scale and the general well-being scale also decreased considerably ($p < 0.0001$) during the period between baseline and follow-up. The fact that two other psychological variables decreased, along with locus of control, is more reason to probe for some kind of explanation as to why control, efficacy and well-being decrease as risk reduction increases. Assertiveness showed no significant change over time.

AIDS locus of control and personal efficacy are highly correlated (0.33, $p < 0.0001$) at both baseline and follow-up, whereas general (psychological) well-being is not correlated significantly at baseline and follow-up with AIDS locus of control. Thus, respondents generally feel worse psychologically while feeling less control over HIV and less personal efficacy, yet make considerable risk reduction efforts during the same time period.

Relationship between Psychological Scales and Risk Reduction Variables

Correlations were performed to identify and evaluate the relationships between the psychological scales and the risk reduction variables. Of the many correlations, a few associations were statistically significant, but the coefficients were small (i.e. under 0.25). Also, no easily interpretable pattern of significant correlations emerged from the analyses. This indicates that the psychological scales and the risk reduction variables may be largely independent of each other.

Specifically, AIDS locus of control is not correlated significantly with any of the injection-related risk behaviours either at baseline or follow-up. It is correlated at baseline with having fewer sexual partners and, with those respondents with multiple partners, having less condom use, but these correlations do not hold at follow-up and they are not highly significant ($p < 0.05$). General well-being and personal efficacy are also not correlated with risk variables at baseline or follow-up in any systematic or interpretable way.

One possibility for the lack of significant findings is that the psychological scales (except for AIDS locus of control) are global measures, while the risk reduction variables are specific variables. Another speculation is that no immediate reward develops from making risk reduction efforts, perhaps causing the respondents to feel that risk reduction is more external, less subject to one's own personal efficacy, and has no relation to feelings of internal well-being. Still another explanation involves the HIV status of the respondents. Many respondents may be HIV positive or have symptoms of AIDS, so that their risk reduction efforts do not have a great impact on the quality of their own lives.

Impact of Intervention
The number of groups respondents attended, or whether or not they attended groups at all, did not yield any significant differences in terms of changes from baseline to follow-up. The hypotheses that those in the enhanced group would show the most risk reductions and the greatest increase in psychological scales were not demonstrated by the data. It could be that since the changes over time were highly significant with respect to risk reduction and psychological scales, whether or not respondents had zero or three groups did not have any additional significant effects.

Discussion and Conclusion

Overall, the women in the study reported substantial risk reduction behaviour change, both before the project began, and from the baseline to follow-up interview. Although reported risk behaviours and reported reductions in risk behaviours were similar for African Americans and Hispanic women, demographic differences on such variables as education level and housing status and significant differences on the psychological scales may have consequences for risk reduction and require further study.

Because risk reduction occurred regardless of type of intervention, this indicates that (a) participation in the interview process itself or even in a minimal intervention is sufficient in itself to lead to risk reduction; (b) other change efforts in the community, including outreach projects and media efforts regarding HIV risk reduction may have contributed to risk reduction across the community; and (c) there were community-wide trends in risk reduction, resulting from the impact of the epidemic itself (including seeing friends and relatives getting sick or dying of AIDS). In addition, socially desirable responses, that is, telling the interviewer what the clients perceived that the project wanted to be told, may have also contributed to the level of reported changes. Analyses of six-month data for the entire sample indicates that this phenomenon, that is, the reported extensive risk reduction, operated for the male as well as the female participants (Deren et al., 1991).

The results of the analyses of the psychological variables indicated that there was an overall reduction in psychological well-being, that is, there was an overall decrease in general wellness and personal efficacy, and a significant movement to a more external AIDS locus of control. Although behaviour change was originally anticipated to correlate with increased feelings of well-being and efficacy, and a more internal locus of control, both these dimensions, that is, behaviour changes and psychological changes, may be associated with changes related to the AIDS epidemic that these women perceived within their own communities. In addition to seeing increased cases of HIV-related illness in their community, many of these women may have themselves, or begun having, AIDS-related symptoms.

Several implications emerge from these data. Although substantial risk reduction was reported, more risk reduction is needed. Furthermore, the simple relationship between psychological 'empowerment' models and behaviour change may not operate in a community in which the day-to-day living has constant reminders of disempowerment and the apparently inexorable spread of a fatal epidemic. Helping women deal with the consequences of the epidemic on their own psychological well-being is also an important issue which requires greater attention. In addition to its consequences for the quality of life of these women and their community, the overall decrease in psychological well-being may result in changes that are short-lived or inconsistently implemented. Intervention programmes which address these psychological issues may be more successful in assisting clients in maintaining behaviour changes.

Acknowledgements

The authors wish to acknowledge the Project Co-investigators, Samuel Friedman and Jacqueline Pascal of Narcotic and Drug Research, Inc. New York (currently known as National Development and Research Institutes, Inc., NDRI), and Janet Mitchell and Sterling Williams of Harlem Hospital Center, New York. Acknowledgement is also made of the contribution of the staff of the Harlem AIDS Project and the outreach staff of the AIDS Outreach and Prevention Bureau at NDRI. This research was supported by grants R18DA05746 and U01DA07286 from the National Institute on Drug Abuse.

References

Bandura, A. (1987) Perceived Self-efficacy in the Exercise of Control over AIDS Infection. Paper presented at the Conference on Women and AIDS: Promoting Health Behaviors, Bethesda, MD.

Bandura, A. (1990) Perceived self-efficacy in the exercise of control over AIDS infection. *Evaluation and Program Planning* 13, 9–17.

Botvin, G.J., Baker, E., Filazzola, A.D. and Botvin, E.M. (1990) A cognitive-behavioural approach to substance abuse prevention: one year follow-up. *Addictive Behaviors* 15, 47–63.

Centers for Disease Control (1991) HIV/AIDS Surveillance. USDHHS, Public Health Service, Centers for Disease Control.

City of New York (1987) Community District Needs: Fiscal Year 1989, New York City.

City of New York (1990) Community District Needs: Fiscal Year 1992, New York City.

Deren, S., Davis, W.R., Beardsley, M., Tortu, S. and Clatts, M. (1991) Reducing HIV Risk Behaviors: Multifaceted Interventions are Needed. Paper presented at the 119th American Public Health Association Annual Meeting, Atlanta, Georgia.

Gambrill, E.D. and Richey, C.A. (1975) An assertion inventory for use in assessment and research. *Behavior Therapy* 6, 550–61.

Guinan, M.E. and Hardy, A. (1987) Epidemiology of AIDS in women in the United States. *Journal of the American Medical Association* 257 (15), 2039–42.

McCord, C. and Freeman, H.P. (1990) Excess mortality in Harlem. *The New England Journal of Medicine* 322, 173–7.

New York State Department of Health, AIDS Surveillance Unit (1991) *AIDS Surveillance Update*. New York.

New York State Division of Substance Abuse Services (1989) The Northern Half of Manhattan: An Assessment of the Drug Abuse Problem. New York.

Paulhus, D. (1983) Sphere-specific measures of perceived control. *Journal of Personality and Social Psychology* 44, 1253–65.

Tucker, B.M. (1982) Social support and coping: applications for the study of female drug abuse. *Journal of Social Issues* 38, 117–37.

Veit, C.T. and Ware, J.E. Jr (1983) The structure of psychological distress and well-being in general populations. *Journal of Consulting and Clinical Psychology* 51, 730–42.

Wallston, B.S., Wallston, K.A., Kaplan, G.D. and Maides, S.A. (1976) Development and validation of the health locus of control (HLC) scale. *Journal of Consulting and Clinical Psychology* 44, 580–5.

4

Tossin' and Tweakin': Women's Consciousness in the Crack Culture

E. Anne Lown, Karen Winkler, Robert E. Fullilove and Mindy Thompson Fullilove

The spread of HIV is primarily related to three means of transmission: sexual activity, injection of contaminated blood products (through transfusion or needle-sharing), and maternal–fetal transmission. Drug use has been a prominent factor in the spread of HIV, primarily because intravenous drug users share injection equipment. The emergence in the early 1980s of a new form of cocaine called crack introduced not only a new substance onto the drug market, but also a new connection between drug use and HIV transmission. Crack users, even those who do not use needles to inject drugs, face an increased risk of HIV infection.

Introduced in 1981, crack was limited to a few cities until about 1986. Since then, it has become a major force shaping life in US cities, leading the *San Francisco Chronicle* (Gordon, 1989) to warn that the crack epidemic was threatening the city with bankruptcy and the Chief Justice of the New York State Supreme Court to title the years 1985 to 1990 'The Crack Years' (Wachtler, 1990).

We first began our research on the crack epidemic in order to understand its effects on sexual behaviour, and its implications for the spread of sexually transmitted diseases (STDs), including HIV. Our interest in the crack–HIV connection began with the US Centers for Disease Control's observation of marked increases in syphilis and gonorrhoea in cities reporting large numbers of crack-related arrests (Goldsmith, 1988). Studies reported over the past four years have provided increasing evidence that crack use is associated with dramatic increases in the national incidence of sexually transmitted diseases (M.T. Fullilove et al., 1990b; Rolfs et al., 1990), including HIV (Sterk, 1988). The practice of bartering sex for drugs has emerged as a particularly important STD/HIV risk behaviour that may facilitate transmission of disease to non-crack users.

Crack addicts, irrespective of gender, consume the drug during periodic binges in which the pursuit and use of crack outweigh other concerns, including personal safety, hygiene, nutrition and family or occupational responsibilities (Griffin et al., 1989). The crack high is an intense experience of euphoria that users are desperate to recapture once the high abates. Addicts will use whatever they have to obtain more crack. When money and possessions are depleted, they may be forced to barter sexual favours for a 'hit on the pipe'.

The barter of sex for drugs, though considered a form of prostitution, differs dramatically from the street walking, call girl and escort service forms of prostitution that were well established before the outset of the crack epidemic (Sterk and Elifson, 1990). First, this sex for drugs exchange (SDE) is carried out for very small sums of money in comparison with more established forms of prostitution. For example, in an SDE, vaginal intercourse might be traded for a $3 vial of crack, but a street walker or call girl would charge $50 or more for the same sexual service. Ironically, in many cities this 'price war' has severely undercut the ability of established, non-SDE prostitutes to maintain their usual level of income (Sterk and Elifson, 1990).

Secondly, since the power to negotiate what will occur in this sexual exchange is much less than that possessed by those involved in other forms of prostitution, many women feel powerless to resist requests to perform, for instance, acts of bestiality or multiple acts of oral sex, in order to obtain a small amount of crack.

Thirdly, SDEs are viewed as degrading to the sexual provider. Depending on the vernacular of a given community, women who participate in SDEs are called 'crack hos', 'skeezers' and 'toss-ups', all terms that carry a derogatory connotation. Women SDE participants perceive this behaviour as a mark of personal degradation and are frequently horrified by the specific acts they have performed.

In the course of our work examining the link between crack and STDs, we became convinced that the crack epidemic posed a particular threat to women. The involvement of women in this epidemic has been of special concern for a number of reasons. First, in other drug epidemics – for example, the heroin epidemics of the 1960s and 1970s – women have been a distinct minority of those affected (Rosenbaum, 1981). In this epidemic, there is evidence that women may comprise at least one-half of all users (US General Accounting Office, 1991). Secondly, crack use is most common among women of reproductive age. Use by pregnant women poses a serious threat to the health of the infant (Chasnoff et al., 1990; Cherukuri et al., 1988; Neerhof et al., 1989). Thirdly, given the critical role that women play in maintaining the tenuous social networks of many poor neighbourhoods (Susser, 1982; Stack, 1984), crack use by women has formidable consequences for the stability of their communities (Wachtler, 1990).

We propose here to examine the following assertions:

1   The existence of SDE in the crack culture affects the status of all women living in crack-affected communities, the status of those who do not use the drug as well as those who do.
2   The sex for crack exchange is best understood as a form of coercion.
3   Women's entrance into crack use has undermined women's traditional gender roles in many communities.
4   Women's use of crack as a method of liberation from overwhelming problems and traumas occurs within a context of massive community decline.
5   The daily survival strategies enforced within this traumatic environment severely compromise women's ability to protect themselves from HIV.

In exploring these issues, we will present research conducted in black communities in San Francisco and Oakland, California (R. Fullilove et al., 1990) as well as from New York City (M. Fullilove et al. 1992). We will present stories collected from men and women users. We plan to explore the language of the crack world, illuminated in expressions such as "tossin'", which describes the sex for drugs exchanges, and "tweakin'", an expression for the peculiar twitching that accompanies the crack high. We will report material that is descriptive of the crises in African American communities in the inner city, but also of other poor, ethnic minority areas in the United States that are burdened by drugs and poverty.

Methods

In order to examine SDEs in greater detail, we conducted several focus groups in a variety of urban black communities. In each setting we interviewed several women participants individually. In California, subjects were recruited by leadership networks in the community to represent homogeneous categories defined by such factors as age, gender, drug use and recent history of gonorrhoea. Data reported here were collected in seven groups with a total of 32 participants. All participants were teenagers from lower- and working-class backgrounds.

In New York, two drug treatment centres providing out-patient care for women crack users were selected as sites for focus groups and interviews. Both facilities are located in poor, inner-city

neighbourhoods characterized by the severe economic disintegration that has been termed 'urban ecological collapse' (Wallace,
1988). Thirteen women in various stages of recovery from addiction
participated in two focus groups; 51 participated in a 'rap group'.

Focus groups of this type are called social sexual history (SSH)
groups. SSH groups are semi-structured group discussions of sexual
behaviours and attitudes, which examine such experiences as first
sexual intercourse, history of sexual and romantic relationships,
sexual orientation, current sexual practices, participation in sex for
drugs exchanges, and drug use. The group format of these
interviews allows individuals to share their sexual life story within
the constraints imposed by the group's rules of public discourse on
sexual behaviour. These rules vary dramatically across gender, race,
age and sexual orientation. We have found that, by comparing
groups to each other, it is possible to understand how the rules of
discourse on sexual behaviour vary from group to group. Moreover,
by paying careful attention to the content of each group session, it is
possible to understand, at least on its public face, critical facets of an
SSH participant's life story and worldview (M. Fullilove et al.,
1990a).

The Toss-up and the Girlfriend

The following dialogue, taken from a series of SSH groups
conducted with teenage boys and girls in San Francisco, reveals
many of the key features of the 'public' images of the toss-up.

> *Leader:* Why do you think people use the word toss?
> *Man:* 'Cause that's what she is. She's a toss.
> *Leader:* How did she get like that?
> *Man:* It's a toss here. A toss there.
> *Man:* 'Cause everybody havin' sex with her. Everybody has sex and she
> just toss.
> *Man:* She don't stay with one man.
> *Man:* It's like I can toss her and I guess I call her a toss 'cause I toss her
> to my buddy. You know, it's like a toss.
> *Leader:* How would it start, though? Why would people be tossed?
> *Man:* 'Cause some girls like it.
> *Man:* I guess 'cause they like it just like boys. Some boys, well I guess all
> boys like it. But you know, I don't think girls should really, not
> like they do it. They just do it.
> *Man:* They like to be with this nigger with the fast car, shit, you get
> tossed her, then another nigger come up and she lookin' for a little
> fresh variety.

The objectification of the toss-up, in the young men's experience,
was bidirectional. The toss-up was looking for material gain and 'a

little fresh variety' – not a relationship – and the man was looking for sex. This is perceived as a contemptible exchange – 'girls shouldn't really do it' – but perhaps a fair one. That the exchange is not fair, but rather a form of exaggerated dependency, was expressed over and over by female teenage participants in other SSH sessions. One young woman, in discussing the young girls who use crack, described such dependency in stark terms.

> Girls do things with guys just for the dope, you know. A lot of 'em, to support their habit; they be hungry or whatever and then, you know, every drug is a mind altering thing. So, you know, a lot of them won't be in their right mind. They do things that they wouldn't of done if they wasn't high.

A young man described the interaction with the toss-up as 'everybody throwin' little kibbles and bits to her . . .'. 'Everybody' in that sentence refers only to men. The woman gets 'kibbles and bits', a reference to a brand of dog food. The animal image was underscored in another context by a young man who, though he confessed to wanting to try sex 'doggy style', said that he would do this with a 'sidekick' or toss-up, not with his steady girlfriend.

A young woman, describing why she broke up with her boyfriend, told us:

> I called his house and this girl answered the phone and I asked him what she was doing over there and he was playing with me, talkin' about bein' a toss. You know what I mean. Something about she was gettin' tossed and how that's my life. How can a 'hubba ho' get so bold? It came out, she kinda like a tossup and I couldn't find out if it was the truth. And I wanted to go over there and fight her and everything.

This final set of images is critical to understanding the social position of the toss-up. She is 'gettin' tossed', the object of the act, not an equal participant; she is a 'hubba ho', not a respectable steady girlfriend; and she is used by the young man to frighten his girlfriend. The 'toss-up' becomes the object of the girlfriend's rage: 'I wanted to go over there and fight her.'

The triangulation of man–girlfriend–toss-up has many implications. Through the sexual relationship between the man and the toss-up, the girlfriend becomes connected to all the sexual contacts in the toss-up's network. This type of intrusion of outsiders, perhaps many outsiders, into the steady relationship is all too often announced by the girlfriend's discovery that she is infected with a sexually transmitted disease. High rates of STDs represent an indirect measure of HIV risk dispersed throughout interlinking sexual relationships in the community, among drug users and non-users. Though the girlfriend most clearly has the 'innocent victim' role in this triangle, each of them – man–girlfriend–toss-up – is an 'actor' and follows a script in which sexual roles and opportunities are clearly defined. In this script, women are censored for liberal sexuality but men are empowered by it. In sum, then, the exchange between the man and the toss-up is not a fair exchange: the toss-up loses.

Sex for Drugs: No Way Out

Women crack users in New York confirmed the images expressed by the teenagers in San Francisco. In SSH groups and individual interviews, women who described their own participation in such sex-for-crack exchanges were clear that they were driven to these acts by their desperate need for crack. A woman told us:

> I sucked his dick, right, and he came in my mouth and I was spitting out – and he gave me $4. I was crying and shit because I knew how bad I [had] gotten. I was like, oh my god, $4 and I was out there beggin for a fucking dollar. Before, I would never do that shit [fellatio], and I was doing it for nothing.

Another woman describes the change in personal standards in her first exchange of sex for drugs:

> He wanted me so I had sex with him, you know, so, I, we got high and shit – he ain't asked me to suck his dick or anything – if he did, I don't remember and I probably told him no anyway . . . I wasn't in too deep . . . I had a little pride, you know, left. I wasn't all fucked up in the head yet.

The unremitting desperation and humiliation was seen as an inescapable fact of a woman's life within the crack culture. 'You have to understand the situation. You have a crackhead, unemployed, who's on welfare and that's the only thing. All you've got is you ass', we were told by one informant.

The dramatically altered norms of women's sexual behaviour were acutely observed by participants. 'They're doing everything' reported another woman:

> I see them having oral sex in the park, in the elevator . . . And one night this girl, right, she, I have a chain on my door, and I leave the door open and I put a thing there, you know, so my cat won't go out. And I heard this young girl, and I swear to God I'm not lying, this young girl said – she walked up and down the hall, and she said, 'I need 75 cents, anybody down?' And this dude said, 'here, need one in the bathroom.' I'm not going to go into explicits, okay . . . She went to the bathroom and she said, 'I want to give somebody some. Anybody I got. I'm going to give somebody some head. Just 75 cents. I need 75 cents to get a tray [a $3 vial of crack].

Women described seeing crack-related sex everywhere. 'There is no boundaries and they don't care where they do it, or who they do it with' explained one group participant. Another woman responded, 'Right, let's go fuck in the car. I don't give a shit if there's 20 people over there having a birthday party.'

There is universal agreement among the women we interviewed that women who smoke crack are held in contempt. 'Men . . . they put crackheads down, I mean, if you smoke crack, you ain't, you know, worth a damn penny.' Women report sexual harassment and public humiliation as everyday occurrences. 'You can be walking with your husband, you can be helping an old lady across the street . . . and they'll say, "Yo, baby, who's got that thing, yo, baby."'

The shame related to participation in SDE was so intense that it was difficult for women to reveal such behaviour in the public setting of a social sexual history group. In one of our SSH groups in New York (the only group of those we are describing here where women were willing to discuss their own participation in SDE) an explosive situation developed because one woman insisted that SDEs were not part of her own drug dependency: as she put it emphatically, 'I never did *that*.'

By contrast, most of the women in this group candidly described their participation in SDEs. The one hold-out qualified her involvement in these activities. She insisted, 'I only did it with someone I knew, never with strangers.' The other women in the group challenged her position, contending that a sex for drugs exchange with a friend was no different from one with a stranger. The participants became very tense, women talked simultaneously, and their voices became louder and louder. The six who had acknowledged sex with strangers accused the seventh woman of 'being in denial' and refusing to admit that she, too, had been degraded by the addiction. The seventh woman, who felt increasingly attacked and misunderstood, continued to assert that she had not fallen to this level of degradation.

At issue here is the proposition that Hell has levels. The woman who always had her own money for drugs may, indeed, have been spared the dehumanization experienced by the woman who had to – as she described it – 'suck eight men's dicks to get a hit'. But the grim reality that confronts any woman who is caught up in crack addiction is that a sudden change in circumstances can force even the most independent of women into a situation in which the need for crack will become so great that no behaviour will be too outrageous. The feeling of independence is an illusion.

Crack, in fact, is in control. The drive to obtain it will take precedence over the drives for food, water and self-preservation. It will take precedence over the user's desire for public approval (or anonymity). It will take precedence over the user's instinct to nurture the young, and it will take precedence over the wish to be attractive, clean and decently attired. It will overwhelm a woman's capacity to protect herself sexually, both from abuse and from HIV infection.

Degradation and Gender Role

There is a critical element of coercion involved in the degradation associated with crack addiction. This has important parallels with rape and torture, where the victim has been forced to perform acts that violate personal standards for human behaviour. Torture is successful because human beings cannot endure unlimited amounts of pain and dehumanization. Despite the fact that torture and rape present forces beyond human capacity for resistance, victims of such traumas are likely to feel intense guilt and shame. Those broken under torture may be ostracized by those who have been betrayed and who view the transgression as an unforgivable act; those women victimized by rape may find themselves isolated by silence and fear, or may become the object of suspicion and public humiliation.

In the case of women driven by crack addiction, the 'unforgivable act' is not just the participation in SDE. The source of their stigmatization is the loss of 'womanliness' as defined by cultural ideals. In the SSH groups and in individual interviews, women described their struggles to fulfil gender-role expectations: to care for their children, to maintain sexual integrity, and to preserve a sense of physical attractiveness. For the most part, they described losing battles in which crack overwhelmed their capacity to be the 'women' and 'mothers' that they were expected to be.

More often than not, these users failed to provide adequate care for their children. They would use food stamps for drugs instead of food, would leave infants and young children unattended while going 'on a mission' to obtain more crack, and could not keep their children clean and sheltered during intense binge periods. One woman, who repeatedly left her one-year-old son in his room alone while she went to get crack, described her reasoning:

> Your son can wait, he's not going to starve to death, just a few more hours. Then you can accumulate the money, you can get the milk, you can get the Pampers, and you can get the food, but just wait. Let me take this hit. That's how it affects you.

In response to having her children taken away by the local child welfare agency, this same woman said, 'It hurts, it really hurts because you really want to do it. You really want to take care of your children and everything, but the drug is – just constantly – its like a monkey on your back. I want it, I want it, I want it, I want it.'

For the addicted mothers, the shame and humiliation of failing to care for their children was a constant source of pain. One woman told us that as they took away her child, 'I started screaming, and breaking, and that's when I really started smoking heroin . . . then it was crack . . . and then every time I would smoke, I'd think about my daughter, crying, crying.'

Women also struggled to protect themselves from incessant victimization. 'Manipulation' of men was described as an important tactic in their efforts. One woman described saying to a man, 'Don't you want a hit first?', knowing that he would share that first hit with her and that, once high, he would lose interest in sex. Thus, she got high without having to 'give it up'. These efforts at manipulation were not without peril: women who do it know that they risk being beaten, abducted, raped or even murdered.

Finally, women were embarrassed by the deterioration in their physical appearance while they were using crack. As one woman described it, 'I ain't care about nothing and my hair was all messed up. I was this skinny. I was hungry every day.' Another woman echoed this sense of apathy: 'They don't care about nobody. They don't even care about themselves.'

In sum, the evidence from our SSH groups and individual interviews suggested that women users had lost respect for themselves as women: their behaviours violated all of the standards of womanhood as defined by the cultures in which they had grown up. They had been humiliated through the sexual barter economy. Many had been raped, beaten or otherwise brutalized. They had been rendered unable to care for themselves or their children by the combined effects of addiction and trauma.

We believe that negative self-perception creates problems for crack-using women in therapy – many believe that their past actions have rendered them beyond redemption and beyond hope – and problems for women who are struggling to 'get out of the life'. These women experience their degradation as a pain that is only relieved by another hit of crack. Each act performed in pursuit of the drug and each trauma that occurs because a drug deal 'goes wrong' increases the need to relieve the pain through more of the same. In short, one of the features of extreme addiction is that it continually drives the user to place herself in danger in order to obtain the relief that the drug briefly provides.

It is difficult to imagine a more difficult challenge for the therapist who wishes to assist the user to begin recovery or for the health educator who hopes to 'reason' with women engaged in SDE so that they will understand their HIV risk and adopt other, less destructive, behaviours. On the continuum in which 'reasoned action' represents one extreme, the behaviours of such women in support of their addiction represents the other. The many kinds of trauma to which they are continually and routinely subjected renders reason irrelevant.

Coping with Trauma

In order to understand the traumatization and victimization of women crack users, we visited the Women's Rap Group at the Lincoln Hospital Substance Abuse Division, in the South Bronx, New York. We asked the 51 women there, the majority of whom were crack users, to review the list of categories of trauma developed for use in the National Vietnam Veterans Readjustment Study (questions M13–22 of that protocol) (Kulka et al., 1990). Participants were asked to check any of the categories of trauma that had affected either their own lives or the lives of friends or family members. The checklists were completed anonymously. Participants were also asked to comment on the categories contained on the list. Members of the research team recorded women's comments. Finally, women were asked to answer the question, 'What do you think is the reason you got into using drugs?'

Table 4.1   *The trauma spectrum: Types of trauma checked in response to the question: 'Has _____ happened to you or someone you know?'*

Type of trauma	No.	%
War-related trauma	8	20
Transportation accident	17	43
Serious fire	18	45
Work-related accident	3	8
Natural disaster	10	25
Physical/sexual abuse	26	65
Witness murder or attack	20	50
Life-threatening situation	21	53
Life-threatening situation of loved one	29	73
Other trauma	18	45
Trauma can't tell us	14	35

$n = 40$.
Median no. of types of trauma = 5.

As shown in Table 4.1, each of the eleven traumas on the list was checked by at least one person. Almost all of those completing the survey (90 per cent of those in attendance) checked at least one type of trauma; half checked more than five. 'Life-threatening situation of a loved one' was the most common trauma checked (73 per cent), followed by 'Physical/sexual abuse' (65 per cent), a category that includes childhood sexual abuse and rape.

Sixteen of the 40 respondents also wrote responses to the question, 'Why did you start to use drugs?' The women may have foregrounded trauma somewhat because of the preceding discussion of trauma; however, it is also likely that the discussion gave them language to describe their experiences. They did not talk solely about trauma, mentioning liking the high, curiosity and wanting to fit in as other reasons for drug use. Nevertheless their answers, given here in the women's own orthography, suggest that trauma and pain contributed significantly to the onset of drug use:

'The event that I had was a serious elbow accident [permanent scarring from a traffic accident] and to excape reality [suicide].'
'I use to like getting high now I feel go not hight.'
'I used drug becouse I felt depress with losing my kids.'
'I was using drug when my husband died.'
'When may father Died his death was very hard for me.'
'Just to fit in.'
'I like getting high. I enjoyed the feeling it gave me.'
'It start first being around with my friend them my sister die so i went back out on that matter and them for my seft because went you start it is hard to just walk away from the shit you get in to.'
'My reason for using drug was because I never had any motherly or fatherly attention. No one too really love me or guild me so the street became my parent with that came the crack.'
'All about drugs.
1. I used drug's cause I like it.
2. I used drug's as a copout.
3. I used drug's out of criousedy.
4. I used drugs cause it made me feel good. I like the high.'
'My next door negibor son died at the age of 6 weeks old from Infant death very sad I went to the babies funeral.'
'I started picking up drugs at the age of 14 yrs old. I was lonley, curious about using. I want it to be accepted with the crowd that I was hanging with.'
'I really don't know why I started using it but I guess some of it is to blame on the pressure that my parents put me through.'
'My reason for using drugs is I had alot of emotional problems. I had always been a neglected child by family, I felt as thou no one loved me. So I looked for love out of drugs.'
'In my childhood I was raped by my uncle and lived in a active house my mother drink my father use drugs.'

'I stop because my sister got killed November 2 and every since that I haved not used drug *since*.

One woman, for example, showed us a massive scar on her elbow, the result of a bus accident. That trauma, she wrote, precipitated her drug use. The woman who wrote, 'All about drugs . . .' offers a fairly complete analysis of the role of drugs in her life: they offer an escape, they are interesting and they make her feel good.

Drugs which alter mood provide an alternative to lives that are enmeshed within a web of trauma and chores. We believe that trauma is related to drug use in a number of ways. Traumatic events in childhood or young adulthood may predispose women to drug use. Trauma may, in some cases, even precipitate the drug use, as in the case of the woman injured in the bus accident. Traumatic events characterize the life of the woman crack user, including – perhaps especially – the traumas associated with loss of status as a woman. But the drudgery of everyday life as a poor woman trapped by circumstance and lack of education – that, too, can contribute to drug use. Addiction is a devastating side-effect of this coping strategy, and AIDS may be a disastrous consequence of the addiction. Ironically, crack-addicted women, whose drug of choice is smokable rather than injectable, may consciously avoid HIV transmission via shared needles only to succumb to HIV infection via increased sexual risk-taking in their pursuit of crack (see also Cindy Patton, Chapter 8, for a discussion of education aimed at drug injectors that neglects the message of safe sex).

Women and the Crisis of the Ghetto

The aetiology of the crack, sex for barter economy is intimately connected with the economic fortunes of the black community. Crack would never have gained such force within the black community had it not been for a pattern of dramatic changes in the economic infrastructure of these communities during the 1980s. Previously, blacks could compete for unskilled jobs but such employment has all but disappeared from the inner city, supplanted by the 'knowledge industry'. Blacks – whose level of educational attainment is far lower than that of whites – are poorly prepared to compete for jobs in the 'information economy'. So, despite the fact that these are the jobs currently available in the urban areas where blacks are most densely concentrated, a mismatch has been created between human and economic resources that has had serious consequences for the economic structure of black communities.

As black males have been increasingly marginalized and displaced from the mainstream legitimate labour market, many have gained employment in the underground economy of drug sales. The sex for drugs bartering system has been virtually institutionalized as an integral part of this crack-based economy.

The economic shifts in the black community have important implications for family life. Bowser (1986, pp. 23–4), in an excellent description of the link between family and economic structures, wrote:

> As the community declines, the family is a key institution which will reflect it. As the nuclear family has become the normative structure for participation in advanced industrial society, Afro-Americans have had to devise or maintain alternative social units in order to survive on the edge of advanced industrial society. The alarming rise in divorce, separations, female-headed households and children born into single-parent households indicates community decline.

The effects of women's crack addiction exacerbate this decline, as children are removed from maternal care *en masse* by the foster care system, and as ever greater numbers of families are convulsed by the loss of members to AIDS.

As vast changes in economy, family structure and education have affected life in the American inner city, a concomitant deterioration in the ecology of these communities has accelerated their decline. Wallace (1988, 1990), for example, has examined the destruction by fire of the South Bronx, a poor, minority community in New York City. Decisions to cut fire-fighting services, made at the municipal level, precipitated an epidemic of destructive fires in this community that devastated acres of vulnerable housing. The physical destruction of the community caused a forced migration of the inhabitants into surrounding neighbourhoods. This massive shift in population further disrupted the social and economic networks necessary for stabilizing life in a poor community. Wallace demonstrates a strong association between the physical loss of housing in the South Bronx and dramatic increases in substance abuse, violence, homelessness and HIV infection (Wallace, 1990).

As networks and peer groups are destroyed, and as family structure shifts, women are left in ever-increasing isolation. As the physical destruction of the community proceeds, there is a dramatic increase in the burdens related to women's gender roles, most notably in providing emotional sustenance and maintaining family cohesion. Networking and kinwork are not only important tasks women perform for the family, they are also important coping strategies for women themselves.

This pattern of disintegration creates conditions of unprecedented crisis in the lives of women, and produces a climate in which crack use and high rates of addiction are likely. A final problem is that such addiction is also linked to behaviours that increase the likelihood of both infection with and dissemination of HIV.

Conclusion

The crack epidemic has flourished in the decaying communities that house groups marginalized from the dominant society. Young, poorly educated inner-city dwellers, with little hope of legitimate employment, turn to crack as a solution to poverty and as a salve for anguish. Crack, however, unleashes an extraordinarily powerful set of forces that deepens the crisis of the community. Women, we have suggested, are at great risk in the world that crack has created. Pursuit of the drug includes tremendous sexual risk-taking to procure crack and a failure to fulfil what are perceived as appropriate gender roles. As the health and social status of crack-using women declines, the entire community suffers.

We have suggested that, in crack-infested neighbourhoods, this suffering has led women down a path of destruction that begins with crack use and intensifies as addiction to the drug drives women into a vicious circle of drug-seeking, SDE, trauma, pain, and a need to repeat the cycle of use in order to escape the pain that such a life creates.

This trauma must be treated. It is at the source of many addictions and is the engine that drives the user to remain drug dependent. Trauma is not merely an unfortunate side-effect of the addictive disorders of many users, it is frequently both the cause and the effect of such addiction. Until this trauma is treated, our best-intentioned HIV risk behaviour prevention efforts are likely, in all too many situations, to fail.

It also seems clear that the neighbourhoods where crack use is most prevalent must undergo transformation as well. Crack sales and use are symptoms of a larger collapse of the economic and social structures of these communities. Until these neighbourhoods achieve some stability, they will continue to be breeding grounds for crime, trauma, addiction and illness. Crack users cannot hope for recovery if the neighbourhoods to which they return are 'toxic' and likely to promote both relapse to drug use and a return to sexual risk-taking.

Healing – on the community as well as the individual level – must be undertaken. Drug abuse and HIV infection are two sides of the same coin and our prevention and treatment strategies must include an understanding of the individual and ecological forces that are at the heart of these epidemics. The stabilization of inner-city communities must become, therefore, our top public health priority.

Acknowledgements

This work was supported in part by Center Grant MH42549, UCSF Center for AIDS Prevention Studies, and by Center Grant 5-P50-MH4352, HIV Center for Clinical and Behavioral Studies. We wish to thank our colleagues in San Francisco: Charlotte Tillman, Phebia Richardson, Jocelyn Nazareno, Richard Martinez and the Crack Users Interview Team. And in New York: Samantha Kaplan, John Forrester, Warren Barksdale, Michael Smith, Nancy Smalls and Evan Richardson. Without their help, this work could not have been accomplished.

References

Bowser, B. (1986) Community and economic context of black families: a critical review of the literature, 1909–1985. *American Journal of Social Psychiatry* 6, 17–26.

Bowser, B. (1988) Crack and AIDS: an ethnographic impression. *MIRA Newsletter* 2, 1–2.

Chasnoff, I.J., Landress, H.J. and Barrett, M.E. (1990) The prevalence of illicit-drug or alcohol use during pregnancy and discrepancies in mandatory reporting in Pinellas County, Florida. *New England Journal of Medicine* 322 (17), 1202–6.

Cherukuri, R., Minkoff, H., Feldman, J., Parekh, A. and Glass, L. (1988) A cohort study of alkaloidal cocaine ("crack") in pregnancy. *Obstetrics and Gynecology* 72 (2), 147–51.

Fullilove, M.T. and Fullilove, R. (1989) Intersecting epidemics: black teen crack use and sexually transmitted disease. *Journal of the American Medical Women's Association* 44, 146–53.

Fullilove, M.T., Fullilove, R.E., Hayes, K. and Gross, S. (1990a). Black women and AIDS prevention: a view towards understanding the gender rules. *Journal of Sex Research* 27 (1), 47–64.

Fullilove, M.T., Lown, A. and Fullilove, R. (1992) Crack 'hos and skeezers: traumatic experiences of women crack users. *Journal of Sex Research* 29 (2), 275–87.

Fullilove, M.T., Weinstein, M., Fullilove, R.E., Crayton, E.J., Goodjoin, R.B., Bowser, B. and Gross, S. (1990b) Race/gender issues in the sexual transmission of AIDS. In P. Volberding and M.A. Jacobson (eds), *AIDS Clinical Review 1990*, pp. 25–62. New York and Basel: Marcel Dekker, Inc.

Fullilove, R.E., Fullilove, M.T., Bowser, B.P. and Gross, S.A. (1990) Risk of sexually transmitted disease among black adolescent crack users in Oakland and San Francisco, Calif. *Journal of the American Medical Association* 263 (6), 851–5.

Goldsmith, M.F. (1988) Sex tied to drug = STD spread. *Journal of the American Medical Association* 260 (14), 2009.

Gordon, B. (1989) Crack's incredible cost to SF: City could go broke over drug. *San Francisco Chronicle*, p. A1,12,13.

Griffin, M.L., Weiss, R.D., Mirin, S.M. and Lange, U. (1989) A comparison of male and female cocaine abusers. *Archives of General Psychiatry* 46, 122–6.

Kulka, R.A., Fairbank, J.A., Jordan, B.K. and Weiss, D.S. (1990) *Trauma and the Vietnam War Generation*. New York: Brunner/Mazel.

Neerhof, M.G., MacGregor, S.N., Retzky, S.S. and Sullivan, T.P. (1989) Cocaine abuse during pregnancy: peripartum prevalence and perinatal outcome. *American Journal of Obstetrics and Gynecology* 461 (3), 633–8.

Rolfs, R.T., Goldberg, M. and Sharrar, R.G. (1990) Risk factors for syphilis: cocaine use and prostitution. *American Journal of Public Health*, 80 (7), 853–7.

Rosenbaum, M. (1981) Sex roles among deviants: the woman addict. *International Journal of the Addictions* 16 (5), 859–76.

Stack, C.B. (1984). *All Our Kin*. New York: Harper and Row.

Sterk, C. (1988) Cocaine and seropositivity. *Lancet*, 1052–3.

Sterk, C. and Elifson, K. (1990) Drug-related violence and street prostitution. *NIDA Research Monograph* 103, 208–21.

Susser, I. (1982) *Norman Street: Poverty and Politics in an Urban Neighborhood*. New York: Oxford University Press.

US General Accounting Office (1991) *The Crack Cocaine Epidemic: Health Consequences and Treatment* (Fact Sheet for the Chairman, Select Committee on Narcotics Abuse and Control, House of Representatives No. GAO/HRD-91-55FS).

Wachtler, S. (1990) *The State of the Judiciary, 1990*. State of New York, Unified Court System.

Wallace, R. (1988) A synergism of plagues: 'planned shrinkage,' contagious housing destruction, and AIDS in the Bronx. *Environmental Research* 47, 1–33.

Wallace, R. (1990) Urban desertification, public health and public order: 'planned shrinkage,' violent death, substance abuse and AIDS in the Bronx. *Social Science and Medicine* 31 (7), 801–13.

Wallace, R. and Wallace, D. (1990) Origins of public health collapse in New York City: the dynamics of planned shrinkage, contagious urban decay and social disintegration. *Bulletin of the New York Academy of Medicine* 66 (5), 391–434.

PART III
WOMEN PROVIDING AIDS-RELATED SERVICES

Many women are closely involved with HIV and AIDS as carers for friends or relations, as volunteers working with AIDS service organizations, or as paid professional workers in HIV/AIDS services. Little research has been done on women working as carers within the community, although a number of personal accounts and how-to books have appeared (Eidson, 1990; Peabody, 1987; Rieder and Ruppelt, 1989). There are also some studies of caring professionals' problems when working with women around AIDS (Macks, 1988), but the professionals' own gender is not at issue in these studies. Some psychologists have, however, started to investigate women workers within AIDS volunteer services and in AIDS-related areas of the caring professions, examining their relationships to the men and women who are their clients and co-workers, and to the organizations that employ them. The chapters in Part III are examples of such work.

Halina Maslanka, in her account of women volunteers at Gay Men's Health Crisis (GMHC), New York (Chapter 5), describes the assumed female, middle-class nature of volunteering in the US and a reality of volunteering which is somewhat different, since it also includes women, often working-class women and black women, who see their work as a form of community activism. The chapter examines how the experience of GMHC's increasing numbers of women volunteers differs from that of the male volunteers, and how it expresses these two perspectives on women volunteers. Maslanka describes how the women volunteers at GMHC, like the men, identify with the organization's politics to a large degree and see their work as making a social contribution. But the women report less personal involvement than the men, and less sense of being able to challenge the organization. Frequently of socioeconomically lower status than the male volunteers and more often working professionally as carers, they see volunteering as contributing to their careers in a way the men do not. They do not articulate that female subjectivity of care which both traditional notions of 'volunteers' and more recent work on the female caring ethic (Gilligan, 1982) might lead us to expect.

How do the white middle-class heterosexual women who comprise the majority of volunteers in AIDS service organizations (ASOs) address the issues of the 'different' gender, sexuality, drug use history, socioeconomic status and 'race' of many of their clients? Little work has emerged so far on this topic. Perhaps this neglect is partly because the bigger and better-funded volunteer-led ASOs, begun in the gay community, have found it difficult to reach the rest of the HIV community. But drug users, people of colour and poor people are nevertheless constituting an increasing proportion of the clients of ASOs founded in the gay community. Many women and men recruited as volunteers by such ASOs stipulate, at least initially, that they do not want to work with drug users. Maslanka explores the problematic relationships between women volunteers at GMHC and these new clients, and between the women and the established client group of middle-class gay men.

Some women volunteers are lesbians, but many lesbian feminists and other feminists, arguing that the gay HIV community is already relatively well resourced, have moved out of large ASOs like GMHC to work with smaller organizations, more orientated towards the concerns of women and people of colour, and often more activist. The growing profile of women volunteers in organizations like GMHC runs parallel, then, with the depoliticization of these rapidly growing ASOs which had political origins in the lesbian and gay community but have now become professionalized. This depoliticization is particularly noticeable when women volunteers have no definite feminist perspective on their work (Patton, 1989; Schramm-Evans, 1989; Solomon, 1989).

What is the place of women when they acquire the status of professionals in what is often called the 'AIDS industry'? (Patton, 1989). Jane Ussher, in Chapter 6, develops a feminist critique of conventional clinical psychological approaches to AIDS and HIV, and relates this to the complex but now-common situation of women psychologists working with gay men affected by AIDS. This situation is particularly salient in Britain where those affected by the epidemic are still very largely gay men.

Ussher points to the clinical advantages a feminist perspective provides in addressing gay clients in a non-pathologizing and empowering way but also acknowledges the limitations of this perspective. Feminist clinical psychologists are themselves embattled, part of a highly conventional profession which finds it hard to countenance its increasing numerical dominance by women (American Psychological Association, 1992; Humphrey and Haward, 1981; Morris et al., 1992), let alone feminism. Like other workers involved with psychological issues around HIV, feminist psychologists may be uneasy about the overlap of their work with social service issues and may use psychopathologizing or simply psychologizing explanations (Silverman, 1989). Feminist psychologists may also make too-easy assumptions of community with gay male clients that ignore the historical and political particularities of male homosexuality. Such clients may in turn, like many male clients, be misogynist.

Ussher dissects the intellectual and emotional involvement of women clinical psychologists in AIDS-related work: their pleasure in dealing with highly articulate, reflective, middle-class gay men and the problematic aspects of this pleasure; their voyeurism, hearing about an 'other' sexual culture; their guilt and sadness as clients die; and their need for a support that the professional discipline of clinical psychology does not offer. It is true none the less, as Ussher says, that AIDS-related psychology is less institutionally fixed than many other specialisms and so may offer opportunities for critical interventions, including feminist interventions. Such feminist initiatives have the potential, she argues, to provide more politically sympathetic and personally supportive services to PLWAs than does conventional AIDS-related psychology.

References

American Psychological Association (1992) Task force examines issues raised by feminization of field. *Monitor*, American Psychological Association, 23 (February), 47.

Eidson, T. (1990) *AIDS: A Caregivers' Handbook*. New York: St Martin's Press.

Gilligan, C. (1982) *In a Different Voice*. Cambridge, Mass: Harvard University Press.

Humphrey, M. and Haward, C. (1981) Sex differences in clinical psychology recruitment. *Bulletin of the British Psychological Society* 34, 413–14.

Macks, J. (1988) Women and AIDS: countertransference issues. *Social Casework*, 340–7.

Morris, P., Cheng, D. and Smith, H. (1992) How and why applicants choose to study psychology at university. *The Psychologist* 5, 247–51.

Patton, C. (1989) The AIDS industry: construction of 'victims', 'volunteers' and 'experts'. In E. Carter and S. Watney (eds), *Taking Liberties: AIDS and Cultural Politics*. London: Serpent's Tail.

Peabody, B. (1987) *The Screaming Room*. New York: Avon.

Rieder, I. and Ruppelt, P. (eds) (1989) *Matters of Life and Death: Women Speak about AIDS*. London: Virago.

Schramm-Evans, Z. (1989) Responses to AIDS 1986–7. Paper presented at the Third Conference on Social Aspects of AIDS, London, February.

Silverman, D. (1989) The AIDS 'Crisis' and its Impact on Professional–Client Relations: the Social Origin of Counselling. Paper presented at the Swedish–British Medical Sociology Workshop, May–June, Stockholm.

Solomon, A. (1989) Doing well or doing good? *Village Voice* 35, December 12, 31–2.

5

Women Volunteers at GMHC

Halina Maslanka

In the US, AIDS is affecting increasing numbers of women. By 1987 it was the eighth leading cause of death in all women aged 15–44 and was among the top five leading causes of death in that group in 1991. The sharp increase in cases among women mirrors the pattern that AIDS took among the gay male population in the early 1980s. Furthermore, AIDS among women is increasingly linked with other factors like minority status, drug usage or poverty. While women of colour account for 18 per cent of the total female population in the United States, they account for 74 per cent of women with AIDS. At the local level in New York City, AIDS is the leading cause of death for women aged 25–44 (GMHC, 1991). The 1991 fiscal crisis in New York City has led to minimal cuts in state or federally run AIDS services but very little increase in their availability, making it difficult for many to get access to necessary services.

The beginning of the epidemic focused upon gay transmission. Indeed initially, HIV was called Gay Related Immunodeficiency Syndrome. The focus upon one particular group by the media and public at large permitted a number of frightening attitudes to emerge. Despite the reasoned arguing of public health officials, attitudes of the public remained hysterical about gay men and about sex education. This hysteria created denial about an individual's own level of risk. The routes of transmission were known early on. Clearly the message was that heterosexuals were at risk, that adolescents were at risk, that sex workers were at risk – in short, that all individuals could be at risk.

The denial that has marked reactions towards AIDS has focused attention not on changing heterosexual male behaviour but on women as 'vectors' of infection: 'One of the obstacles women confront in relation to condoms may be their lack of information regarding appropriate usage' (Miller et al., 1990, p. 96). Since men are the individuals who need to use condoms to prevent transmission and since they have historically been resistant to doing so, women are at high risk but are also charged with being responsible for preventing transmission. Ambivalent attitudes towards women, and especially towards women's sexuality, have led to ambivalent reactions towards women as a risk group. Women are both the caretakers of gay men who are HIV positive and promiscuous prostitutes; they are both 'innocent victims' and irresponsible mothers, giving birth to possibly HIV positive children. These attitudes have led to a range of reactions from denying that lesbians are at risk (in the 1990 report from the National Research Council they are discussed only in terms of recruitment for blood donors thus 'protecting the safety of the blood supply', Miller et al., 1990, p. 303), to insisting that pregnant women must abort their fetuses and that women must be responsible for condom usage. The effects of such denial will be felt in the coming years.

Gay Men's Health Crisis has shown a commitment to the AIDS crisis over the first 10 years of the epidemic, a commitment that has been consistent and well documented in the press and has made it well known outside its original gay male constituency. The organization is relatively independent of federal funding with most of its operating budget raised from private donations. This places the organization in a unique position in the AIDS crisis. For its members are not only the experts, they are also advocates for the rights of PLWAs and they have achieved organizational stability in a much-needed area. This position also places the group in jeopardy as it faces increasing numbers and increasingly diverse populations in need of help. For many gay men and increasingly for women, community-based volunteer organizations like Gay Men's Health Crisis (GMHC) are the first option for information and help.

This chapter will look at the motivations for volunteering and the experience of volunteers at GMHC as they relate to issues of race and gender. The comments made are based on data obtained from volunteers as they arrived for orientation meetings at the agency and from focus group interviews with longer-term volunteers at the agency. While research on AIDS volunteers is starting to appear in the literature, some on volunteers at GMHC (Chambre, 1991) and some on volunteers at other agencies (Hooyman et al., 1988; Omoto and Snyder, 1990), there is little that looks specifically at the impact of gender on the work that is being done.

The Gay Men's Health Crisis was formed in 1981 in reaction to AIDS and the public reaction to AIDS. The development of the AIDS crisis has continued to fuel its growth and development. As the organization approaches its tenth anniversary it has grown from a small group of concerned upper middle-class gay men to a structured organization of over 180 staff, 2,000 volunteers and 3,000 clients. The original group's purpose in meeting was to raise money for research on AIDS (in the first year of operation $60,000 was raised) but it became obvious that there was an immediate need for information. The first AIDS Hotline was opened immediately, offering information about AIDS, and it soon became apparent that people living with AIDS (PLWAs) had other needs not being met within existing health organizations.

A system of functional volunteer roles evolved to deal with the reality of living with AIDS: buddies (to replace and/or supplement family members) who were there to do anything from shopping to escorting PLWAs for hospital visits; crisis intervention workers for when PLWAs were in psychological, medical or legal crises; lawyers to advocate for insurance and social security payments, and drawing up wills; the Hotline itself to deal with any and all questions concerning AIDS. Volunteers now at GMHC are also involved in work that aims to help shape policy in favour of PLWAs and, through their education department, to help educate hard-to-reach populations about AIDS. These functions are best summarized through GMHC's mission statement:

> Gay Men's Health Crisis, Inc. (GMHC) the first organization created in response to the AIDS epidemic, founded by members of the gay community and committed to the practice and realization of multicultur-alism, whose services are provided principally by volunteers, has as its purposes: to maintain and improve the quality of life for persons with AIDS, persons with AIDS-related complex and their carepartners; to advocate for fair and effective public policies and practices concerning HIV infection; and, through education, to promote awareness, under-standing and prevention of HIV infection. (GMHC, 1991)

The mission statement makes clear the roots of the organization and the pride it feels in the accomplishments of the individuals who founded it. It is interesting to note the inclusion of the term 'multiculturalism' in GMHC's mission statement as a testament to both the changing face of AIDS and the changing face of those who constitute the organization. GMHC has grown rapidly with a staff of over 180 individuals, 27 per cent of whom are women. Such an organization in effect combines both aspects of service delivery and advocacy work and women have been a part of that organization for some time. Women, including women of colour, are increasingly represented throughout the agency serving as directors and staff members, on various voluntary committees and, finally, as volunteers. The tensions arising from GMHC's organizational history and the future it faces creates an uneasy space within the organization in which the position of women as volunteers is not particularly clear. These tensions are focused around issues of sexuality (gay versus straight), gender (men versus women), race (white versus black, Latino or Asian) and class (middle class versus working class) as the staff, client base and volunteer base shift in the next phase of the AIDS epidemic.

Kayal, in surveying the volunteer population at GMHC in 1986, found that 17 per cent of the volunteer base were women. In the early 1990s, women volunteers constituted 40 per cent of the volunteer pool and in increasing numbers the pool of clients at GMHC. As the pool of volunteers changes, the assumptions underlying an organization based in the gay community like GMHC are questioned. Donated labour still maintains the core of services provided by GMHC but, as the focus of the agency broadens to include other populations, the issue of the volunteer pool becomes increasingly important. The traditionally gay, middle-class male AIDS volunteer may well feel differently about helping a minority member, a drug user or even a straight male than he would about helping someone perceived to be of the same class, background or sexual orientation.

The structure of volunteer agencies is not only relevant to services provided but also to the experience of volunteers in the work they do. Rubin and Thorelli (1984), for example, have depicted the general role of volunteers as one in which:

> They receive meager recognition and repeatedly encounter the disparity between popular conceptions . . . of appreciative clients who dramatically resolve their problems through peak experiences and the reality of ambivalent, resistant clients whose progress, if any, is difficult to see and who may resent or otherwise be unable to express gratitude to the volunteer.

More specifically, individuals volunteering with PLWAs have documented the emotional stress faced by, for example, group therapists: 'Conducting an AIDS group dramatically demonstrates our own inadequacies, ineffectiveness, powerlessness and helplessness – feelings that are rarely as powerful in other psychotherapy groups' (Tunnell, 1989, p. 9). Such stresses can lead to a loss of emotional objectivity on the part of the therapist and consequent drop in the quality of work done by such volunteers. The supportive organization is seen as a way of ameliorating the stress that volunteers will experience through their work without interfering with the work they do. To provide such an organization the connections between volunteers and organization are necessarily loose. However, such looseness of the organizational interface with volunteers may create additional stress leaving individuals unclear about organizational policy and satisfying the needs of their client.

Women as Volunteers

Kaminer (1984) conducted in-depth interviews with women volunteers challenging the assumptions about the nature of women's volunteer work. For many years volunteering has been seen as a respectable way for middle-class women to combine their role as mothers and housewives with a 'career', albeit unpaid. In the 1950s, for women, 'Volunteering had been a kind of halfway house between the family and society. It may not have gained her the world, but at least it made her a part of it' (Kaminer, 1984, p. 5). Feminist critics of volunteering feared in the 1970s that: 'Career volunteering denied women their capacity to be self-sufficient and also their right to run things. Social policies, often carried out at the lowest levels by women volunteers, were usually set by men' (Kaminer, 1984, p. 3).

The position of women in US society has radically altered over the past 30 years. Today, over 60 per cent of women between the ages of 18 and 64 are in the workforce (Christensen, 1989), and it is estimated that by 1995 women will comprise almost half of the total workforce in the US. As a part of the workforce, women have marketable skills which they bring to volunteering. This position, one would assume, would make it unlikely that their volunteering would be seen today, as it once was, as 'public housewivery' (Kaminer, 1984). Women who volunteer today are more likely to have already embarked on a career so that volunteering no longer serves the need of creating an *ersatz* career. Volunteering today might be assumed to serve a different function for women and might cause the experiences of female volunteers to look somewhat different. However, the question remains whether women who volunteer at an organization established by men, where the policies have been set by men, can achieve a status consistent with their skills and interests.

While traditionally volunteering has been seen as a natural extension of women's more caring orientation towards the world (Odendahl, 1989), there are for many women very concrete achievements to be gained. Odendahl's findings on wealthy female philanthropists who volunteer shows the way in which women can transform the power of their status and wealth into a position of authority in their volunteer work. The women Odendahl researched are the white upper middle-class women one traditionally associates with 'good works'. Kaminer's interviews with women volunteers cover this traditional female volunteer base but she also extends the definition of volunteers to include minority volunteers who might more correctly be called community workers. These, typically, minority women saw their volunteer work as directly contributing to the development and improvement of resources in their community. Their work was, however, no less voluntary in that they did not receive payment for it. These volunteers interviewed by Kaminer felt that the traditional female pool of charitable workers ignored the pressing social problems faced by many in society. For this group of volunteers, advocating for change was critical to their work but even more critical was the fact that they provided necessary services. In impoverished, minority communities 'The volunteer work they did on the side was essential to the health and welfare of their communities; if they didn't take care of their own, no one else would' (Kaminer, 1984, p. 9). This view of volunteer work is very similar to that taken by those who volunteered in the first years of the AIDS epidemic. Those who worked at organizations like GMHC were gay male community organizers, providing information, educating other members of their community about safer sexual practices and providing services. The effects that their work had were dramatic.

As the AIDS epidemic reaches its tenth year GMHC as an organization appears to many to have moved away from both that early politicizing experience and radical philosophy. The increase in staff has led to a consequent increase in professionalized services offered by the agency but it may not have led to a more democratic dispersal of services. Over the past five years the criticism of GMHC's advocacy position has led to the founding of ACTUP (AIDS Coalition to Unleash Power), an organization whose prime role is to advocate on behalf of PLWAs. This has led to an interesting symbiosis between the two organizations with some staff members of GMHC participating in ACTUP and with ACTUP adopting the unique stance of being independent of, but critical towards, GMHC.

Volunteers at GMHC

The comments that follow draw on two different sets of data. The first is gathered from people who came to GMHC to volunteer during 1990–91. Nine hundred and sixty people arriving at the agency agreed to complete brief questionnaires that asked about their reasons for volunteering and also covered demographic information. The second set of data is drawn from volunteers who had been at the agency for at least six months and who were asked to participate in focus group interviews covering their experiences as volunteers. Comments and observations from those interviews are used in this chapter.

The motivational scales completed by individuals when they arrived at the agency to volunteer are taken from Maslanka et al., (1990) (see also Wong et al., 1991). These scales use items derived from motivation scales found in the literature and from motivations cited by GMHC volunteers themselves. The scale consisted of 26 items taken from a 40-item pilot scale which was subsequently factor analysed producing six sub-scales. These sub-scales cover such motivations as:

1. *Affiliative*, e.g. 'To feel close to others'.
2. *Career-related*, e.g. 'To enhance your career exploration and development'.
3. *Ideological*, e.g. 'To make some response to the AIDS crisis'.
4. *AIDS-general*, e.g. 'To help gay friends do something about AIDS'.
5. *AIDS-specific*, e.g. 'To do something besides worry about getting sick'.
6. *Self-development*, e.g. 'To provide a kind of satisfaction you no longer feel in your paid work'.

Thirty per cent ($n = 285$) of the individuals contacting the agency to volunteer and agreeing to complete the initial questionnaire were women. This figure differs from the percentage of active women volunteers at the agency for two possible reasons. Individuals who come to the orientation session at GMHC do not necessarily go on to volunteer and there tends to be an immediate drop-out after the orientation. This may be due to a lack of openings in particular volunteer opportunities or to people feeling unsure that they can commit to the amount of time required to be a volunteer. Those who drop-out are differentially represented by men and specifically men of colour. It appears that women having made the decision to come to the agency to volunteer are more likely to carry out that decision.

Demographic variables do not differentiate the groups except in one instance. Both in terms of age and education, male and female groups are very similar. The instance in which they do differ is not of particular surprise: women are earning significantly less than the group of males who decide to volunteer ($p < 0.05$, d.f. 894). Individuals coming to the agency to volunteer were also asked about their knowledge of the agency and their experience of AIDS itself. Men and women do not differ in the number of people they know at the agency and, in fact, very few individuals did know either a volunteer or a staff member prior to volunteering. Only 18 per cent of the total sample knew one or more staff members while over two-thirds (69 per cent) did not know any of the volunteers at the agency. As the agency moves away from being a small grass-roots organization to becoming a larger professional service agency, it is less likely that people will be introduced to the work and GMHC through a friend who is already there. Increasingly, the agency brings in volunteers through advertising, through outreach efforts and individuals who have heard about the agency through the media. The benefit of such routes lies in the agency's ability to target particular groups and in diversifying the pool of volunteer skills.

For the past decade the face of AIDS in America has been changing. It is less likely to be seen as a 'gay disease' than as a disease that can and does affect everyone. Kaminer (1984) stated that volunteers in her study picked issues in which their interests and their prior experiences converged. Increasingly, women who volunteer know someone who has tested positive for AIDS, making the disease more pertinent in their lives. While men cited an average of five acquaintances who are known to be HIV positive, women cited an average of two HIV positive acquaintances. While these numbers are obviously very different, it is interesting to note that only a little over one-third (35 per cent) of the total sample had not been touched by the disease. In recent years the epidemic has directly impacted on more and more people in New York. For some, this is also a reason not to volunteer. As one volunteer, interviewed in the focus group, pointed out, a close friend had been diagnosed as being HIV positive and also as having AIDS shortly after she had decided to volunteer. The decision to volunteer at that point became moot. Her first priority was to support him. For the men who come to the agency to volunteer, given that they know more HIV positive acquaintances, one would assume that this would also dissuade them from volunteering and that may well account for the early drop-out. However, for far more men this appears to be a cue for volunteer work for reasons that will be explored below.

There were significant differences between men and women on several of the motivational scales. Men scored higher on the sub-scales measuring *AIDS-general* and *AIDS-specific* motivations for volunteering. GMHC's traditional volunteer base has been gay males who were concerned about AIDS and so one would expect to find such motivations rating high among that group of prospective volunteers. On the *AIDS-general* scale which asked questions such as 'To respond to the death of a friend', men scored higher than women ($p < 0.01$, d.f. 907). On the *AIDS-specific* sub-scale consisting of items like 'To do something besides worry about getting sick', again men scored higher than women ($p < 0.001$, d.f.

888). Clearly, though AIDS is making inroads in other populations, its impact is still perceived by males to be in the gay male population and it is this perception that motivates their volunteer work at the agency. This was further emphasized when potential volunteers were asked how they perceived their level of risk of becoming HIV positive. On average, women saw their risk as being far lower than men ($t < 0.000$, d.f. 877), although this score is inflated somewhat due to the fact that 88 males knew already that they were HIV positive. The face of the AIDS crisis is perceived differently by men and women.

Women were clearly differentiated on the scale measuring *Career* motivations ($p < 0.01$, d.f. 919) consisting of items such as 'To enhance your career exploration and development'. Women volunteering at the agency see professionalization continuing beyond achieving a career and it is this desire for career development that motivates their volunteerism. The sub-scale on which women scored highest was that of *AIDS-activism* which consists of items like 'To make some response to the AIDS crisis'. Women endorse this scale significantly higher (albeit marginally so) than men ($p = 0.06$, d.f. 918). This suggests that for women AIDS is seen as a critical epidemic though felt somewhat less personally than it is for men. Their reaction to AIDS operates at the level of a social issue about which they feel strongly, whereas for men it is a direct and personal threat. Given the difference in the number of HIV positive people that male volunteers know as opposed to the number that women know, this makes sense. Women may have contact with HIV positive individuals but not to the devastating extent that gay males have and they do not perceive their own personal risk as high. While they may all be volunteering at the same agency, the routes by which male and female volunteers arrive are somewhat different.

The further question is whether women at GMHC resemble earlier generations of volunteers or whether, as Kaminer suggests, women have moulded a new and different role for themselves. Some women volunteers at the agency do bear a resemblance to older generations of women volunteers in that they are looking to do something useful and have found themselves with time on their hands. They tend to be older women who are settled and secure in their lives. However, even this generation differs from previous volunteers in that they are professionally qualified, do not wish to sit stuffing envelopes to pass the time but rather have skills that they wish to continue to use. For them volunteering represents a chance to continue developing and growing both professionally and intellectually.

Women are more likely to volunteer in the areas relating to client services, that is, the direct help and support of clients. On the one hand, this would appear to be a traditional female role to take. On the other hand, it also reflects the skills that women have acquired (for example, as social workers and mental health professionals) and therefore wish to continue to use. As one clinically trained volunteer put it: 'I had been asked to volunteer elsewhere but it usually involved answering telephones or not doing professional work so I came here . . . I liked it and decided to stay.' For others, the crisis of AIDS is seen as a logical extension of the work they perform during the day and one in which they could offer something meaningful:

> Having had a great deal of professional experience with the [health] profession I knew that the next great task before us would be dealing with AIDS and having done a certain amount of work previously with cancer patients I decided that I had something . . . to offer.

Another manifestation of individuals developing their career motivations is shown by women who perform volunteer work that differs from their paid work. These women choose a different forum for their volunteering, something which extends their careers into new areas. One such volunteer, for example, was a lawyer and had a lot of experience in AIDS discrimination cases but decided that she wanted to volunteer in an area which, while challenging, limited the extent of her emotional involvement with clients. By choosing to work on the Hotline she found that she could be effective in helping others but did not have to deal with the emotional duress associated with working face to face with a person with AIDS. Further, she saw her volunteer work as extending her expertise into an educational or counselling role.

For those women looking to expand their skills such work frequently has unexpected rewards providing a challenging and richly rewarding sphere:

> There were many group meetings where there was such trust, such personal strength and pride, such initiative, and such integrity that group members as well as the therapists seemed to behave as though they could successfully meet any challenge. (Tunnell, 1989, p. 10)

Or again: 'My ignorance continues to be challenged by the clients' (Tunnell, 1989, p. 10). Other areas of volunteer work relate to less involved and less skilled forms of working; for example, packing condoms, preparing literature for mailing, etc. For those individuals who volunteer to do this form of work there are other compensations in the form of friendships and socializing.

Experience of Volunteering

In focus groups conducted separately with men and with women there were some clear differences in experience. The focus of the groups was a longer questionnaire that covered individuals' experiences of volunteering at the agency from when they began, through stresses that they faced in their volunteer work, to support experienced from the agency.

Volunteers at GMHC are encouraged to work in groups to reinforce the idea that AIDS work cannot and should not be done alone. They are supervised by a volunteer who has more experience to ensure that special problems can be dealt with. Volunteers are encouraged to see the agency as a source of information and an advocate for clients but the primary source of support for volunteers during their work remains the team within which they work. In terms of service delivery this system is highly effective and direct but it may lead to problems as volunteers feel a basic disconnection between themselves and the staff members of the agency. This model is one that has been increasingly used by AIDS organizations in other developed nations (for example, The Netherlands, England) primarily because of its effectiveness (Morin et al., 1984). As an organizational model it allows flexibility in getting help to PLWAs with minimal interference from an organizational structure. As Cindy Patton (1989) has pointed out, it is also a model that draws on feminists' work in the health care field.

Men in the groups appeared to feel more entitled to complain or make suggestions for changes in the agency. This did not imply that their experiences of volunteering were negative. On the contrary, they were uniformly positive when talking of the work they did. However, they felt that there were areas that could be improved through changes in the way that volunteers were managed. Women, on the other hand, were far more hesitant in discussing changes they wanted to see at the agency. This appeared to arise as much from their sense of loyalty to the agency, as it did from a sense of not wishing to rock the boat.

Typically, a woman at the focus group would say that everything at the agency was satisfactory 'but well, maybe', as this woman does in discussing the orientation sessions offered:

> It's like a wall of people that you walk into but at the time it can make you feel very enthusiastic because here are all these people and they are all here for a specific purpose. Granted the session itself might have been better organized but I don't know if that would have made it more effective.

Men, on the other hand, were forthcoming with suggestions for improvements for the volunteers including tours of the agency, and informationally based get-togethers where volunteers could trade notes. It was not that men or women viewed the focus groups as gripe sessions. Both men and women discussed the benefits they got from volunteering and the rewards they found in the work. It was rather that men felt that they were entitled to play a part in the direction that the agency was taking. Women did not feel that that was their domain. This relates partly back to the history of volunteerism among women, which may lead them to see themselves as carrying out the policies set by others, but also harks back to the motivations they cited as being important. If one's motivations relate to helping in a cause one feels is important yet does not, as yet, directly impact on one's own well-being then criticism will be felt as somewhat inappropriate given the lesser degree of personal involvement. Or again, if one's motivations relate to developing career options one assumes that those with whom one works are the experts who can help in that development. In this sense, although professionally women may be experts, they may well feel that they are, in the sphere of AIDS, still novices. As one woman said of the training, 'technically it really acquainted me with aspects of the illness of which I had no concept.'

In discussing the training, the women spoke of how well it covered all aspects of HIV infection and the issues that they would face. There were clearly issues that were specific to women's needs or perhaps more specifically heterosexual women's needs. Issues covering gay men's lifestyles, the detailed information about the progression and transmission of HIV infection, the psychological impact of HIV, were issues of which many women had limited understanding or knowledge and which were found to be extremely helpful. One older participant stated, 'there is clearly a politic to this and there is also a medical politic and the two are in conflict.' Such reappraisals of previously held views and the introduction of new political ideas was common among the female volunteers interviewed. Aspects of the training which covered issues of gay men's lifestyle and emotional issues that would be faced were commented upon as being important if, in the latter case, they were also intimidating: 'there was one session that was an acting session [role playing] . . . I found it horrifying, it frightened me so much, though yes, it was useful.'

The way that the agency acts towards its volunteers is clearly important in integrating and making volunteering rewarding for these women. Annual parties were cited, as was the agency's handling of interpersonal conflicts, as being important for making volunteers feel connected and encouraging them to stay. For men, while they acknowledged the use of annual parties they were more interested in them for providing information updates on HIV issues. For some, such parties were clearly felt to be inappropriate as they were seen as catering to a younger population of volunteers. It was also clearly the responsibility of individual volunteers to connect with others to maintain that sense of association. One volunteer talked repeatedly about how important her 'friends' were in helping her with her volunteer work. These 'friends' were other volunteers who had become more than colleagues and with whom she socialized frequently. All felt that one of the most important factors maintaining their volunteer work was the support they felt for the work they do. If they were not given a formal support network into which they could fit, they created one and endorsed the importance of that support for what they were doing.

There appeared to be no difference between men and women in the lack of detailed knowledge they had of the agency itself. For many volunteers their main connection with the agency remained the department in which they worked. Beyond that, individuals had little understanding of where different departments were or what those departments actually did. Furthermore, volunteers did not appear to be clearly informed about meetings at the agency that were designed for their participation. Some of this follows from the nature of the work they do. Some volunteers are not required to come into the agency on a regular basis and their main contact may be either by telephone or through their team. On the other hand, faced with trying to maintain a well-trained volunteer corp to deal with a changing epidemic, this lack of connection may create a sense of alienation in the volunteer. It is important to remember that the volunteers interviewed were happy in their work and had managed to negotiate the organizational system at the agency. Those who were not happy or were unable to negotiate GMHC were not likely still to be volunteers or to take part in a focus group.

As hinted at earlier, problems of sexuality or of difference are faced by women. Men calling the Hotline were reported sometimes to be reluctant to talk to a woman about highly personal sexual practices, gay male group participants were said to resent having a woman as a group leader. One particular interviewee had had problems when she started running her support group for PLWAs and had faced a lot of hostility from members of the group. Some of their anger related to their diagnosis but it was directed at her. When a new co-group leader was being discussed the group specifically asked that the position not be filled by a young, attractive woman. Given that many of the group leaders are women, these are problems faced by many of them. However, as the client base at GMHC changes, the problems faced by female volunteers also change. For whereas with the majority of gay men volunteering at GMHC there are at least educational or class similarities, and sometimes a shared community of sexual orientation, with the traditional client the differences may predominate for those volunteers when they are faced by women, or men of a different sexual orientation, different social class or different habits.

The image of AIDS as gay cancer has meant that many straight individuals have been reluctant to face their own risk behaviours:

> People are clueless but when straight men and women call they are asking the basic transmission questions that gay men knew about years ago, and they don't want to change their sexual behaviour.

A clear difference is felt by volunteers facing such individuals which goes beyond sexuality or gender. Volunteers feel themselves when faced by these differences to be separated by experience. Women volunteers at GMHC feel themselves to be part of an educated, caring group who have made it their business to know about HIV transmission. Those who don't know or don't wish to know are perceived to be 'other', echoing the frustrations felt early in the AIDS crisis by gay male educators.

How Different are Women Volunteers?

The differences between men and women volunteers at GMHC are clear and tend to relate to their experience and understanding of AIDS and HIV. However, it should also be pointed out that in many ways women do not differ that much from their male counterparts nor from women volunteers in the past. They are middle class and educated and for the most part ethnically homogeneous. Eighty per cent of individuals who come to the agency to volunteer and who completed the questionnaire give their ethnicity as white. When one looks at the sample of individuals who remain as volunteers, this number goes up to 83 per cent. They are well able to discuss their experiences and detail their feelings about their volunteer work.

Women have been involved for some time in the agency as volunteers and appear to have been assimilated within the structure of the agency. They share its aims, if not necessarily its gay political stance. This assimilation does not necessarily occur at the client level and illuminates the route and problems to be faced by GMHC. One woman interviewed discussed the problems faced by the introduction of a female client to a PLWA group: 'A woman interviewed to enter the group and the clients are very closed mouthed about it which means, I think, they are having a problem with it.'

The problems of difference are what now faces an agency predicated on difference. On the Hotline women must also face the problem of difference when men call and wish to ask sexually explicit questions. Specific training is given in how to handle such calls. Both of these are problems that women volunteers know how to resolve. The differences that are more problematic are those that relate to cultural differences. Volunteers are facing the introduction of new clients who are less informed than gay men about safer sex guidelines and HIV transmission but in many ways are unversed in how to negotiate organizational systems. Volunteers are going to face problems in dealing with clients who are drawn from a different class and frequently from a different race. Assumptions made about the present client base cannot be made about future clients. While outreach programmes attempt to educate and inform new groups that are harder to reach, these clients may well be faced by volunteers who have little experience or understanding of the problems they face and who may have difficulty in communicating and empathizing with them.

References

Chambre, S.M. (1991) Volunteers as witnesses: the mobilization of AIDS volunteers in New York City, 1981–1988. *Social Service Review*, 531–47.

Christensen, K. (1989) Flexible staffing and scheduling in U.S. corporations. Conference Board Research Bulletin 240. New York.

GMHC (1991) *The First Ten Years* Annual Report. New York, NY: GHMC.

Hooyman, N.R., Fredriksen, K.I. and B. Perlmutter (1988) Shanti: An alternative response to the AIDS crisis. *Administration in Social Work* 12 (2), 17–30.

Kaminer, W. (1984) *Women Volunteering: The Pleasure, Pain, and Politics of Unpaid Work from 1830 to the Present*. Garden City, New York: Anchor Press, Doubleday & Co. Inc.

Kayal, P. (1986) GMHC: Volunteer Survey. Unpublished report of findings.

Maslanka, H., Cassel, J.B., Wong, L.M. and Ouellette Kobasa, S.C. (1990) AIDS Volunteering: Links between Experiences, Motivation, and Choice of Work. Poster presented at American Psychological Association Convention, Boston, Mass., August 10–14.

Miller, H.G., Turner, C.F. and Moses, L.E. (eds) (1990) *AIDS: The Second Decade*. Washington, DC: National Research Council.

Morin, S.F., Charles, K.A. and Malyon, A.K. (1984) The psychological impact of AIDS on gay men. *American Psychologist*, November. 1288–93.

Odendahl, T. (1989) *Charity Begins at Home: Generosity and Self-Interest among the Philanthropic Elite*. New York, NY: Basic Books.

Omoto, A.M. and Snyder, M. (1990) Basic research in action: volunteerism and society's response to AIDS. *Personality and Social Psychology Bulletin* 16 (1), 152–65.

Patton, C. (1989) The AIDS industry: construction of 'victims', 'volunteers' and 'experts'. In E. Carter and S. Watney (eds), *Taking Liberties: AIDS and Cultural Politics*. London: Serpent's Tail.

Rubin, A. and Thorelli, I.M. (1984) Egoistic motives and longevity of participation by social service volunteers. *Journal of Applied Behavioral Science* 20 (3), 223–35.

Tunnell, G. (1989) Complications in Working with AIDS Patients in Group Psychotherapy. Paper presented at the American Psychological Assocation Annual Meeting, New Orleans, LA.

Wong, L.M., Ouellette Kobasa, S.C., Cassel, J.B. and Platt, L.P. (1991) A New Scale Identifies Six Motives for AIDS Volunteers. Poster presented at the Third Annual Convention of the American Psychological Society, June 15, Washington, DC.

6

Paradoxical Practices: Psychologists as Scientists in the Field of AIDS

Jane M. Ussher

'Paradoxical practices' is the phrase that springs readily to mind to describe the role of feminist women working as clinical psychologists with gay men in the field of AIDS – a role I occupied myself for nearly two years. Yet, apart from the allure of alliteration, why do I call these practices paradoxical?

First, there is the paradox of feminism and psychology. The professional identity of a feminist clinical psychologist working in the National Health Service in Britain is still fraught with contradiction and confusion. Psychology, at its crudest, positions feminism as outside, as esoteric and irrelevant, because 'political'. Yet, at the same time, feminist theory often positions psychology as irrelevant – as reductionist and oppressive (for example, Kitzinger, 1990; Miller, 1973). So psychology and feminism may seem a contradiction in terms, for all concerned. To seek alliances and allegiances in both worlds demands both an ability to cope with an almost schizophrenic existence, and the strength to ignore vilification and incomprehension from both sides. But it is possible.

The second paradox is that, although considerations of issues such as gender and sexuality would seem an essential part of the working agenda of anyone involved with AIDS,[1] in the main these are issues considered to be irrelevant within positivistic psychology, and consequently marginalized. Sexuality itself is invariably framed as deviancy or dysfunction within psychology (Ussher, 1993), decontextualized, or ignored. Equally, women are invariably invisible within the official discourse of clinical psychology: the psychologist as scientist practitioner is stripped of her sex.[2] The questions which may seem to be of central importance to women working in AIDS will find no place in the professional discourse, the questions which beg to be answered are silenced by science, that which regulates the legitimated discourse of clinical psychology.

The third paradox is that of the juxtaposition of (often heterosexual) women workers and gay men; for while clinical psychology in

Britain is largely populated by women (Nicolson, 1992), those with AIDS in Britain are still predominantly gay men.[3] This potentially raises many issues for both the women clinicians, and for the gay men themselves. For example, the fact that the majority of gay men prefer to see a woman psychologist (George, 1992; Ussher, 1989)[4] is certainly cause for comment. Equally, the question of why women are attracted to such work could be begged. In the clinical context there may be conflicts around differences in gender, sexual preference, and potentially sexual politics -- misogyny is not confined to heterosexual men. At its crudest and most simplistic, feminism positions men as the 'other', as women have for so long been positioned themselves[5] within the phallocentric discourse. To work clinically solely with men may thus provoke conflict for the feminist psychologist.

The fourth paradox is that of feminism and AIDS. For while it might seem at first a contradiction to work from a feminist perspective with a predominantly male client group, the feminist perspective most clearly places considerations of gender and sexuality high on the agenda. For while the perspective of others, such as gay men, has certainly been influential in raising considerations of gender and sexuality within disciplines other than psychology (i.e. Dollimore, 1992; Weeks, 1985), it appears to be the lone voice of feminists raising these issues within psychology.[6] Ironically, in my own experience, the fields of AIDS is the area where feminist theory can most easily be reconciled with clinical practice. This is partly because of the absence of traditional ossified professional structures in this new field of psychology, and partly because the majority of gay men I saw in AIDS psychology were far more politicized than those with whom I have previously worked, and were themselves lobbying for many of the things which have formed the central tenets of feminist therapy: such as open access to information, equality within the therapeutic relationship and the use of therapy as an empowering process. The fact of being able to work as a feminist clinician with gay men, when it is difficult to work from a feminist perspective with *women* in mainstream clinical psychology if one wishes to escape vilification, is certainly ironic.

This chapter will examine many of the issues behind these paradoxes and contradictions, and outline the implications they have for women working in AIDS from the perspective of British clinical psychology. This will be, to some extent, an analysis grounded predominantly in the British experience of AIDS and AIDS care, but many of the conclusions have far wider implications, for other professional groupings within the field of AIDS, and for psychologists, be they feminist or not, working in other arenas.

No Sex, Politics or Subjectivity – We're Scientists

I started work in AIDS as a naive practitioner, filled with the rhetoric of efficacy and scientific utility which my clinical psychology training had provided. I carried my proverbial bag of tricks, my knowledge about the course of psychological problems and the appropriate means of intervention, before me, like an armour. I was a professional. I could interview, assess, diagnose and hopefully cure. Like many other professionals, I was shielded from scrutiny by my mask of accomplishment, but perhaps I was also shielding myself from any true realization of the cause of difficulties in those with whom I was working, and perhaps shielding myself from offering anything other than superficial intervention.

While I was buttressed by my training as a 'scientist practitioner', skilled in many techniques and therapies, many of those truths I had been trained to trade in rang hollow. The professional rhetoric suggests that psychological techniques can ameliorate anxiety, deal with depression. That research and practice are closely intertwined. In the textbooks it seems so simple. In reality it is not. Sometimes I felt as if I was blinkered – not allowed to address many issues which seemed central to the experience of working in AIDS, or not able to find the answers within the psychological agenda. The official discourse of clinical psychology failed as it did not allow the space to even set the many questions out, never mind to face the implications of such issues, as part of the professional agenda.

To demonstrate this conundrum, I will begin with a few brief case descriptions, which demonstrate the idiocy of the notion that sexuality or gender (or issues such as class or ethnicity) could be ignored[7] – as they presently are within the positivistic paradigm.

Thomas

Thomas was 26, newly diagnosed as HIV positive, and referred for psychological intervention because he was 'depressed'. He was angry. He had been celibate until he was 22, only starting to enjoy an open gay lifestyle after having moved to London. He felt that he had been shown the door to the garden of Eden and then had had it slammed in his face. Referred for 'anxiety management' and for help with his growing depression, I examined his negative cognitions, his belief that he would soon die and that there was no hope, and spent time talking to him about the fact that he might not develop AIDS. But after a month his face was disfigured with the red glare of Karposi's sarcoma. My encouragement to him to continue his social life as he had before seemed futile and useless. Would I go out with such marks, I was asked? How could I honestly say yes. Thomas was angry with me – and he showed it. I could couch it in psychological terms, realizing that he was transferring his aggression to an easy and willing target, that I was helping him to release his pent-up emotion. I could change from the cognitive approaches to depression and anxiety which I had been practising to supportive counselling, to listening. But it was not this simple. I felt guilty for my health. For the fact that I was at minimal risk of HIV infection through my being in a monogamous heterosexual relationship – something known to Thomas. For my clear skin. These feelings did not seem to fit with my conception of what a clinical psychologist *should* feel – what use my scientist practitioner training here? Thomas was not experiencing irrational thoughts easily ameliorated by cognitive therapy when he told me there was little hope, that everyone stared at him, that friends shunned him, and that he felt like giving up now rather than go through the pain. He died three months later, few friends at his funeral, perhaps proved right.

Sarah
Sarah had recently discovered that her husband of 20 years had AIDS. He had lived a double existence for years, active on the gay scene, but maintaining his marriage and family, Sarah being unwilling to question too much because she thought she would lose all. I was the only person she could talk to – acceptable to her because I was a professional, known to her because I had also worked with her husband. She cried. She felt bereaved before her husband had died, betrayed in the most fundamental way, and unable to turn to her friends and family for help. She described a life to me that was full of deceit. While she was depressed, I felt her anger. How could her husband have paraded his duel sexuality to her for years, allowing her to see glimpses of his other life through photographs and phone calls, yet still command her loyalty and secrecy now? How could this woman, who had no sexual life, no social life, and who feared the stigma of AIDS as much as her husband's death, continue? What could I offer? I felt angry with him, but also bound by professional obligations, as he was also my clinical responsibility. His sexist comments, his assumptions of female loyalty at any cost, were often difficult to bear.

Philip
Philip was referred for psychological support after a series of negative HIV tests, which were carried out because of his anxiety about AIDS. It became clear that his frequent testing was motivated by his having been repeatedly sexually abused as a child. Philip met

with me once a week for three months and discussed in detail the sexual abuse perpetrated by his father. He had not disclosed it to anyone before, and was racked with guilt, as well as anger. He attributed his homosexuality to this abuse, and had a very negative sexual identity. The fact that there is a dearth of research or training for work with adults who have been sexually abused, within psychology as well as many other professions, resulted in my feeling unprepared for the avalanche of emotion the disclosures created in myself. I was also faced with a situation where extremely distressing details of abuse were being presented week by week, juxtaposed with lurid descriptions of Philip's later adult sexual activities. Some were fantastic and shocking – even to someone by then used to discussing sexuality on a daily basis. I could not deny my interest in such discussions, my sometimes wonderment at whether such things described were physically possible. Was I voyeuristic? Could I merely react as the impartial scientist practitioner I was trained to be? What were the implications of Philip's obvious sexual arousal in such discussions, and his insistence – to a woman psychologist – that he was no longer gay?

I could go on – case after case where there were central issues, particularly those associated with sexuality and gender, within the therapeutic encounter where I felt that my training as a psychologist did not equip me to help. I looked hard for the answers – for a place to lay out the questions. Individual colleagues could provide support, could share their own experiences, but these discussions remained outside of the public domain, and so were not 'real', not reified by the appearance in academic journal, conference proceedings or psychology text. Clinicians working in this field may have had many of the answers I sought. But they were not publishing – they were seeing individual clients day after day – the dictates of the theorists far from their minds, the reality of the individual need for care uppermost in their minds.

But perhaps it is not surprising that these practitioners had little time for the research or the theory, because when I turned to the official (because published) discourse of psychology, to see what psychologists had to say about AIDS, I found a very different set of concerns.

Science as the Solution to AIDS

Since the early 1980s there has been a boom in scientific research on the subject of AIDS, with protagonists in academic debates rivalling each other for claims of ownership to ideas, theories and inventions.[8] The discipline of psychology has been no exception.

From a dozen or so published papers per year at the beginning of the decade, there were many hundreds published in Britain between 1989 and 1991. There are certainly more research papers on AIDS published in Britain than there are individuals with AIDS. More eager researchers than PLWAs. It is easy to see why many PLWAs have become cynical and bitter about what appears to be an 'AIDS industry', which seems to operate irrespective of their needs.

In the early years the funding seemed almost limitless, for after an initial refusal on the part of politicians and scientists to acknowledge the existence or implications of AIDS for the population at large, preferring to position it as an irrelevant 'gay plague', the governments of Western industrialized countries woke up to the need for research. In the continuously competitive and increasingly fund-starved world of academia and clinical research there was a realization that a new cherry had arrived to be bitten. And bite they all did, as the growth in publications indicates. The expertise of the various disciplines was brought to bear on the question of AIDS, which journals and international conferences were spawned to promulgate.

Academic and research psychologists have investigated a whole range of issues in relation to AIDS, including AIDS and depression, neurology, anxiety, sexuality, education and group behaviour, invariably framed within the positivistic framework. Yet the most popular subject is attitudes. For example, in random analysis of 130 papers published between 1989 and 1990,[9] 81 were concerned with attitudes. The main focus of research appears to be undergraduate students (for example, Connors and Heaven, 1990; Witt, 1990), with other clusters of papers appearing on attitudes of medical students, dental students, adolescents, doctors and nurses. It is interesting that psychological research which focuses on those directly affected by AIDS is certainly in a minority (2 out of 130 in this sample).

Research on attitudes to AIDS is certainly important, but is it not odd that this seems to be the main focus of concern? Is the research agenda not incredibly narrow? Does this type of research tell us any more than how people respond to questionnaires about AIDS? Psychometric indices are developed (for example, Shrum et al., 1989; Vest et al., 1990) with great care in order to establish practices acceptable as 'good science', valid and reliable quantitative measures. Group discussions and interviews are taped and transcribed, showing the (unsurprising) fact that undergraduate students have mistaken and negative beliefs about AIDS, and do not believe it will affect them. Then the results of these various studies are accepted and interpreted almost unquestioningly, adding to the mountain of publications accumulating. This work may command professional and academic credibility, it may be simple (and quick) to carry out, but it seems divorced from the reality of AIDS, treating AIDS and the PLWA as merely another variable in a carefully executed research project. One might cynically comment that in the morass of research on attitudes, researchers have conveniently substituted AIDS for issues such as unemployment, a favourite in the 1970s.

Looking back on the 1980s one might expect these myriad research studies to have yielded excellent data which have been integrated into services and policy to improve our knowledge and treatment of AIDS. We might have expected direct benefits for people with AIDS, and their carers. We might have expected leaps in theory and practice not always possible in areas of psychology where the established *Zeitgeist* creates a stranglehold. But no.

It seems as if the psychologist, following the ideal of objectivity, reduces the aspect of AIDS he or she is studying to a few cut-and-dried epithets, ignoring the complex ambiguities of human conduct or the context in which the behaviour is occurring or being observed, simplifying complex issues in order that they fit into the research agenda, and thus making many of the research questions which were addressed meaningless. This means missing the opportunity to move outside the narrow boundaries often created and maintained by tradition (see Healy, 1990) and making the research irrelevant to PLWAs, or to those working in AIDS – the discipline letting us down.

The AIDS Bandwagon

As the research is limited in its implications, and is often of questionable validity because of the narrow agenda it operates on, it can be seen as a missed opportunity, and a sad loss to opportunism in many cases. In the 1980s AIDS became the area guaranteed to attract research funding, publication opportunities and rapid promotion, as well as a higher public profile than most researchers generally achieve. Whether many of these individuals will continue to work in AIDS when the spotlight has dimmed is doubtful. And while there certainly are those who have carried out work of a consistently conscientious and useful nature, who have not merely jumped on the bandwagon of AIDS opportunity (see Mednick, 1989, on bandwagons in psychology), those who *have* profit from the general assumption in psychology that what we need is more data, more empirical work, more 'findings'.

Yet this empiricist view is naive in assuming that more findings equal more knowledge, 'rather like pebbles which, if stacked up in sufficient quantity are bound to reach the ceiling eventually' (Ingleby, 1981). This view is also both deceptive and destructive, preventing real innovation and discovery. We don't need more findings now, we need a reappraisal of explanations and theories in AIDS psychology, and a clear analysis of the type of research needed to ameliorate the difficulties of all those affected by AIDS. But as 'fact finding' and the collation of empirical research publications are regarded as the goal within psychology research circles, this is unlikely to happen. While psychological success is increasingly judged in terms of the number of published papers (and often never mind the quality feel the width), or acquisition of research grants, it is not surprising that theoretical and conceptual sophistication, or acknowledgement of issues such as gender and sexuality, are sacrificed at the altar of empiricism; or that researchers choose to look to the easily quantifiable subject of attitudes, rather than to widen their agenda and ask many of the questions which would be more useful. Do we not now know enough about the attitudes of undergraduate students (the psychologists' favourite subjects) towards AIDS?

Yet this attempt to achieve mastery by science, and insistence on confining debate within the narrow bounds of positivism, is not limited to academic psychology. The *ideal* of objectivity is as rife within clinical psychology, as I found to my own cost (see Ussher, 1992, for a more complete discussion of this).

Science and Psychology: The Emperor has No Clothes?

At the same time as the researchers were building up their mountain of (naive) empiricist research, clinical psychologists were increasingly seeing people with AIDS and those who were HIV positive in their practice. And, like academic psychology, clinical psychology is nothing if not a science. The modern profession which reaches out its tentacles into areas as disparate as AIDS, ageing and organizational psychology has its roots in the work of the experimental psychologists of the early twentieth century, of Galton, Pearson, Spearman and Burt (Pilgrim and Treacher, 1992). In Britain, as in North America, the professional and academic rhetoric of clinical psychology is still that of the scientist. Journal articles, professional documents (Scientific Affairs Board, 1989) and reviews of the profession (for example, Management Advisory Service, 1989) clearly portray the same message: we are all 'applied behavioural and social scientists with a clinical role' (MAS, 1989, p. 45). We are all experts. The power and prestige that this invariably bestows is unstated; but it is clear to all.

In Britain, clinical psychologists are products of this positivistical-ly biased training system, which continues to be advocated and publicly advocated (Ussher, 1992). As the recent report on the profession declares:

> Scientific method and systematic enquiry determines the way in which [clinical psychologists] practice. Hence characteristics of their approach are hypotheses testing, collection of evidence to confirm or deny a hypothesis and thorough evaluation of their intervention. (MAS, 1989, p. 45)

The budding professional is schooled in the rhetoric of efficacy which will stand her in good stead in the competitive arena of health care, where she must compete with the great (the psychiatrists) and the good (the social workers and counsellors). Her scientific standing allows her to hold her own in the market-place of madness[10] and claim jurisdiction over those in distress, as her predecessors turned to science to lift them from the mire of lay practitioners in the nineteenth century (see Pilgrim and Treacher, 1992).

For it is positivism which positions the issue of AIDS as apolitical, the clinician and client as de-sexed, as gender neutral, stripped of class, age, ethnicity. It is positivism that encourages the clinician to categorize and diagnose, to research and treat objectively. The theories and therapies which form the official discourse of clinical psychology are constructed within a causal deterministic framework, where it is implicitly assumed that observations can be collected from a neutral stance, where the relationship between the clinician and her client is irrelevant. The elevation of this scientific method to the status of objective truth serves to excommunicate those who are not 'proper scientists', the most lowly of these being the 'lay person' imbued with nothing but untutored subjectivity. So it is as reified experts, buttressed by the rhetoric of positivism, that clinical psychologists enter the realm of AIDS.

The positivistic discourse did not allow for many of the issues central to my clinical work on AIDS. How to deal with Thomas's anger at his illness, my guilt and the conflict provoked by my being healthy and heterosexual while he died. How to deal with the anger I felt towards Sarah's husband, the futility of her lost life, the contradiction of my need to help her husband and my ambivalence towards his sexual politics. The horror and fascination around Philip's disclosures, and the implications of his views of his changing sexuality. I could frame these 'clients' simply and succinctly within one or other of the models offered within the official positivistic discourse of clinical psychology: as anxiety (treated cognitive behaviourally), as depression (cognitive therapy), as reaction to sexual abuse (psychodynamic therapy), but each would involve the adoption of artificially constrained frameworks which emphasize the efficacy of theory at the expense of the individual.

For in reality it seems to me that the emperor has no clothes: the rhetoric of psychology occludes the failure of the scientific method to provide the answer to the pain of the individual men and women living and dying with AIDS. It fails to answer many of the fundamental questions which might have produced significant developments in theory and practice. The bandwagon is full of those jumping desperately for career progression and prestige through pronouncing on the new epidemic of the eighties, but the polemic rings hollow. I would not doubt that many individual practitioners are miraculous in their ability to provide comfort, care and concrete solutions for psychological difficulties. But whether it is their training as scientific practitioners which equips them with these skills is debatable.

For while there *is* a body of literature within AIDS psychology which examines issues such as counselling (Green, 1986; Miller, 1986), therapy (Carballo-Dieguez, 1989; Lomax and Sandler, 1988) and the relationship of general psychosocial factors to behaviour and symptoms (Martin and Vance, 1984), this stands in stark contrast to that which is deified within the scientific regime. The former is invariably published in review form in edited volumes, or in unrefereed journals, and thus often not recognized as 'real science' within the dominant discourse of psychology, and therefore ignored.

The Challenge to the Scientist Practitioner

In other fields of psychology (with the exception of feminist psychology), the disassociation from politics and values, the insistence on viewing the individual as a rational unitary object, the denial of the importance of sex and sexuality, or issues of age, class or ethnicity, invariably goes unnoticed. In AIDS it stands out as a nonsense, because these issues are at the forefront of the agenda for many of those directly concerned with AIDS. While high patient power has resulted in positive benefits in terms of services, it has also produced a highly articulate and very aware client group (as well as many campaigning carers). Thus the charade cannot continue unchallenged for long.

As has been outlined by many critics, one major flaw inherent within the positivistic paradigm within clinical psychology is the emphasis on the individual, or at most the family, at the expense of sociopolitical or institutional discourse. This applies to those operating therapeutically in the different denominations, from the behavioural or cognitive through to the humanistic. Problems are located in the private domain, rather than the domain of the public or the political. I would not argue that we should ignore the individual, but we cannot see anyone in a social vacuum, stripped of sexuality, class or race, which seems to be what clinical psychology attempts to achieve.

A further problem in the positivistic approach to therapy is that it is based on the assumption of the individual as 'ill' (Ingleby, 1981): the PLWA thus has symptoms which can be classified and identified as distinct from 'normal' human conduct, thus requiring intervention based on the scientific principles in which we have been steeped. In this model, there seems to be an implicit assumption that illness, AIDS, equals psychological difficulties. But why should pneumonia, or Karposi's sarcoma *necessarily* cause psychological problems? And if physical illness does equate with psychological difficulties, why are there not such large numbers of psychologists working in other spheres of physical medicine, where patients are suffering from leukaemia, cancer or heart disease? For while there certainly are psychologists working in general medicine, they attract less public attention, less funding (both research and clinical). There is no scientific reason for the proliferation of both clinical and research psychologists in AIDS and their relative absence in many related spheres. Their presence is a result of political (i.e. funding and glory) not scientific factors. Setting up specialist AIDS posts certainly acts to assuage public demands for government action.

But even if we put the problematic causal explanations aside, there is a question hanging over the very notion of diagnosis and classification implicit within a psychological analysis, as there is clear evidence that both diagnosis and classification are notoriously unreliable (Busfield, 1986), with heavy gender (Broverman et al., 1970; Ussher, 1991) and cultural (Littlewood and Lipsedge, 1982) biases. So the anger of gay men at their treatment in society, at the initial neglect of AIDS, at their marginalization as homosexual, can be translated into a pathology and dismissed. As gender stereotypes have been shown to be used in the diagnosis of problems and pathology in women (Broverman et al., 1970), they can also be used with gay men. For it is deviation from prescribed gendered roles which is often seen as the basis for diagnosis of pathology (Chesler, 1972; Ussher, 1991). I personally observed a considerable number of gay men sent for psychological intervention because they were openly expressing grief, because they were crying, or because they were blaming themselves for their illness: some even described as 'hysterical'. All these behaviours were 'normal' for women, but seen as incongruent in men. Were these men keeping a 'stiff upper lip' and coping with a diagnosis of AIDS calmly and coolly they might not have been seen as in need of psychological intervention. Yet were these symptoms not understandable, even healthy reactions to their situation, to being HIV positive? To being physically ill? If so, should we offer psychological intervention at all?

One other issue central to the neutral stance adopted by the scientist practitioner is the refusal to examine the subjectivity of the clinician, and the associated fact that clinical psychologists are not required to undergo any form of therapy or counselling themselves as part of their training. For a scientist this is understandable: why should the objective overseer of carefully validated interventions delve into their own feelings and fears? But the nonsensical nature of this approach was never more clear to me than when working with the life and death issues always to the fore in AIDS. Feelings about sexual abuse, about sexuality, about heterosexuality and homosexuality, about adultery or betrayal, about death and illness, could not be merely examined on an abstract level, removed from the experience of the individual clinician. Like many colleagues, I could address these issues through engaging in therapy on a personal basis, but this experience (central to my coping as a clinician) remained unrecognized within the official discourse of psychology. I again felt sadly let down by the dominant paradigms of the profession within which I had trained.

The Reluctant Positivist

Many clinical psychologists would throw up their hands in horror at this analysis, saying that they aren't labelling, diagnosing, medicalizing. That they aren't imposing themselves on unwilling victims, but that individuals come to them for help. That they aren't treating 'ill' individuals, but those with 'problems in living'. This view of psychology has been called the 'therapy of normality' (Rose, 1986, p. 80). Yet, as Rose argues, is not the therapist merely transposing difficulties of living on to a psychological register, psychopathologizing the individual, and thus ensuring that any difficulties are seen as amenable to particular expert technologies, which maintain the role of the expert and remove the responsibility from the individual person or the society. The liberal psychologist who cares and kindly cossets his or her clients may not be so different from the traditional medic whose power and prestige were reified by the scientific discourse, even if the epistemology and treatment offered are different. The solutions offered are all within a narrow domain:

competing explanations and theories always ignored as they may provide a challenge to the expert.

While positivism positions the person with AIDS as the neutral subject, it is the individual scientist practitioner who continues this charade, and who is thus culpable. The individual practitioner *may* deviate from the mould of the scientist practitioner in her work, developing empathic and empowering practices, but this does not detract from the fact that the official front of psychology is that of a science – the expert reified. To talk of the damaging effects of the scientific discourse of psychology in gatherings of clinicians is to invite the response: 'it's not like that in practice'. This may be the case. Individual practitioners *may* move away from the position of neutral observer; the profession may be less homogeneous than the experts would allow (or admit). But empowering individuals, adopting a different discourse behind closed doors, is not enough.

A Conundrum

So this is the conundum. On the one hand, an awareness of the desperate need for support and help on the part of those with AIDS – evidenced by the phenomenally high referral rates to clinical psychologists within the few hospitals which specialize in such care in Britain (as well as the low rates of drop out, unusual in psychology, and perhaps testimony to the effectiveness of the individual practitioners). On the other, an awareness of the many contradictions within the professional discourse, and the impossibility of addressing (never mind answering) many central issues within the current psychological agenda. The simplicity and naivety evident in much of the psychological research on AIDS is thus matched by the apparent rigidity and narrowness of the official clinical psychology discourse, which leaves many questions unanswered. One solution would have been to ignore the contradictions, to develop an empowering practice on an individual basis, using informal networks and 'unofficial' (because not publicly recognized) means of resolving questions around sexuality, class or gender: individual ways of resolving the personal issues arising from such work. Another approach is to find a way of addressing these issues within a different discourse of psychology – which is where the feminist approach is the key.

Feminism and Clinical Psychology

The implications of feminist psychology for this discussion may not seem at first glaringly obvious. Yet the debates which have been raging in feminist psychology, around issues of oppression, powerlessness, stigmatization and the pathologizing of anger and unhappiness, are of central relevance for women working in AIDS. The feminist approach allows a reconciliation of the critiques levelled at the professional expert with the need of the individual to receive help and support. It also allows for the subjective experiences of the psychologist to be acknowledged – moving away from notions of the rational expert, the blank screen.

Feminist critiques of science (Bleier, 1986; Harding, 1986; Keller, 1985) and of psychology (see Squire, 1989) have resulted in a reappraisal of theories and practice in the light of the claim that the existing order is both phallocentric and prejudicial to certain groups. Science itself has been severely criticized for its gender bias, for positioning the scientist as male, as rational and reasoning, the woman as of necessity outside of the scientific discourse for she is as irrational as she is irrelevent (except as the object of interest, trapped and objectified under the gaze of man). Within a feminist view of science (Harding, 1986) the notion of the objective expert is not reified, allowing an acknowledgement of many of the questions currently denied within the official discourse of psychology.

Feminists have outlined the way in which psychological labels are used to classify behaviour as ill which is a legitimate reaction to oppression or to inequities in the social environment (Chesler, 1972; Showalter, 1987; Ussher, 1991). In feminist therapy or research, there is an acknowledgement of the importance and validity of lay explanations for behaviour, as the division between the expert and the subject or patient is seen as less important, with a refusal to use 'top down' analyses, which only serve to disempower the individual. There is a history of questioning who is research for, whose interests does it serve, which allows for a critical analysis of the politics of AIDS research, examining the utility of such endeavours for the PLWA, in the same way that the use of research on women, but not for women, has previously been questioned. This may mean a demise in the ubiquitous 'attitudes to AIDS' research, which might not be a bad thing.

Feminism also easily accepts the role of campaigning groups within the discourse which informs practice, rather than emphasizing professional boundaries and the uniqueness of the psychological training found within mainstream clinical psychology (see the recently published MAS report for examples of this). Yet while criticisms of existing psychological frameworks are at its fore, feminist analysis does not necessarily exclude psychological involvement or intervention; it merely advocates a wider therapeutic agenda, epitomized within feminist therapy. This marks out the feminist analysis as different from many of the other critical analyses of psychology (such as that of the traditional anti-psychiatry model) as positive alternatives to orthodox treatment are advocated.[11]

Feminist Therapy

Feminist therapy,[12] perhaps somewhat ironically, provided me with a positive framework within which to work with gay men in an AIDS setting. It could not provide all of the answers to my questions, but at least it allowed them to be addressed. As I have argued elsewhere (Ussher, 1991), feminist therapy is a perspective, rather than a technique, as those who practice under the umbrella of feminist therapy draw on very disparate techniques and theoretical paradigms, drawing on the theoretical positions of the different feminist groups (such as radical, liberal, socialist or black feminists), or drawing on frameworks evolved by the mainstream theorists: such as the psychoanalytic, behavioural, cognitive and humanistic. But through the use of therapy as a 'rich and inclusive political practice' (Ernst and Goodison, 1981, p. 303), feminists have attempted to reconcile the problems in traditional expert interventions and the structural and political problems in society with the needs of individuals to receive help.

This perspective is potentially as valuable in work with gay men as it is with women. It allows an acknowledgement of distress, but recognizes that this cannot be divorced from social or political factors, and that problems do not arise because of an inherent weakness within the individual. Therefore it is possible to acknowledge that being HIV positive may create psychological difficulties, but also to move away from a framework wherein the individual is not seen as helpless in the face of some internal flaw. The social root of despair in the face of AIDS is perhaps more readily accepted within a feminist approach than it is within the traditional (invariably cognitive behavioural) frameworks beloved by clinical psychologists in Britain, yet feminist therapy can be beneficial, through providing some support, and ideally empowering individuals to seek solutions.

For example, power is of central concern within feminist analyses, and critiques of the abuse of power in therapy are central themes in therapy. The 'madness' for which individuals are treated is seen as often being in response to powerlessness, whether it be manifested in depression, self-harm or anxiety. Feminist therapy attempts to allow individuals to speak in ways other than through their bodies, or through pain, or thwarted protest, 'making explicit the social processes that delimit women's use of, and access to power . . . enabling the lessening of shame or blame women may feel about the power they use' (Watson and Williams, 1992).

Some may argue that this analysis is not appropriate for work with gay men who have AIDS, as these men often have more access to power than the average woman because of their privileged position in terms of gender and class (the men I worked with were predominantly middle class). It is true that the HIV status and sexuality of these men which might have marked them as 'other' often went unrecognized: biological sex (womanhood) being generally a more obvious signifier than sexual preference or HIV status. However, homosexuality and AIDS do act as signifiers which may position certain groups of men outside the patriarchal order as firmly as many women have traditionally been, making relevant the feminist perspective here. Heterosexist society may be as central to the gay man's experience of his illness as the fact of living in a patriarchal society is to a woman's (see Ussher, 1991, for an analysis of the latter).

As feminism does not define intervention within the narrow agenda within which mainstream psychology operates, a wider spectrum of ameliorative efforts can be offered. In practice, this means that a regular and acceptable part of the therapeutic agenda could be lobbying for the rights of the individual PLWA within health and social services. It means being able to exercise care outside of the formal confines of the therapeutic setting, facilitating a reconciliation of the professional and voluntary side of care, as the campaigning, the politics, the social action and intervention can work alongside therapy. These aspects of intervention are normal and accepted areas of work for those psychologists who practice in AIDS, but this part of their work is currently invisible, not recognized within the rigid constraints of the positivistic framework and completely denied by those who promulgate the research rhetoric. Perhaps this is because if it were recognized psychologists would no longer be able to claim to be apolitical, to be experts, to be unique. To be scientists.

Conclusion

Psychologists working in AIDS are in many ways in a unique position, within a field where traditional hierarchies and methods of working do not exist. New innovative methods of research and practice are possible in this context, with normally marginalized issues, such as gender or sexuality, firmly on the agenda. If psychologists in AIDS miss this opportunity, they only have themselves to blame.

While many of my own observations are based on the two years I worked as a clinical psychologist with gay men who were living and dying with AIDS, it is relevant to this debate that I no longer do this work. The pain and the sorrow of watching those I had grown to care about die was too much. Individual support from colleagues was not enough: institutional recognition from the profession was needed to prevent burn-out. I could no longer reconcile my professional veneer with the sense of uselessness in the face of the realities of AIDS. And I could no longer reconcile my feminist beliefs with the professional practice I was involved in, however much I spun webs of wonderful theories to convince myself of the boosts the men with whom I was working were receiving from my beneficent care. However much I attempted to adopt a feminist perspective, I had to be a closet feminist in my professional practice, as the men with whom I was working felt that their sexuality, and their HIV status, had to be concealed from colleagues and friends. Yet the contradictions and incongruities were too easily translated into feelings of personal failure and inadequacy, which only in retrospect can I see as reflections of structural and professional hypocrisies: hypocrisies which still confine women (and men) working in AIDS today.

Yet the other side to this argument is that working with the population of gay men whose lives were affected by AIDS was a stimulating and enriching experience. To work in a setting where theoretical discussions of life and death were on the daily agenda, where political and emotional awareness made analyses of relationships both sophisticated and stimulating, was nothing if not unusual. And, despite the sorrow often intrinsic to the situation, there was a great deal of humour in the individual clinical sessions, which made them often enjoyable, and fulfilling. Jokes against the pressures to perform in a patriarchal heterosexist society made the reality of the situation (of being a woman, or a gay man) more bearable. Many colleagues similarly enjoyed their clinical sessions, but this is rarely spoken about in the public arena. This enjoyment may compensate for the tragedy of the death of clients, again an unusual experience for the majority of clinical psychologists. It may also explain why so many continue in this work. Yet, more negatively, it might mean that other groups of individuals affected by AIDS are ignored, as they are not as appreciative and articulate as the the the middle-class gay men I worked with were.

From the safe distance at which I now stand I can look back and contemplate the difficult position in which many women psychologists working in AIDS are placed, at the dangers in their ignoring or denying the many contradictions in order to cope with the daily grind and grief. To look back in abstract contemplation may to many still working in this area seem a safe way of rationalizing a route out. To myself it seems as if only now can I see what it was really like, and how if things do not change significantly, neither psychology, nor well-meaning women workers, will be wanted or welcome in AIDS. It is paradoxical that *feminist* psychologists might.

The Future

I would like to end on a positive note, predicting that many of the paradoxes facing women (or men) who are attempting to reconcile the professional discourse of psychology with the reality of AIDS, or the contradictions of feminism and psychology, can be overcome. Unfortunately, the future does not look rosy, as the agenda of clinical psychology in Britain seems *more* wedded to science professionalization and paternal patriarchal (often heterosexist) practice as we move towards the end of the twentieth century, heralded by the new era of professionalized practice and changes in the British health care system towards a 'market force' approach. Perhaps this is an overly pessimistic view. For women and men whose lives are touched in whatever way by AIDS, I hope so.

Psychology does have much to offer. As researchers, psychologists have the potential to offer much in terms of theoretical and empirical analysis, if only the simplistic quick–return project can be usurped by that which carries more weight in terms of theoretical and methodological sophistication. In clinical practice, psychologists are skilled in many different therapeutic approaches, can work at many different levels of service delivery (see Ussher, 1990), and can in many instances act to integrate and complement the skills of other workers, both paid and voluntary. But if psychologists continue to practice within the model of the rational scientist – even if only within the official discourse of the profession – they will inevitably find themselves replaced by those who are more open to the direct needs of those who look for help; individuals who may also be more in touch with and open about their own needs and weaknesses.

But this is the future: when psychologists may climb off the positivistic pedestal, and be open to the complex historical, social and political context of the lives of the individuals with whom they work. In its present framework psychology is still short-sighted and limited. Only through continuous challenges of the professional and scientific discourse can it be made useful, and the paradoxes in AIDS, as other areas of psychological practice, become a thing of the past.

Notes

1 Both because AIDS is often sexually transmitted, and the gender of therapist and client in AIDS is often different.
2 In all, her biological sex, her gender and her sexuality – as I will outline below. See Ussher (1992).
3 This analysis applies to 1988–1989. Now, the rate of HIV transmission is increasing in the heterosexual population, but not in the gay population. In Scotland, because of needle-sharing practices in the past, there are high rates of HIV and AIDS in the heterosexual drug-using population.
4 In preference to a heterosexual man.
5 This is particularly so within the radical feminist analysis, such as that of Daly and Dworkin, whereas liberal or socialist feminists (Friedan and Segal) advocate working with men.
6 There are certainly others, not identified as feminists, raising gender and sexuality as important issues, but not in the same theoretical context.
7 These cases have been altered to prevent identification of the individuals. Each of the people involved has given permission for their story to be told in this context.
8 For example, there has been battle over the naming of the HIV virus as HTVLV or HIV, variously termed by French and North American medical researchers, culminating in battle over the discovery of the virus and the possible antidote, AZT, with millions of dollars at stake.
9 This search was carried out using Psychlit, the computer search, of recognized (because refereed) psychological journals. There undoubtedly are a number of papers published which would have not been included here, but the range of papers is certainly representative of the type of research, which is the focus of the present argument.
10 See Ussher (1991) for a discussion of madness.
11 See Ussher (1992) for a more complete discussion of this.
12 In this context, I did not directly refer to my individual work as 'feminist therapy' because of the misunderstandings this might have led to, associated with the misconception of 'feminism'. This is also invariably the case with feminist therapists working with women.

References

Bleier, R. (ed.) (1986) *Feminist Approaches to Science*. New York: Pergamon Press.
Broverman, K., Broverman, D., Clarkson, F., Rosenkrantz, P. and Vogel, S. (1970) Sex role stereotypes and clinical judgements of mental health. *Journal of Consulting and Clinical Psychology* 34 (1), 1–7.
Busfield, J. (1986) *Managing Madness: Changing Ideas and Practice*. London: Hutchinson.
Carballo-Dieguez, A. (1989) Psychotherapy with AIDS patients. *Psychotherapy in Private Practice* 7 (3), 85–9.

Chesler, P. (1972) *Women and Madness*. Garden City, New York: Doubleday.

Connors, J. and Heaven, P.C. (1990) Belief in a just world and attitudes toward AIDS sufferers. *Journal of Social Psychology* 130 (4), 559–60.

Dollimore, J. (1992) *Sexual Dissidence. Augustine to Wilde, Freud to Foucault*. Oxford: Oxford University Press.

Ernst, L. and Goodison, L. (1981) *In Our Own Hands: a Self Help Guide to Therapy*. London: Women's Press.

George, H. (1993) Sex, love and relationships: issues and problems for gay men in the AIDS era. In J.M. Ussher and C. Baker (eds), *Psychological Perspectives on Sexual Problems: New Directions for Theory and Practice*. London: Routledge.

Green, J. (1986) Counselling HTLV-111 sero-positives. In D. Miller, J. Weber and J. Green (eds), *The Management of AIDS Patients*. London: Macmillian.

Harding, S.J. (1986) *The Science Question in Feminism*. Ithaca: Cornell University Press.

Healy, D. (1990) *The Suspended Revolution*. London: Faber and Faber.

Ingleby, D. (ed.) (1981) *Critical Psychology: The Politics of Mental Health*. Harmondsworth: Penguin.

Keller, E.F. (1985) *Reflections on Gender and Science*. Yale: Yale University Press.

Kitzinger, C. (1990) Resisting the discipline. In E. Burman (ed.), *Feminists and Psychological Practice*. London: Sage.

Littlewood, R. and Lipsedge, M. (1982) *Aliens and Alienists: Ethnic Minorities and Psychiatry*. Harmondsworth: Penguin.

Lomax, G. and Sandler, J. (1988) Psychotherapy and consultation with persons with AIDS. *Psychiatric Annals* 18 (4), 253–9.

Management Advisory Service (1989) Management Advisory Service to the NHS. Review of Clinical Psychology Services.

Martin, J. and Vance, C. (1984) Behavioral and psychosocial factors in AIDS. *American Psychologist* 39 (11), 1303–8.

Mednick, M. (1989) The politics of psychological constructs: stop the bandwagon, I want to get off. *American Psychologist* 44, 1118–23.

Miller, D. (1986) Psychology, AIDS, ARC, and PGL. In D. Miller, J. Weber and J. Green (eds), *The Management of AIDS Patients*. London: Macmillan.

Miller, N. (1973) Letter to her therapist. In P. Brown (ed.), *Radical Psychology*. London: Tavistock.

Nicolson, P. (1992) Gender issues in the organisation of clinical psychology. In J.M. Ussher and P. Nicholson (eds), *Gender Issues in Clinical Psychology*. London: Routledge.

Pilgrim, D. and Treacher, A. (1992) *Clinical Psychology Observed*. London: Routledge.

Rose, N. (1986) Psychiatry: the discipline of mental health. In P. Miller and N. Rose (eds), *The Power of Psychiatry*. Oxford and Cambridge: Polity Press.

Scientific Affairs Board (1989) The Future of the Psychological Sciences. Report prepared by the Scientific Affairs Board of the British Psychological Society.

Showalter, E. (1987) *The Female Malady*. London: Virago.

Shrum, J.C., Turner, N.H. and Bruce, K.E. (1989) Development of an instrument to measure attitudes towards acquired immune deficiency syndrome. *AIDS Education and Prevention* 1 (3), 222–30.

Squire, C. (1989) *Significant Differences. Feminism in Psychology*. London: Routledge.

Ussher, J.M. (1989) Sex and Marital Therapy with Gay Couples. Paper presented at the British Psychological Society Annual Conference, St Andrews, April.

Ussher, J.M. (1990) *The Role of Clinical Psychologists in HIV and AIDS*. British Psychological Society, Leicester.

Ussher, J.M. (1991) *Women's Madness: Misogyny or Mental Illness?* Hemel Hempstead: Harvester Wheatsheaf.

Ussher, J.M. (1993) The construction of female sexual problems: regulating sex, regulating women. In J.M. Ussher and C. Baker (eds), *Psychological Perspectives on Sexual Problems: New Directions for Theory and Practice*. London: Routledge.

Ussher, J.M. (1992) Science sexing psychology. Positivistic science and gender bias in clinical psychology. In J.M. Ussher and P. Nicolson (eds), *Gender Issues in Clinical Psychology*. London: Routledge.

Vest, M.J., O'Brien, F.P. and Vest, J.M. (1990) Perceived consequences of employing AIDS victims: development and validation of a scale. *Psychological Reports* 66 (3), 1367–74.

Watson, G. and Williams, J. (1992) Feminist practice in therapy. In J.M. Ussher and P. Nicolson (eds), *Gender Issues in Clinical Psychology*. London: Routledge.

Weeks, J. (1985) *Sexuality and its Discontents: Meaning, Myths and Modern Sexualities*. London: Routledge.

Witt, L.A. (1990) Factors affecting attitudes towards persons with AIDS. *Journal of Social Psychology* 130 (1), 127–9.

PART IV

REPRESENTATIONS OF WOMEN AND AIDS

This fourth Part looks at representations of women and AIDS in the popular media, and in scientific and policy discourse. This is an important area of investigation since AIDS has generated such an extensive signification 'epidemic' (Treichler, 1988). For psychologists, the particular value of work on representations of HIV and AIDS lies in the powerful effects such representations have on how women and men understand and experience the conditions.

Psychologists have done relatively little work on popular representations of AIDS and HIV. Most psychological research on representations of AIDS has focused on what people say about the conditions. The chapters in this section were indeed written not by psychologists but by scholars and activists in the popular media and AIDS. Including such work in a book on 'psychological perspectives' is a way of foregrounding the importance for AIDS-related psychology of such complicated and wide-ranging analyses of representations.

The contributors to Part IV look in detail at the representational control of women. Alexandra Juhasz (Chapter 7) analyses television presentations of AIDS, and their documentary, 'horror-movie' and scientific narratives. She explores the relationship between these narratives of scrutiny, knowledge and conquest, and discourses of masculinity and heterosexuality. Women are, she suggests, oppressed by television representations of them as objects of journalistic, scientific or horror-struck fascination, as they are by more obvious discrimination against them around, for instance, HIV antibody testing or treatment access. But her argument goes further than this: the objects of scientific documentaries on AIDS are feminized, she says, even where they are not female, by being constituted as passive and innocent, ignorant or unthinking. When we get pleasure from looking at such representations, we are adopting the spectator positions conventional to the representational genres of journalism, horror, and science, which are generally coded as masculine.[1]

Cindy Patton (Chapter 8) gives an account of shifting media coverage of women in relation to AIDS from 1981 to the present, and of the representations of women in AIDS research, policy and education. She discovers parallel patterns of invisibility, victimology and pathologizing. Indeed, she notes that a generalized 'queering' of women is displayed in the representations affecting not just 'junky prostitutes' and 'AIDS mothers' but the most apple-pie 'wives of bisexuals' and women 'transfusion recipients'. Drug-taking, non-white ethnicities and poverty are easy for the media to demonize, but homosexuality too remains culturally disturbing, albeit half-assimilated, and women's associations with it are ubiquitous in AIDS discourse. Patton points out that many women are distanced from the 'coming out' models of lesbian or gay, and ex-IVDU identity, and proposes that, instead, lesbians' and gay men's newer formulations of their identities and communities around safer sex could be taken up by heterosexuals. Indeed, the prevention of HIV among women who define themselves as heterosexual depends, she suggests, on a queering of sexual identity among men who call themselves heterosexual: a decentring of intercourse, and a willingness to use condoms when it occurs.

Alternative media have constructed different, oppositional repre-sentations of women and AIDS in different and oppositional forms. These alternatives are visually sophisticated, clever, funny and – importantly for Juhasz – angry. In the US at least, they have gained some guerrilla footholds within the flow of mainstream AIDS representations. Among those directed at women, video examples are Alexandra Juhasz and Jean Carlomusto's 'Living with AIDS: Women and AIDS', Jean Carlomusto and Maria Maggenti's 'Doctors, Liars and Women', and Greg Bordowitz and Jean Carlomusto's 'Current Flow', for women who have sex with women. Diane Niemacher, stamping the slogan 'find a cure' over a highly conventional advertising image of white heterosexual leisure, ironizes it. Tessa Boffin creates a fantasy photographic narrative of the evolution of a lesbian angel of AIDS-generated melancholia into an 'angelic rebel' of lesbian safer sex. Books like Patton's and Kelly's (1987) *Making It* represent safer sex for women in diverse, engaging and affirmative ways. Of such work, Simon Watney (1990) says that it constitutes a new form of engagement between politics and representation: a new activist aesthetic. But, as Juhasz points out, even mainstream media science is not homogeneous in its representations of women and femininity. Some documentaries are less objective than others. And the kind of queered representation Patton discusses happens in mainstream media as well as on their margins. The careful sorting out of diverse representational positions and interests that characterizes this section is also part of feminists' 'alternative' take on representations of gender and AIDS.

Note

1 Such gendering of visual objects and spectators can seem oversimple and is controversial; for a good recent overview of the theoretical impasse it presents to feminist work on visual representations, see de Lauretis (1991).

References

de Lauretis, T. (1991) Film and the visible. In Bad Object-Choices (eds), *How Do I Look? Queer Film and Video*. Seattle: Bay Press.

Patton, C. and Kelly, J. (1987) *Making It: A Woman's Guide to Sex in the Age of AIDS*. Ithaca, NY: Firebrand Books.

Treichler, P. (1988) AIDS, homophobia, and biomedical discourse: an epidemic of signification. In D. Crimp (ed.), *AIDS: Cultural Analysis/Cultural Activism*. Boston, Mass: MIT Press.

Watney, S. (1990) Representing AIDS. In T. Boffin and S. Gupta (eds), *Ecstatic Antibodies: Resisting the AIDS Mythology*. London: Rivers Oram Press.

7

Knowing AIDS through the Televised Science Documentary

Alexandra Juhasz

A car is driving down a dark and lonely country road. It pulls to a halt at a security booth. A sloppy cinema-verité camera catches the back of an officer as he says, 'Driver's licence, please.' There is a cut to the face of the driver, grotesquely lit so that his white face is barely outlined. He has probably escaped from a mental hospital, and is sneaking by the officer so as to rape, molest and maim the unsuspecting woman at road's end.

A narrator enters: 'US Army, Fort Dietrich, Maryland. Once renowned for its biological warfare experiments.' The car pulls forward. In slow motion, mist wisps about mysterious tanks: 'More AIDS virus is produced here than anywhere else in the world.' Danger! They're creating biological warfare at Fort Dietrich. Those tanks are full of deadly AIDS virus!

But no, this is quickly revealed to be a set up. The narrator returns. He explains instead that here 'an intense scientific effort to unravel the complexities of this strange and deadly virus' is being waged. Only then does the camera cut to a clean and well-lit scientific lab. But why the mysterious car and driver? Why the build-up with its threat of apocalypse? Why all the codes (and fun) of the fiction film in what is – surprise! – the first sequence of a *science documentary*: a 1986 *NOVA* programme, *Can AIDS be Stopped?*

In this chapter, I intend to think critically about the ways in which AIDS is represented in the mainstream media as one approach to understand better the culture in which women suffer HIV infection. Somehow AIDS has become just one more systematic oppression for the already oppressed in our society, exaggerating and multiplying the compromised positions under which many women already live their lives (Sabatier, 1988). This can be explained, in part, by the ways that AIDS has been *represented*. It is my belief that the structures and ideologies under which the representations of AIDS have been organized are the same systems which have long permitted power and pleasure in our culture, most typically to the detriment of women.

I will analyse two science documentaries about AIDS – *Can AIDS be Stopped?* and the Winter 1990 segment of WGBH's *AIDS Quarterly, The Trial of Compound Q* – so as to understand better the ways that science is reported and the effects that such systems of representation have over the ways in which AIDS is known and lived, particularly by the real female bodies that are infected with HIV, or that are perceived to be. My close textual analysis of these two programmes could have been performed on other mainstream science/AIDS documentaries with similar results: it is the typical structure and presentation of these programmes which makes them my subject of study.

The historically gendered structures used in the work and representation of science means that AIDS is usually conceptualized within already current and oppressive rubrics. Evelyn Fox Keller (1985, p. 18) writes in her book on women and science: 'one of the most common metaphors in Western history for such [scientific] mediation has been the sexual relation: knowledge is a form of consummation, just as sex is a form of knowledge.' Her metaphoric description of the work of science has a basis in the real: the acquisition of knowledge has often been obtained by the sexualized scrutiny of women's bodies (Harding, 1986; Jacobus et al., 1990).

But such metaphors also imply that even when men scrutinize nature, other men, the HIV virus or knowledge in general, this activity is already codified by tropes of gender, sexuality and power: the seer is a man, that which is seen is a woman, and the act of seeing is sexual. In her book on primatology, Donna Haraway (1989, p. 179) explains that even when the scientist is a woman, which is often the case in her field, she is constructed and understood as 'female male'. How does this always-male scientist look at science? In his book on postmodern theories of televised culture, Gregory Ulmer (1989, p. 7) writes: 'Knowing, in the modern paradigm is scopophilic. Regardless of gender, sex, class, race, or orientation of the knower, the one who knows, the subject of knowledge in the mind of science, is in the position of the voyeur.' And, I would add, the object of the gaze is in a passive position, a position codified as female.

Thus, in this paper I am less interested in how AIDS science documentaries see *women* (see Juhasz, 1990), as I am in the way that documentary and science invoke paradigms of looking at *AIDS' bodies* as if they were women. The structure for seeing the science of AIDS places the subject of representation into an already codified position – one of subjugation. The effects of this are very real for female, and male, PLWAs.

Pleasure/Power and Access to Vision in the Science Documentary

> Pleasure and power do not cancel or turn back against one another. They are linked together by complex mechanisms and devices of excitation and incitement. (Foucault, 1980, p. 48)

Mainstream science documentaries gain power and pleasure through knowing the subject of AIDS. Televised science documentaries take up the same truisms that have long organized both the institutions of science and documentary:

To see is to know.
To know is to control.
To control is a pleasure.

Both institutions rely on visualization and visualization technologies – the microscope, the film camera, the computer – to gain access to knowledge about the invisible virus AIDS. Both institutions claim the authority of rationalism and therefore are authorized to control what they see. This control brings satisfaction and mastery . . . it feels good.

In *The History of Sexuality: Volume I* (1980), Michel Foucault writes of the particular kinds of pleasure which arise from visual conquest. Taking up this analytic project, feminist theorists of science think critically about the ways that looking has been used by those people who have historically had the privilege of vision: 'some have singled out reliance on vision as a key culprit in the scrutiny, surveillance, domination, control, and exertion of authority over the body, particularly the bodies of women' (Martin, 1990, p. 69). I will argue that AIDS is envisioned in science documentaries in a manner that invokes Foucault's 'complex mechanisms and devices of excitation' (1980, p. 44). The consequences are a further 'domination, control, and exertion of authority' over the body with HIV disease: bodies of people already disenfranchised, already ill, already punished. For instance, the fear that is constructed in *NOVA*'s narrative is easily displaced on to *people* with AIDS (or perceived to be) rather than focused on the HIV virus (AIDS Discrimination Unit, 1987). In a society where femininity or homosexuality are often considered diseased states in themselves, this is an especially easy displacement. The way that AIDS is looked at in the science documentary condones the further domination and control of people, often women, who are already so seen.

Most televised AIDS documentaries naturalize and therefore authorize the power and pleasure they acquire in their study of this particular infected body of knowledge. It is in their blood. The form (documentary) and content (science), each work to confirm the validity of the other by naturalizing their underlying assumptions to the point of invisibility. The scrutinizing gaze of science is condoned by the scrutinizing gaze of the documentary camera; the technologically enhanced vision of the scientist is infinitely reflected in its technologically enhanced documentation. In the science documentary, the path from seeing to knowledge to power and pleasure – so common as to pass unnoticed in many cultural institutions – becomes twice transparent. Yet, theorists of documentary have argued that this use of the filmic apparatus has no greater claims upon the truth than does fiction film (Lazere, 1987; Minh-ha, 1990; Nichols, 1981; Rosenthal, 1988). Documentary 'truth' is discursively constituted, and is a social relation like any other form of culture (Hall, 1977). More generally, it is argued that science and documentary are subjective and political, because scientists and film-makers have their own opinions, because the institutions themselves embody dominant 'concepts, values, and ideologies', and because these institutions can be big business motivated by economics and politics (Aronowitz, 1988; Foucault, 1977; Nelkin, 1987; Rosenthal, 1988).

Feminist interpretations of science, while also discussing science as discursive, subjective and economic, emphasize that culture has been primarily the field of white, middle-class, heterosexual men: 'The dominant categories of cultural experience (white, male, middle/upper class, and heterosexual) will be reflected within the cultural institution of science itself: in its structure, theories, concepts, values, ideologies, and practices' (Bleir, 1986, p. 2). When I analyse these two PBS programmes on AIDS, I begin to consider how 'dominant categories of cultural experience' are reflected in the 'structure', 'values' and 'ideologies' of these specific science documentaries. I consider how the cultural experience of 'white, male, middle/upper class and heterosexual' men inflect the representation and knowledge of AIDS, and then, the lived experiences of female (and male) PLWAs.

The Three Routes to Pleasure and Power

NOVA offers the spectator three related routes to the pleasures of knowledge and power, all constructed through the privileged relationship to sight which define science and documentary: the powers and pleasures which are associated with control over the subject of study, with participating in a narrative which follows a vanquishing superhero, and with taking up a permitted gaze over the 'other'.

First, *NOVA*, like most documentaries, invites the viewer to identify with its own controlling vision over its weekly content. The viewer can take on the role of the omnipotent and omnipresent, unnameable, and unseeable force which constructs, organizes, interviews, makes music and images, and tells it like it is. Secondly, the structure of the horror film is appropriated to order the programme into a narrative about scrutiny, knowledge and conquest. *NOVA*'s episode *Can AIDS be Stopped?* allows the spectator a second site for power-and-pleasure-through-vision: the adventures of the superhero-scientist out to conquer the monster AIDS. Finally, a third system of delight is produced by assuming the gaze of the conquering scientist: the permitted and uninterrupted study of others. In *NOVA* and to a lesser degree in *The AIDS Quarterly*, the spectator can take up the scientist's gaze as he probes, examines and ultimately knows the monster AIDS, in all of its cultural manifestations: sexually exotic Africans, prostitutes, homosexual men.

All three of the structures set in place in *NOVA* rely upon gender: the metaphor of sexuality organizes scientific study and authority, gender roles underlie narratives of power and control, and women's bodies are always allowed to be looked at in compromising ways in our society. With this in mind, the printed scroll read by the narrator at NOVA's beginning can be seen less as a warning than as a tease about the good stuff to come: 'The following film contains graphic illustrations of human anatomy and sexual behaviour. Viewer discretion advised.'

The Construction of Pleasure through Control

AIDS is a scientific puzzle unsolved, a frightening example where nature has yet to be contained by science. 'Nothing could be more meaningless than a virus', suggests Judith Williamson, explaining the tremendous energy expended trying to define AIDS. 'It has no point, no purpose, no plan; it is part of no scheme, carries no inherent signification' (Williamson, 1989, p. 69). Yet, *NOVA* and its booming, male, unidentified voice-over make a coherent flow out of *representations* of AIDS: interviews with scientists, trips to labs, images of beakers and test tubes, national statistics about infection, and scientific explanations of the virus. The show's basic structure becomes a first example of the trajectory from visualization to pleasure and power. The authority and success with which the programme organizes its own sound and image bites replaces the incoherence of the phenomenon upon which it reports.

An alternative to this uncontestable and tautological force can be seen in *The AIDS Quarterly*. This science documentary takes a different approach to the construction of authorial control. Rather than relying on an unidentified and omniscient narrator, the programme is written and narrated by well-known TV personality, Peter Jennings. Jennings stands in a carpeted studio and chats with the home-audience. The feeling is familiar, friendly, informal. Unlike *NOVA*, which constitutes a single, logical narrative for the disparate events in its hour, *The AIDS Quarterly* takes up a structure that need not connect the complex issues surrounding AIDS under one over-arching, and over-simplifying plot. Instead, narrative coherence resides in Jennings' position as 'anchor'. The programme returns to him after each segment, and *he* is the necessary segue into the next AIDS story. If one disagrees with the show, one disagrees with Jennings. The very logic of the nightly news makes this difficult to do, according to Margaret Morse (1986, p. 58) who writes: 'Today it seems as though the anchor speaks on his own authority as an overarching presence, as a subject of the news who vouches for its truth.'

Although this method of documentary narration seems more ideologically 'honest' than that of *NOVA* because it identifies the location of its opinions, it is not outside the powers and pleasures of authority. Jennings demands the tremendous respect that nightly news anchors are afforded in our society, and more. For he is not working for ABC News here, he is working for the public good – one of Bush's 'thousand points of light'. We trust him because his heart is in the right place *and* because we already trust the news. This system of seeing, emanating from Jennings, although different from *NOVA*'s impersonal stare, is in this case difficult to contest because of the emotional and moral pulls of loyalty and philanthropy.

It is difficult to challenge *NOVA*'s authority for another reason: the strategy of tautology. *NOVA* constructs its authority through a mastery of vision which is enforced by its creation and presentation of expensive computer generated images of science. At the show's beginning, the narrator describes a 'strange and deadly virus'. The image which accompanies his lecture is a fuzzy sphere, a bit like a tennis ball. There is a thin horizontal line descending the field of the image, making a beep, beep sound like an electrocardiograph monitoring the heart of a patient in intensive care. The image moves closer and closer, the lines move faster and faster, and the beeps get louder and quicker. Then, there is a cut in image as the voice says: 'Littering its surface, hundreds of virus particles are budding forth ready to spread disease. This is how AIDS begins.' With 'magnification' we see 'how AIDS begins': the tennis ball is covered with countless, symmetrically placed pimples.

This is only the first example of a series of four such science-pix which repeat during the show. Simply through the repetition of these imaginary visions of invisible and hypothetical events is their status as real explanations of real events constructed. The viewer becomes familiar with these meaningless graphics, and grants them a credibility by virtue of recognition: ah yes, the T-4 cell's outer membrane . . . .

This is *NOVA*'s tautological system of science presentation: image confirms voice and voice confirms image. It is also Jean Baudrillard's vision of the postmodern world:

> The real is produced from miniaturized units, from matrices, memory banks, and command models – and with these it can be reproduced an infinite number of times. It no longer has to be rational, since it is no longer measured against some ideal or negative instance. It is nothing more than operational. In fact, since it is no longer enveloped by an imaginary, it is no longer real at all. (Baudrillard, 1984, p. 254)

These less than real sequences are always followed by a statement from a doctor or scientist who confirms the information and image constructed by *NOVA*. Knowledge is confirmed by vision; vision is empowered by knowledge.

For instance, Dr William Haseltine says: 'What we're finding is truly astounding. It's as if this virus comes from the depths of the seas encrusted with new biological organisms that we've never seen before in all of biology.' Midway through his interview, a visual insert of the rotating image of the blue orb, symmetrically dotted with pulsing white pimples, is shown. *NOVA* lets the home viewer *see* what 'we've never seen before', what even Dr Haseltine cannot: the cells, membranes, and viruses of AIDS. The first truism of 'science and documentary – to see is to know – is thus in *NOVA*, artificially, but forcefully, assured by technology which manufactures images of the things that *NOVA* says it knows. 'The territory no longer precedes the map, nor survives it. Henceforth, it is the map which precedes the territory' (Baudrillard, 1984, p. 253).

The Pleasures and Powers of Narrative

Dr Haseltine's words serve another function. His rhetoric is part of the second system of pleasure through vision and knowledge which is put into place by *NOVA*: the AIDS-as-monster-that-ate-Manhattan narrative structure of the programme. This second strategy make sense of the incoherent or unknowable (unseeable) phenomenon of AIDS by fabricating, and in the case of documentary, making visible, a story. '*NOVA* dramatizes scientific endeavor, with the scientist engaged in a race against various threatening forces to gain mastery over some aspect of a malevolent universe', writes Hornig in her analysis of the show (1990, p. 21). Narrative gives coherence, structure and pleasure to the random and frightening phenomenon of AIDS because it permits closure and it allows conquest. According to Nelkin (1987, p. 71), this coupling of closure and conquest is often the form that the media takes in its coverage of science: 'the message is our ability to win over the forces that besiege us. Order is restored.'

At the opening of the show the dramatis personae in the story about to unfold are introduced. The first image is of innocent victims – a young man and woman ice-skating hand in gloved hand at Rockefeller Center. The narrator says, as we watch them spin: 'Bruce and Bobbie – a young married couple at the beginning of their life together. There's only one problem. Bobbie has AIDS.' Can't anything be done to save Bobbie? Who will come to the rescue? 'In the face of this new and deadly epidemic', answers our narrator, 'science is engaged in a desperate fight to understand and overcome the AIDS virus.' There is a cut to Dr Haseltine, who makes his sea-monster comparison: 'What we're finding is truly astounding. It's as if this virus comes from the depths of the seas . . . .'

It is specifically, and importantly, the patterns of the horror movie which organize, visualize and make pleasurable this acquisition of knowledge about AIDS. For the horror film is not only a structure where good ultimately triumphs over evil, but one in which the distinction between good and evil, scientist and monster, self and other, is clearly and carefully delineated (Carroll, 1990; Kuhn, 1990). The function of the horror text is precisely to construct an other, a *Monster*, that embodies that which is not wanted in the self: 'the monstrous which narrative splits off from the self is a projection of unacceptable parts of the self – and indeed, of society' (Williamson, 1989, p. 77). The monster is the 'locus of the most primitive' (Newton, 1990, p. 85): sexuality, impurity, irrationality and, most importantly for this analysis, femininity. Feminist theorists of the horror film have maintained that the monster stands in for 'that area over which the narrative has lost control' (Creed, 1990, p. 214). This is the 'space' of the feminine. Noel Carroll (1990) argues that horror is defined by both fear and disgust. He writes that the envisioning of 'fantastic biology' plays a large part in the formation of these feelings: seeing bodies that are impure, that 'transgress categorical distinctions' (Carroll, 1990, pp. 43–4). Our society has long felt such feelings towards particular bodies and biologies. Women and gay men, for instance, transgress into the 'space of the feminine' – those places unknown, uncharted, irrational.

Early AIDS media were quick to isolate risk of HIV infection into communities – 'risk groups' – of others: homosexual men, Haitians, IVDUs, prostitutes (Treichler, 1988). It seemed clear who was safe and who was sick. Yet, by this 1986 *NOVA* production it was evident that all people, depending upon their behaviour, of course, were at risk (Treichler, 1988). Boundaries were dissolving and, according to Williamson, this made people anxious: 'the virus threatens to cross over that border of Other and Self; the threat it poses is not only one of disease but one of dissolution, the contamination of categories' (Williamson, 1989, p. 78). *NOVA*'s narrative re-clarifies boundaries in a real world where things are not nearly so simple. With perhaps too much simplicity, too much finality, *NOVA* identifies the good guys and the monster.

This eerie mood, wherein sea-monsters arise to snatch young skating couples away from Rockefeller Center is continually constructed throughout the show. A sense of threat, fear and mystery is manufactured to build anticipation before the conquest of the monster by science. But this mood is also constructed so that the resolution of the narrative (and the AIDS crisis, the show suggests) can be articulated within the discourse of horror. It should be no surprise, then, that this show manufactures a *visual* image where 'answers' are stored. To see is to know. But in this mythic narrative, things can be seen – like answers – which are not so visible in the real world. Answers are said to be in what the narrator calls the 'magic box' of possible cures.

Of course, hidden behind the box's spell-encrusted top are not only the magic serums which will cure Bobbie, but the programme's more political and economic agenda, which is to present pharmaceutical cures and medical research as the magic resolutions which will solve the crisis as *NOVA* has constituted it. The show is split into two equal halves: the laying out of the problem (can AIDS be stopped?), and solutions to this problem (Yes, it can, with magic, i.e. medicine). The sequence which introduces the 'magic answers to AIDS' opens on black. A light enters the screen because a door opens: the camera is inside a refrigerator. Unidentified hands enter the space, and grab something that has been resting inside the refrigerator. It is a box. An Asian scientist picks up the box, and carries it to a table. The narrator says: 'They've tested hundreds of substances and narrowed the search to the contents of what is known as the "magic box."'

The scene which follows depicts Bobbie's experimental treatment with AZT. After having been on AZT for several months and seeing a weight gain and stabilization of her fevers, Bobbie says to her doctor: 'You don't know how pleased we are. I mean we are so happy right now.' Dr Samuel Broder responds: 'But you have to understand that although I'm extremely gratified about your response, I can't be sure that it's the drug that we gave you that did this.' Bobbie concludes the scene with: 'I attribute it to the drug, though. I do. I don't care what anybody else says, it's the drug.'

The scene carefully ends with Bobbie's unfounded faith in her drug, not her doctor's more cautious advice. But this is necessary in the terms of a mythical narrative that presents magical answers to difficult problems. Unlike horror films, where the monster will be vanquished in two hours, the crisis of AIDS can not be reduced to the search for a cure, nor will the problem be solved when and if a cure is found. The ills of AIDS are not just physical, but economic, social, cultural and political (Sabatier, 1988).

The oversimplification of the search for medical cures forecloses accurate reportage on the complexities of medical research, the politics and economics of the pharmaceutical industry, and the negative (as well as positive) effects of particular medications. Furthermore, a focus on magical medical cures means little attention to the politics of *who* is predominantly affected by AIDS and why, means little attention to holistic and other non-Western responses to illness, and means little attention to those who *do not* have access to experimental studies or expensive medication. For example, as this show pictures the science of AZT, there is no suggestion of, or analysis about, why women have been continually discriminated against in access to experimental drugs and clinical trials.

The AIDS Quarterly's, *The Trial of Compound Q*, on the other hand, is about the scientific, economic, political and moral complexity of medical and pharmaceutical research. The sequence monitors two drug protocols – one legal, the other illegal – for a Chinese 'abortion and cancer drug', Tricasanthin, known as Compound Q. At the segment's beginning, Martin Delaney 'one of the most important AIDS activists', approaches Dr Alan Levin to see if he will run a speeded up drug trial to analyse the effects of Compound Q. Dr Levin agrees, but cautions, 'the odds are good that someone is going to die. This is not a magical panacea.' Then the show weighs the verbal testimony of people on the other 'side' of this case. Dr Volberding, who is conducting the 18-month official study of Compound Q, explains why things need to progress slowly.

The segment follows three gay men. Unlike *NOVA*, this show names the subjects and interviews them about their feelings and motivations throughout the study. It chronicles the death of two of them perhaps as a result of the study, and shows Dr Levin and Delaney making the difficult moral and medical decisions about whether they should continue the study, and at what dose level. The conclusions of the segment are presented with ambivalence. Tandy Belloo, the only survivor of the original study, is much improved after a bout of AIDS dementia, caused most probably by the Compound Q. He is taking Compound Q for a second time: 'I was disappointed when it wasn't a miracle cure . . . But I think its working.' Delaney is now leading an official protocol with the FDA.

The speakers in the programme, and the programme itself, conclude that there are no easy answers. It is unclear who was right and who was wrong, and if the two studies got anyone anywhere. Yet, if there is anything that is celebrated here, it is the search for knowledge itself, by the male scientists and PLWAs, and by *The AIDS Quarterly*. There is a narrative structuring this programme, but it is not that of horror. Rather, the structure of the trial system of liberal democracy is engaged – there are two sides to be heard, listen to them, weigh them, draw your own conclusion, vote. 'In this way television does not favour one point of view,' explains Stuart Hall. 'But it does favour – and reproduce – one definition of politics and excludes, represses, or neutralizes other definitions. By operating balance *within a given structure*, television tacitly maintains the prevailing definitions of political order' (Hall, 1988, p. 359).

Permitted Looking

In both of these science documentaries, one final system allowing the acquisition of pleasure is set in place: the delightful activity of watching those whom scientists study. Throughout the programmes, the audience is allowed permission, like the scientist, to watch the strange and curious lives of all kinds of social 'perverts'. In *The AIDS Quarterly*, this is handled with some grace by allowing the objects of the study to speak for themselves, yet the camera pries into several private moments. For instance, when Tandy Belloo, who is suffering from side-effects of AIDS dementia from his use of Compound Q, is confused, cannot form sentences and is ultimately brought to tears, the camera rolls and rolls, and this footage is included in the final programme.

This is only one example of a probing into the lives and bodies of others that often occurs in the science documentary. The particular power and pleasure of this form is that the viewer of scientific activity is a *permitted* voyeur – the voyeur who gave himself permission to look. Unlike the conventional Freudian voyeur, whose pleasure is in seeing without being seen, knowing without being known (even if he may ultimately 'accidentally' reveal himself), the scientist, the documentary camera and the home-viewer who is offered identification with both of these sites, authorize their act in the names of Science, Knowledge and Truth. They proudly announce their presence and flash their licences to be there.

For example, the *NOVA* programme ends with a sequence presenting a gay male PLWA. The man, identified not by name but by sexual preference, is participating in an unspecified study. But, the narrator does say some things with great precision: every year 'he' arrives at 'Ward 86' at 'San Francisco General' for his part of the study. He gets a medical examination ('stick your tongue way out' instructs the doctor, as we see this less-than-dignified moment of the patient's visit). The narrator concludes: 'The medical exam is only the beginning. Volunteers are also asked to reveal the history of their sexual lives. What they did, with whom, how often, and with what protection.' The real need to understand the relationship between sexual behaviour and HIV infection seems somehow lost in this sordid inclusion of the study's demands about private sexual practice but not of the study's purpose or results.

Earlier, in reporting a study on heterosexual transmission, *NOVA*'s camera lingers on the spaces and bodies of the sex industry. Although the study considers three groups of heterosexual women, *NOVA* only covers one aspect of the study. The narrator says: 'the project's field workers go into the streets recruiting from those groups of women.' Simply the use of the loaded statement 'in the streets' is enough to identify *NOVA*'s interest in only one of 'those groups' of women. But to make it crystal clear, his voice is accompanied by a lurid montage of images of the red light district: Live! Live! Live!, Erotic Nude Show!, lights blink, seedy men enter shaded doors. Only one short segment of an interview with a prostitute is included: she is asked to calculate how many partners she has had in a year. When she can't work out the maths, the narrator does it for her.

The way that *NOVA* reports the work of science and doctors – the knowledge and concomitant sexual pleasure gained from an authorized scrutiny of others' problems and lifestyles – has a long tradition. 'Science is a masculine viewer, who is anticipating full knowledge of nature, which is represented as the naked female body', writes Jordanova (1988, p. 87) in her study of scientific imagery.

Conclusions: Alternative Pleasures

> Sex here is the perfect metaphor for a particular admixture of power and pleasure. (Jordanova, 1988, p. 150)

Power and pleasure are invoked by the conflation of vision and authority. The science documentary affirms its privilege to see and learn at the expense of others – the bodies it 'objectively' views and then objectifies. What are the effects of representations which are based upon a sexualized and gendered gaze? How does pleasure transfigure itself into power? Putting AIDS into the gendered female position has easily translated into policies which treat PLWAs in the same way our culture presently treats those, like many women, who are culturally disenfranchised: perpetuating problems by cutting funds, care, services (ACTUP/NY Women and AIDS Group, 1990; Patton, 1985; Sabatier, 1988). Making AIDS and its bodies the monster has contributed to a culture where PLWAs are actively discriminated against in all aspects of their existence from access to health insurance and clinical trials, to the less blatant forms of discrimination which occur against women and their children in the neighbourhood, workplace and home (AIDS Discrimination Unit, 1987).

But there are other systems of pleasure that can be used to make a documentary or to study science. Rather than a system of distance and control, difference and power, structures of similarity and reciprocity are possible. Perhaps the recent theories of feminist science provides better founding principles for scientific study than the three truisms with which I began this chapter: 'No rigid boundaries separate the subject of knowledge (the knower) and the natural object of knowledge; the subject/object split is not used to legitimate the dominance of nature; nature itself is conceptualized as active rather than passive' (Fee, 1986, p. 47). Furthermore, much alternative AIDS media differentiates itself from work like *NOVA* because it willingly situates itself *within* the object of study: speaks *from* and *to* a position of infection, difference, otherness (Juhasz, 1992). Such work identifies with, instead of gapes at, the subject of study. Such work identifies with, rather than intensifies, the struggles of PLWAs. In AIDS media that are effective rather than punitive, to look is to see and know *yourself*, not the other – an entirely different route to pleasure. Finally, pleasure is not the only emotion upon which representation can be based. Much alternative AIDS media has been rooted in anger: the motivating power of political action.

References

ACTUP/NY Women and AIDS Book Group (1990) *Women, AIDS and Activism.* Boston: South End Press.

AIDS Discrimination Unit of the New York City Commission on Human Rights (1987) *AIDS and People of Color: The Discriminatory Impact.* New York: The Commission on Human Rights.

Aronowitz, Stanley (1988) *Science as Power: Discourse and Ideology in Modern Society.* Minneapolis: University of Minnesota Press.

Baudrillard, Jean (1984) The precession of simulacra. In Wallis, B. (ed.), *Art after Modernism: Rethinking Representation.* New York: The New Museum of Contemporary Art.

Bleir, Ruth (ed.) (1986) *Feminist Approaches to Science.* New York: Pergamon Press.

Carroll, Noel (1990) *The Philosophy of Horror.* New York: Routledge.

Creed, Barbara (1990) Gynesis, postmodernism and the science fiction horror film. In Kuhn (1990), pp. 214–18.

Crimp, Douglas (ed.) (1988) Introduction. *AIDS: Cultural Analysis/Cultural Activism.* Cambridge, Mass.: MIT Press.

Fee, Elizabeth (1986) Critiques of modern science: the relationship of feminism to other radical epistemologies. In Ruth Bleir (ed.) *Feminist Approaches to Science.* New York: Pergamon Press.

Foucault, Michel (1977) *Language, Counter-Memory, Practice: Selected Essays and Interviews.* Ithaca: Cornell University Press.

Foucault, Michel (1979) *Discipline and Punish: The Birth of the Prison.* New York: Vintage Books.

Foucault, Michel (1980) *The History of Sexuality: Volume I.* New York: Vintage Books.

Hall, Stuart (1977) Culture, the media and the 'ideological effect'. In J. Curran, M. Gurevitch, and J. Woollacott (eds), *Mass Communication and Society.* London: Edward Arnold.

Hall, Stuart (1988) Media power: The double bind. In Rosenthal (1988), pp. 357–64.

Haraway, Donna (1989) *Primate Visions: Gender, Race and Nature in the World of Modern Science.* New York: Routledge.

Harding, Sandra (1986) *The Science Question in Feminism.* Ithaca: Cornell University Press.

Hornig, Susanna (1990) Television's *NOVA* and the construction of scientific truth. *Critical Studies in Mass Communications* 7, 11–23.

Jacobus, Mary, Keller, Evelyn Fox and Shuttleworth, Sally (eds) (1990) *Body/ Politics: Women and the Discourses of Science.* New York: Routledge.

Jordanova, Ludmilla (1988) *Sexual Visions: Images of Gender in Science and Medicine Between the Eighteenth and Twentieth Centuries.* Madison: University of Wisconsin Press.

Juhasz, Alexandra (1990) The contained threat: women in mainstream AIDS documentary. *The Journal of Sex Research* 27 (1), 47–64.

Juhasz, Alexandra (1992) From within: alternative AIDS media by women. *Praxis* 3, 23–46.

Karpf, Anne (1988) *Doctoring the Media: The Reporting of Health and Medicine.* London: Routledge.

Keller, Evelyn Fox (1985) *Reflections on Gender and Society.* New Haven: Yale University Press.

164   *Women and AIDS*

Kuhn, Annette (ed.) (1990) *Alien Zone: Cultural Theory and Contemporary Science Fiction*. London: Verso.
Lazere, Donald (ed.) (1987) *American Media and Mass Culture: Left Perspectives*. Berkeley, Calif.: University of California Press.
Martin, Emily (1990) Science and women's bodies: forms of anthropological knowledge. In Jacobus et al. (1990), pp. 69–83.
Minh-ha, Trinh T. (1990) Documentary is not a name. *October* 52 (Spring), 77–97.
Morse, Margaret (1986) The television news personality and credibility: reflections on the news in transition. In Tania Modleski (ed.), *Studies in Entertainment: Critical Approaches to Mass Culture*. Bloomington: Indiana University Press.
Nelkin, Dorothy (1987) *Selling Science: How the Press Covers Science and Technology*. New York: W.H. Freeman.
Newton, Judith (1990) Feminism and anxiety in *Alien*. In Kuhn (1990), pp. 82–90.
Nichols, Bill (1981) *Ideology and the Image*. Bloomington: Indiana University Press.
Patton, Cindy (1985) *Sex and Germs: The Politics of AIDS*. Boston: South End Press.
Rosenthal, Alan (ed.) (1988) *New Challenges for Documentary*. Berkeley, Calif.: University of California Press.
Sabatier, Renee (1988) *Blaming Other: Prejudice, Race and Worldwide AIDS*. Philadelphia: New Society Publishers.
Treichler, Paula (1988) AIDS, gender, and biomedical discourse: current contests for meaning. In E. Fee and M. Fox (eds), *AIDS: The Burdens of History*. Berkeley, Calif.: University of California Press.
Ulmer, Gregory (1989) *Teletheory: Grammatology in the Age of Video*. New York: Routledge.
Williamson, Judith (1989) Every virus tells a story: the meanings of HIV and AIDS. In E. Carter and S. Watney (eds), *Taking Liberties: AIDS and Cultural Politics*. London: Serpent's Tail.
Winston, Brian (1990) Roger and Me and Francois Arago: Documentary and Science. Paper presented at the Ohio University Film Conference, 1990.

8

'With Champagne and Roses': Women at Risk from/in AIDS Discourse

Cindy Patton

> Most of the reported [cases among heterosexuals] clearly involved anal sex or intravenous drugs.
>
> Dr Jay A. Levy of the University of California, San Francisco, reported in *Newsweek* 'Special Report on AIDS', 12 August 1985

> I have only normal heterosexual intercourse . . . but I've become a lot more selective about my partners.
>
> A 'typical single women' quoted in *People Magazine*, 'AIDS and the Single Woman', 14 March 1988

The *People Magazine* of 30 July 1990 featured a full-cover photograph of a hopeful Ali Gertz, with the bold, black headline, 'AIDS: A Woman's Story', above her head. Burned in white type over her dark sweater were the words: 'Her date came with champagne, roses . . . and AIDS. Eight years later, ALI GERTZ, 24, is fighting for her life and warning women that, yes, it *can* happen to you. Inside: Her story and those of six other women living with the deadly disease.'

Though certainly not the first woman in her situation, Gertz, through media attention and her own decision to become publicly involved in HIV education, provided a 'real' referent for the apocryphal stories about 'average' white middle-class young women who contracted the virus through 'ordinary sexual intercourse' with men from their own class. Coming on the heels of the highly publicized Chambers 'love murder' case, in which a young man of Gertz's social class killed his girlfriend during 'rough sex', the Gertz story was able to draw on a re-emerged anxiety that 'nice men' harboured a variety of pathologies.[1] The story manages to romanticize without blaming the spunky, well-to-do socialite infected with a disease of the 'other' through a man as socially emblematic as herself: the moral is that 'ordinary' women are not only at danger if they cross class lines, but also within the tightly guarded bounds of their own class. The ability to embrace as part of the mainstream 'risk behaviours' once associated with an 'other' – 'queers', 'junkies' and 'prostitutes' – is accomplished by covertly deploying class and race to bifurcate the connotations of homosexuality and drug use.

The story mystified how Gertz's boyfriend had become infected. He seems to have had sex with men: ironically, the omnipresence of the well-groomed gay lawyer or doctor with HIV diminished the otherness of homosexuality, as long as such 'deviants' bear upper-class markers. Or, *People* suggests, he might have injected designer drugs for fun. Media accounts had already established these high tech escapes as a problem plaguing yuppies with career stress and puritanical incapacity to pursue simpler forms of leisure. Yuppy 'use' of cocaine was less personally demeaning and socially destructive than the 'abuse' of heroin or crack which was represented as characterizing black or working-class 'street addicts' who were the real targets of the 'war on drugs'.

Despite its reproduction of many class-linked misconceptions about AIDS, the *People* version of Gertz's story was a break from seven years of stories which first sensationalized women's categorical vulnerability then confounded women's ability to identify with risk-reduction advice (largely the promotion of condom use) by shifting focus away from behaviour and on to an identification split between 'women' of the 'general public' versus those 'at risk', visually represented as women of colour, drug injectors, sex workers or as heterosexual women who cannot tell a gay/bisexual man from a 'real (safe)' man.[2]

The Risk that Could not Speak its Name

Epidemiological and media nomenclature were politically charged from the beginning of the HIV epidemic. By the end of 1981, the emerging syndrome was dubbed Gay Related Immune Deficiency (GRID) and the 'gay plague' by researchers and reporters, respectively. The name change to Acquired Immune Deficiency Syndrome (AIDS), adopted both by scientists and the media by early 1983, occurred in part because gay activists objected to the social implications of the term GRID, and in part because researchers recognized that the name was simply inaccurate since a quarter or more of the initially identified cases appeared in 'non-gay' people. Ironically, gay activists' hard-fought battle to be recognized as a community with common cultural values and social identity – to be called a *gay/lesbian community* rather than socially disconnected *homosexuals* whose distinguishing characteristic was a perversion not a counterculture – was hijacked in the name change.

Public health strategies usually use either a risk-based or a population-based strategy, and these are not thought to be compatible. 'Risk' strategies aim at getting individuals to perceive a particular practice as risky, while 'population' strategies seek to transform norms in large groups so that the aggregate practice of potentially problem behaviours is lowered. Because the initial 'risk behaviours' were thought to be the exclusive domain of the 'risk groups', the public health strategies inadvertently fused the two types of approach.

The struggle to establish gayness as more than a sexual practice in part exacerbated the confusion of researchers, the media and even gay men between social identity and risk practice. The collective social identity supported by an elaborate economy of bookstores, bars and newspapers of urban gay men made it relatively easy to 'sell' safe sex through marketing-style risk-education campaigns. However, in addressing men based on identification with the gay community rather than with specific high-risk behaviours, this strategy produced a further conflation of risk practice and identity: not all gay men engaged in anal intercourse, but they were addressed as if they did. Likewise, not all drug injectors shared works and many sex workers had long practised 'safe sex' (either through using condoms, or specializing in acts other than intercourse). The persistent association of AIDS with stereotyped notions of 'deviant subcultures' confused the biology of transmission with the fragmentation into 'target audiences' of likely candidates for education. The 'community'/target audience approach implicitly suggested that gay men and drug injectors were categorically at risk, regardless of an individual's actual practices. There was, and remains, a confusion in the public mind about the distinction between claimed identities ('gay', 'junkie' etc.) and modes of transmission (male to male, or male to female intercourse with ejaculation, transfusion or injection of blood).[3]

If AIDS seemed always to be a possession of groups fractured-off from the mainstream, then women seemed to be the stitches holding the tattering mainstream together (mothers, wives, sisters, volunteers). Capacity to acquire HIV became a signifier of difference: the slide from 'risk' to 'deviance' virtually disabled efforts to direct education towards women, or even to recognize that women had clinical AIDS. Although Centers for Disease Control (CDC) reports included a woman with 'these two conditions [Kaposi's sarcoma and *Pneumocystis carinii* pneumonia] in persons without known underlying disease'[4] in a July 1981 report, and while women are listed in summary epidemiological counts, no full-scale analysis of women and AIDS appeared in CDC reports until well after media accounts of the mid to late 1980s had presented apocryphal and bizarre accounts of women's risk of HIV.[5]

These media accounts first raised the spectre of pervasive infection (as in a 1985 *Life* cover which read, polysemously, 'No One is Safe') and then retreated to assure the public that 'ordinary' heterosexuals were not in danger. In particular, AIDS was early said to result from anal sex itself (independent of any virus), a practice which, according to broad social perception, is 'kinky', a 'primitive form of birth control' or associated chiefly with 'prostitution'. The public discussion of heterosexuals who had contracted HIV might have broken down the homophobia and misogyny latent in the epidemiological labelling. Instead, by fusing the myths that AIDS is caused by anal sex and that 'normal' heterosexuals do not engage in this practice, the category of risk/deviance *expanded* to include 'kinky' heterosexuals. The fundamental bifurcation, evident from the beginning of the epidemic in the research and media terms of 'risk groups' and 'general public', survived unchallenged because heterosexuals with AIDS were re-categorized as nominal 'queers'.

This mystification of risk seemed to work in tandem with a reconstruction of notions of identity: rather than remaining as a kind of silent, invulnerable norm against which the 'deviations' were constructed, the 'general public' began to quantify an identity as white, non-drug injecting and, especially, as heterosexual. Like gay people's oppositional identity construction in relation to the homophobia of the post-war years, 'heterosexuals' seemed to form a more concrete and public identity in opposition to the invocations that 'anyone can get AIDS'. This 'straight' identity worked sometimes to articulate more clearly an inchoate collective desire for 'normal intercourse' with the 'opposite sex', but as often served as a mechanism for distancing from risk of contracting the 'gay plague', and even as a justificatory position from which to advocate draconian measures against 'deviants' or engage in hate crimes.[6]

Once risk-reduction education spelled out the specific hazards of sex, the covert but common practice of male–male sex among non-gay identified men had somehow to be excluded from 'straight' identity. An old category – 'bisexual' – was reinvented to account for those men who seemed incapable of taking up a stable identity and role in either the 'general (heterosexual) public' or the 'gay lifestyle'.[7] Despite the media's new character, the indecisive bisexual, CDC epidemiology and risk-reduction advice grounded in it continued to use the category 'homosexual/bisexual male', leaving a wide interpretive space for men and women reluctant to be hailed by educational campaigns.

If there were ever-expanding ways for men outside the core urban

gay communities to *evade* identification with risk-reduction education, women could barely have recognized themselves in the CDC
accounting if they had tried. The route of transmission for women
drug injectors was considered a closed issue; their sexual practices
were considered redundant or irrelevant to *their* risk, though
important in sketching out the 'pool' of 'vessels and vectors' waiting
to infect babies or men. On charts representing the breakdown of
the officially counted AIDS cases by gender and risk factor the
category 'homosexual/female' was usually marked not zero, but 'not
applicable'. Women who had sex exclusively with women were
considered not at risk, and 'lesbians' were widely considered to be
neither drug injectors nor former (or current) sexual partners of
men. In this same logic, 'bisexual' women were considered at risk
only as the 'passive partner' during 'heterosexual intercourse' and
were thus only counted as heterosexual contacts of men.

Obviously, these 'scientific' categories are deeply influenced by
cultural assumptions about sexuality. Male sexuality is the only site
of agency, so the bisexuality of indecision invoked in the mainstream press can only be a 'male' phenomenon. Women's sexuality
is treated as totally passive and outside any discourse of choice or
will; 'heterosexual' women are understood as partners of men
rather than as agents of their own desires. Sex between women is
simply considered 'not applicable' because it does not count as sex.
The implicit argument here is that the crucial issues of sexuality are
those concerning men, a kind of patriarchal self-obsession that has
still not been able to admit that, biologically speaking, women are
indeed at far more risk of contracting HIV from men than vice
versa.[8]

The association of AIDS with North American forms of deviance
was under siege by the First International AIDS Conference held in
Atlanta in April 1985, this time based on data from African cities.
In these studies, sexual intercourse between men and women was
the most common risk factor among study subjects on that
continent, suggesting that 'ordinary intercourse' might be as
common as homosexual intercourse as a modality of HIV
transmission.[9] Racist beliefs about differences in the conduct of
heterosexuality were invoked to distance further the North American, white heterosexual reading public from this new evidence that
they might be subject to HIV infection. The cultural imperialism of
Western writers prevented them from seeing the real parallels
between the situation of women in 'Africa' and in Euro-America: as
long as writers could blame African men, it was possible to talk
about the plight of women dependent on their male partners.[10]

For example, a *Time* article of 16 February 1987, called 'In the

Grip of the Scourge', provides a narrative framework for a racist view of an 'other' heterosexuality in order to brush away the implication that widespread infection of Western heterosexuals might be possible:

> Josephine is dying because she had sexual intercourse with her late husband. A prosperous trader, he had contracted 'slim disease' . . . thousands of people in her town and the surrounding countryside have already died . . . Townspeople first attributed the mysterious disease to witchcraft. Now they know that their lovemaking is to blame.

Josephine's tragedy is the tragedy of central Africa.

> Once the disease gained a foothold, it spread rapidly among Africans in the same way it has among homosexuals in the US: through sex with multiple partners.
>
> Another key factor in the transmission of the disease is the unwillingness of many heterosexual men to change their sexual practices.

Again, men's sexuality is the concern, and women's 'plight', once mentioned, must be instantly metonymized: her needs and her experience can never be specified or addressed.

Finally, because the original case counting considered male-to-male sex to be the primary route of transmission, men with two or more routes of exposure were represented in statistics as homosexual/bisexual. In the late 1980s, the CDC revised their categories several times to reflect people with multiple exposure routes. The new categories were single-route, double-route etc. with the basic categories remaining: male-to-male, drug injection, blood product consumption, perinatal and partner, a category comprising women.[11] Once this new counting system reorganized the cases, it became clear that people whose sole (and therefore definitive) route of transmission was male–male sex comprised less than half of the total. If drug injection had been the privileged category in the early epidemiology (that is, if men with both homosexual contact and drug injection with more than one risk factor had been listed as injectors rather than homosexual), the 'male-to-male only' category even during the confusing first years would have been closer to 60 per cent. And, since cases among drug injectors and 'female partners' have continuously increased, individuals whose risk is *solely* male–male sex continue to decline as a percentage of total cases. Even among this number, many men do not identify with 'the gay community', especially men of colour, whose ethnic cultures have specific long-standing, if sometimes unnamed, homosexual social roles.

The assumption that those engaging in 'risk practices' constructed for themselves an identity which could be targeted in educational campaigns tended to split AIDS education into two forms: the 'need to know' about risk reduction (aimed at 'risk communities') and the softer knowledge that AIDS cannot be casually contracted (aimed at quelling the hysteria of 'the general public' and, perhaps, promoting 'compassion' towards people living with AIDS). This bifurcation proved fatal when addressing women, who were represented in two ways: the compassionate member of the general public (the 'AIDS volunteer'), and the source of infection (the 'prostitute' or 'junky mother'). The elision of a realistic subject position from which to assess what personal risk meant became the linchpin of the reconstruction of heterosexual identity, first by degendering women who had contracted HIV – pictured as women who shared needles – and second by reinforcing the idea that 'normal' sexual intercourse between 'ordinary' heterosexuals re-quired no modifications, specifically, condoms.[12] Epidemiologists knew that an important percentage of the men infected with HIV were engaging in sex with women (perhaps even half), and that a considerable number of women were infected through male partners who had themselves been infected through needle-sharing. Nevertheless, women were rarely represented as generally at potential risk, only as at risk as needle-sharers or risky as 'prostitutes': that women could be at risk through sex was neatly elided. Education to drug injectors continues to emphasize needle hygiene more than condom use, and the message has been heeded: sadly, it is not unusual to find men who have stopped sharing needles but do not use condoms, or even to find needle-sharing sex partners who bleach their works but do not practise safe sex. Some would call this genocide.

The Representation of Biology

The confusion between identity and practice was shored up through some curious readings of the female body: because the syndrome was associated with 'gay' men, and because such men were stereotyped as having only anal sex, many researchers and most popular writers considered sexual risk to be through anal sex, but not vaginal sex. The reasoning here was tautological: if AIDS was a disease of perverted sex, then heterosexuals who got it must also be engaging in perverted sex.[13] The image of anal intercourse as the culprit was never grounded in any epidemiological data. The only evidence offered for the hypothesized greater risk of anal inter-course was the 'rugged vagina'/'fragile anus' argument (Treichler, 1988) which, while a technically accurate description, ignores the cervix as a portal of entry and rests more on bizarre folk beliefs than any epidemiological evidence or well-reasoned assessment of mechanism of infection. Instead of realizing that anal sex was more common among heterosexuals than popularly believed, the 'danger of anal sex' asserted in AIDS discourse converged with the belief that 'nice girls don't' to produce a fatal bit of folklore among heterosexuals that vaginal intercourse carried no risk.

The disappearance of women into euphemistic or politically charged categories like 'heterosexual', 'partners of', even 'prostitute' and 'IVDU' only reflected on the level of representation what was occurring at the level of research and clinical practice. It is only now becoming public knowledge that women's clinical and social experiences of the epidemic are considerably different from men's. Women are diagnosed later in their disease process because they generally receive less health care than male counterparts and because many physicians still have difficulty imagining that a woman they are treating might be presenting HIV-related symptoms. Doctor's misperceptions are redoubled because a range of seriously disabling or fatal gynaecological sequelae to HIV infection are not counted as 'symptoms' in the CDC's definitional hierarchy.[14] Unlike night sweats or weight loss, once non-definitive, now red flags for HIV infection, persistent vaginal infections or rapidly progressing cervical cancer do not lead most clinicians down the path to diagnosis of HIV infection. Until recently, women generally only discovered their serostatus *after* a male partner's illness, during prenatal care or because she had been identified as at 'high risk' and recruited for study, usually through drug treatment clinics or STD clinics likely to have a client population of sex workers. Even where HIV antibody testing is widely available, women have high rates of not returning for results[15] (Nelson et al., 1990; Norris et al., 1990).

What Women Need

Women's concerns have been erased from AIDS policy and media accounts because women are not considered to be persons. Women, and especially women's bodies, are decontextualized from women's concrete social existence, and treated as of concern only in so far as they affect men or children. To put it bluntly, women are either vaginas or uteruses and, curiously, never both at the same time. It is as if there were a great sea of undifferentiated, but generically male bodies which, at particular moments – 'sex' (always recreational) – or for a particular purpose – procreation (which never involves pleasure) – suddenly take on two different genders. The women who emerge in the context of sex are always considered 'prostitutes' or 'loose women', and the women who become childbearers seem never to engage in 'sex'. A *Newsweek* article of 12 August 1985 relies completely on this split: the left page features a large but fuzzy night shot of 'prostitutes' 'working the streets in New York: some experts fear that prostitutes might turn out to be carriers who could further fuel the epidemic.' On the facing page are smaller photographs of pubescent Ryan White and baby Matthew Kozup; both contracted HIV through blood products. 'Prostitutes' are problematic only as sex partners, not as childbearers: 'Any future argument for unrestrained sexual life will have to take into account that it has dire new consequences – not only for those adults who freely choose it but for children like Ryan White.' The writer seems never to have considered that sex workers are mothers, too; after all, sex work is a reasonably well-paid way to support their children and be home during the day. The writer could have suggested that sex workers' children are at risk from infected 'johns', but this would only have located the source of infection in the one place our culture cannot believe it exists: the wilful refusal to wear condoms on the part of 'ordinary' US men.

The fear of sex workers seems always to precede addressing the needs of women, including female sex workers. The World Health Organization's Global Programme on AIDS produced special official guidelines (October 1988) for the control of HIV transmission between male and female prostitutes and their clients six months before submitting an unofficial advisory paper on 'Women and AIDS' for the Economic and Social Council's Commission on the Status of Women (March–April 1989), the latter of which was completed at the request of another United Nations branch (scc World Health Organization, 1990). There is no division or individual in charge of women's concerns in the epidemic; however, there are posts covering sex workers, men who have sex with men, youth, and the general population.

Media and public health concern for childbearers is less with the welfare of the woman than with that of her unborn child. A *Newsweek* article of 23 September 1985, 'The AIDS Conflict', goes so far as to construct an epidemiological category (mother with AIDS) that has never appeared in CDC counts: 'Most of the cases (among children) represent children who were born to a *mother with AIDS*, a category that seems likely to grow with the spread of the disease among intravenous drug users' (emphasis added). A *Time* article on 27 April 1987, summarizing the CDC's first published report on women and AIDS (which had appeared in the *Journal of the American Medical Association* the previous week:

Time appears to have rewritten a press release for its first major article on women and AIDS) also lays bare the assumptions about the real issues to be addressed in women's risk of HIV:

> Though women account for less than 7% of all U.S. AIDS victims, their cases have a special significance . . . By studying these cases, researchers can get clues about how rapidly the disease is spreading among heterosexuals and among children, most of whom contract AIDS from infected mothers . . . No less striking was the study's finding that more than 70% of AIDS cases in women occurred among blacks and Hispanics. Indeed, a woman who is black is 13 times as likely as one who is white to fall victim, and 90% of infants born with AIDS are black or Hispanic.

If this did not condemn women enough, the *Time* article cites an editorial accompanying the *JAMA* report as claiming that: 'The potential future danger of AIDS is less compelling [to poor, minority women] than the day-to-day problems of poverty and drug use.' It seems impossible to acknowledge that women themselves might need help.

The Always Already Infected

How either the vagina-body or the uterus-body became infected in the first place is never addressed: one is left with the distinct impression that particular, isolated women are somehow always already infected. The reality that it is mostly men – clients, husbands, boyfriends, needle-sharing partners[15] – who infected the women is ignored.[16] When men are mentioned as a danger it is through the invocation of the (exceptional) 'bisexual' man, or as a reminder that a woman (who will, of course, be 'promiscuous') will have to figure out some way to deal with getting him to use a condom. Conversely, advice to men about using condoms centres almost exclusively on the risk to them of sex for hire.

There are a number of striking duplicities here: lists of risk factors in educational material aimed at heterosexuals includes 'having sex with a prostitute', while having sex with 'johns' is absent. There is no admonition to protect sex workers by using condoms, only dire warnings about the danger of being infected in such a commercial transaction. Certainly, community-based organizers and educators emphasize that condom use is to protect the sex workers. However, it is important to recognize the bizarre logic of getting prostitutes to risk their income to get men to use condoms which public health officials view as for the protection of the men. This amounts to a tax on sex workers, or perhaps a rebate to the male client who, for the sake of the epidemic, must purchase supposedly 'inferior' experiences of sex, that is, intercourse or oral sex while wearing a condom. The implication – and in fact, the practice – of public health is to disregard the safety of women sex workers because they are viewed only as sexual receptacles, presumed to be already infected.

When women are not vaginas waiting to infect men, they are uteruses, waiting to infect fetuses. The obsessive concern with preventing conception by HIV positive women, or *any woman who might be perceived at risk of contracting HIV*, is often first invoked through the spectre of millions of infected babies. Most media reports start by invoking horrific statistics of huge numbers of infected babies, usually confusing seroprevalence in newborns tested to discover prevalence rates in women indirectly, with the number of truly infected infants. Because it is easier to obtain permission to test newborns than their adult mothers, most studies citing seroprevalence rates of women giving birth are derived from unlinked testing of their babies. Accurate testing of the serostatus of the infants themselves can occur only later, since it takes about 18 months before the infant has its own immune system.

Once the reader is horrified by the prospect of an 'AIDS generation', as one poster purporting to represent infected infants calls it, a curious tautology is proposed. Without ever suggesting that an HIV positive woman might rationally calculate the risks of pregnancy, and failing to recognize most women did not discover their serostatus until late in a prenatal care process, the media suggest that by virtue of having been wanton enough to contract HIV, a seropositive women is incapable of making an informed and reasonable pregnancy choice. The fact that an HIV positive woman chooses to start or continue a pregnancy is taken as evidence of her immorality. But, certainly, couples in which one or both partners are HIV positive might view the risk of childbearing as a fair one to take. The best recent studies suggest that there is a 20–60 per cent chance of the child being infected.[17] Even worse, when the issue of childbearing decisions by discordant couples (man HIV positive, woman HIV negative) is raised in the World Health Organization's HIV counselling guidelines (aimed principally at developing nations who are the agency's main clients), the counselling issue is identified as that of preventing infection of the child. The possibility that the seronegative woman will also become infected in the process of conception (during 'sex') is ignored. As Chapter 1 by Amaro explains, women and couples often express the desire to have a child as a positive contribution to their community, a legacy, or part of their attempts to maintain their social status and interconnected-ness with their families and communities.[18] Faced with a 40–80 per cent chance of bearing a non-infected child, this does not seem like such an irrational or immoral decision.

When 'People' Doesn't Fit

Women's needs are also elided because they are viewed only as exceptions or variables to generalities about 'people living with AIDS', a term which always implicitly refers to men. We don't, for example, say 'men living with AIDS', or even 'men and women living with AIDS'. We say 'people living with AIDS', and when necessary, specify 'women living with AIDS'. That is, the concerns and issues of people living with AIDS orientate towards men's social situation, men's bodies and men's needs. Women are thought to have 'special needs', and this only when the basic male-orientated model is clearly incapable of meeting their needs. This is in no way to undervalue the importance of the PLWA movement, its conscious attempts to involve women, and its concrete role in improving the lives of women. However, we might ponder how the movement would have been different if it had risen out of women's experience of the epidemic.

One problem is that the PLWA movement is modelled on the 'coming out' process in gay culture, and can accommodate the 'storytelling' process within Alcoholics or Narcotics Anonymous culture, both of which empower the individual by helping them to claim as positive an identity which society labels as bad or immoral. To the extent that individuals can relate to this model, the PLWA movement is empowering. However, women, especially those infected through ordinary intercourse with their husband or boyfriend, have difficulty claiming this new identity – women weren't especially labelled sick, and the conditions of poverty and isolation which many men experience *because* of their AIDS diagnosis are already the lived experience of women. Thus, for women, AIDS usually does not cause the difference in social standing or identity that it does for the self-identified gay man and for some heterosexual men and women involved in the drug culture.

This individual empowerment model has become the trend in most Western counselling and service delivery agencies. The model assumes that the major problem of the person living with AIDS is making the behaviour and attitude changes which 'safe sex' and the patient role require, and assumes that the best way of supporting the person living with AIDS is to provide paraprofessionals and befrienders. This gender-biased model may serve to make a woman's situation worse by encouraging separation from her existing family system and informal women's networks. Where paraprofessionals and befrienders augment a system of supports for men, they may disempower a woman or her support networks by introducing someone with a perceived higher social status and connections to formal public health surveillance systems, especially if the paraprofessionals and befrienders are men.[19]

Why We Can't Talk about Prevention

Perhaps the most deadly erasure of women's needs has been in the area of HIV infection prevention. Certainly, the tendency to view women as either vaginas or uteruses enables educators and policy-makers to avoid the issue of how and why women are infected in the first place. It is hard not to see the workings of an adolescent male sexual psychology in this desire to avoid the idea that sex can lead to conception and, at the same time, to refuse to ask where babies come from. Sex is implicitly reconstituted as a man's right and a woman's obligation, with women responsible both for protecting men from disease and for avoiding the consequences of transmission to a man's child. From the 'active', male perspective, risk is equated with women, not with particular heterosexual practices. From the woman's perspective, a husband or boyfriend may be at risk from someone else (a needle-sharing partner, a 'homosexual' partner or a 'vagina'), and her child might be at risk from her ('uterus'), but the twist in the logic of safe sex which encourages heterosexuals to view unpaid intercourse as 'safe', makes it difficult for a woman to perceive *herself* as at risk. Studies of young heterosexual adults suggest that, with the exception of drug injectors, most women have no perception that the men they have sex with might be infected. As discussed above, women's knowledge of serostatus *often precedes* their realization that they might be at risk because women generally discover their serostatus during pre- and antenatal care or after a male partner is diagnosed with an HIV-related illness. The positive community concern and support for testing among gay men which enables identification of risk, considered decisions about testing and follow-up medical intervention do not exist for most women. Women simply discover, almost by accident, that they have been infected. This is no coincidence, since the media and counselling programmes describe women as either at risk through socially disapproved of 'dangerous' sex and drug use, or as apparently always and already infected. This construction of dangerous sex prevents most women from perceiving themselves to be at risk of HIV infection because when they are having sex with men, they view themselves as engaging in 'ordinary' or 'normal' and, therefore, 'safe' heterosexual intercourse.

A Queer Sort of Resistance

Ironically, the initial societal construction of AIDS as a disease of dangerous sexuality in part *enabled* gay men to identify the mechanisms of change. Through a kind of queer logic, a camp logic, changing to 'safe sex' behaviours constituted a new politically resistive space of identity for gay men. Having already claimed 'pride' in what society viewed as perversion, it was not that hard defiantly to claim pride in a new 'safer' sexuality now that society had used AIDS to condemn homosexuality once again. As a gay man in a Boston, Massachusetts-based organizing project called 'Safe Company' said to me: 'Every time I have safe sex, I feel like I'm getting back at straight society. I have a lot of sex, and I feel like I'm avenging the deaths of my friends. It's like I can say see, I can still be queer and you can't make me die.'

I don't want to idealize the gay male culture, nor underplay the trauma many gay men have experienced as they watch friends and lovers get sick, and as they grapple with the very complex and often painful process of re-establishing identity on the other side of 'safe sex'. But it is important to understand, on the ideological level, why gay men – why gay communities – can still fight back, in order to understand the depth of resistance to change that is far more hazardous to women than to men. Why, at the very core of heterosexual identity, is there an incapacity to understand what is being said about safe sex? I find it baffling that a relatively small change – use of a condom or, at most, shifting to non-intercourse forms of sexual pleasure – is greeted, especially by heterosexual men, as if it were tantamount to castration. Heterosexuals seem to view homosexual personhood, homosexual activities of any sort, even homosexual 'safe sex', as at least partially risky. And yet, heterosexuals only accept that particular *heterosexual individuals* are risky; that is, an act of 'ordinary' heterosexual intercourse is never risky, but having any form of contact with certain heterosexuals – drug users, sex workers, people of colour – is risky. While the logic promoted within gay male culture views *particular acts* as risky and to be modified or avoided, the logic within heterosexual culture remains one that views certain *individuals* as risky and to be avoided. Within gay male culture, there has been a massive effort to re-invent homosexuality and homosexual identity as 'safe sex' while retaining long-standing gay culture values, like the acceptance of promiscuity and experimental sex. The campy button which reads 'safe sex slut' is not viewed as contradictory within gay male culture.

This effort ideologically to reconstruct gay sex as safe sex seems to have partially succeeded; and for heterosexuals, too, since 'safe sex' is now interpreted by many to apply largely to 'kinky', that is 'gay', 'bisexual' or 'promiscuous' sex. By sharp contrast, heterosexuals seem to have gone to great lengths to deny a place for safe sex within heterosexual identity. The very sexual techniques which make *queer* sex *safe* seem to ruin heterosexual sex: 'real sex' is that which does not require any of the techniques or latex accoutrements of 'safe sex'. There is a dichotomy between 'normal' heterosexual sex, and 'safe sex', at least conceptually. Heterosexuals routinely invoke HIV antibody testing as a mechanism to determine when to use a condom and this misperception of testing, promoted by the media and public health system alike, is tragic and fatal for women. In addition, heterosexuals who initially use condoms with a partner seem to abandon them when a 'relationship' – however defined – is established. Studies suggest that there are important disparities between heterosexuals' willingness to use condoms with new or 'suspect' partners versus using condoms in primary or long-term relationships. Ironically, *ceasing to use condoms* may signal trust and commitment for heterosexuals.[20]

Of course, I am not the first person to criticize heterosexual ideology: feminists have long made similar claims about how it prevents women from controlling their bodies and lives. And I want to be clear that I am not suggesting that anyone abandon their cross-gender sexual relations. The typical rebuttal to criticism of heterosexual relations, and especially heterosexual intercourse, is that if men and women stopped 'doing it' it would be the end of the human race. The far right has capitalized on just this argument, but with an interesting twist: Gene Antonio, author of perhaps the best-known right-wing book on AIDS, *The AIDS Cover Up?*, argues that homosexuals should be quarantined because 'safe sex' is a plot not only to allow homosexuals to 'continue their filthy practices' but to cause 'self-extinction of mankind' (Antonio, 1986, p. 148). To counter arguments that he might be homophobic, Antonio argues that gay people, and the CDC, which the 'homosexual lobby' mysteriously controls, are heterophobic and attempting, through promoting safe sex for everyone, to cause dissent between men and women and aversion towards heterosexual intercourse. This seems paranoid and silly, but only displays in relief a much more pervasive but less articulated fear which undercuts the efficacy of risk-reduction education. Pop sexology gurus Masters and Johnson pulled out all the stops when they wrote their *Crisis: Heterosexual Behaviour in the Age of AIDS* (Masters et al., 1988). The fundamental difference between gay sexuality and heterosexuality lies not in the gender of object choice, but in attitudes towards the meaning of safe sex. Instead of safe sex being a form of liberation from fears of infection, a practice of pleasure, safe sex is presented as something to be dreaded, which turns sex into a confrontation with danger. It turns out that safe sex = queer sex, and the fear of perversion is transformed into a fear of safe sex. This queer calculus allows Masters and Johnson to conclude with a bizarre formulation that opposes *safe* and *natural* sex. They are particularly disgusted by the technical implications of safe sex, and never even consider the non-intercourse practices, which might constitute safe sex as potentially satisfying elements in the hetero-sexual repertoire. The following section from their book reveals the deep-seated fear of the *cultural* danger of safe sex:

> Sex partners of uncertain [HIV antibody] testing status could . . . wear disposable plastic gloves during all intimate moments. These gloves, after all, aren't too different from condoms. Yet we are unwilling to seriously entertain such an outlandish notion – right now, it seems so unnatural and artificial as to violate the essential dignity of humanity. (Masters et al., 1988, p. 118)

Pretty strong objections to a little latex. And doubly ironic given that Masters and Johnson have long preached the malleability of human sexual behaviour. Why is a latex glove any more unnatural or undignified than performing daily exercises to tighten vaginal muscles, or step-by-step exercises to help men learn to delay ejaculation? Masters and Johnson propose that heterosexuals do any act they choose, as long as they have obtained three (yes, specifically three) negative HIV antibody tests, spaced three months apart. Of course, they note, heterosexuals must abstain from sexual intercourse during this time in order for the test results to be valid. For Masters and Johnson, safe sex is a kind of punishment for those who 'fail' or refuse to take the test, or who can't abstain for the nine months which they view as sufficient to eliminate the possibility of test errors. This not-too-subtly redraws the line between a homosexuality which they themselves once studied and deemed normal, and a heterosexuality which they now want to preserve as natural. Even condoms are unacceptable, not only because they are not 100 per cent 'safe', but because while 'many couples find the post-orgasmic glow a time of tenderness in which they want to lie quietly with their genitals still in union, they run a distinct risk of having just such spillage [of the semen from around the now "receded" penis] occur' (Masters et al., 1988, p. 116).

On one side we have a 'natural' heterosexuality which has no limits, but can accept no latex. On the other side, we have all those people who, because they are truly queer or merely nominally queer, are condemned to safe sex, that latex-ridden set of activities which dehumanizes its practitioners. This barely concealed homophobia sweeps even aberrant heterosexuals under the banner of perversion, and naturalizes the condomless heterosexual intercourse which women need to be challenging. Masters and Johnson invoke precisely the terms which have always been used to describe both non-submissive women and homosexual sex: dehumanized, unnatural, artificial, not to be taken seriously.

The heterosexuality which I am invoking here is, I think, recognizable to all of us: either because it is the beacon by which we gauge our inadequacies, or because it is the monument against which we define our difference. It is a heterosexuality that is not new, but is newly dangerous for women. After a two-decade attempt to wrest control over our own bodies by fighting *for* legalized birth control and abortion, organizing *against* sexist violence and sexual harassment, and working to achieve women's agency and freedom to seek sexual pleasure, all this is in jeopardy again because the logic of safe sex under the sign of AIDS has once again constituted heteromasculinity as exempt from change. The terror at the heart of men's willingness to wear a condom is equalled only by the power heterosexual men have to make someone else – usually a woman – protect them from themselves. But while we may all feel sympathy towards the men who have fallen victim to that trap called heterosexual masculinity, the fact is that while men fear for their sexual identity, their women partners need to fear contracting HIV. It is easy to find fault with men who lie about their past to their wives and girlfriends, but it is not just a few unredeemed men who are the problem. At fault is the continuing construction of heterosexuality and specifically heterosexual intercourse as 'safe by nature' which prevents women from protecting themselves. Until heterosexuality means more than intercourse, and can always accommodate a condom, women will be forced to make case by case, situational demands on men. The paradox is this: heterosexual identity can only be reconstructed as truly 'safe sex' when heterosexual men are just *queer enough* to wear a condom.

Notes

The last part of this chapter also appears in Wilkinson and Kitzinger (1993).

1   The emergence of the 'new American Gothic' genre, inaugurated with David Lynch's *Blue Velvet*, reflects a shift away from the spectre of a pathological female who destroys men or makes them destroy her. *Fatal Attraction* was supplanted by films like *Internal Affairs*, perhaps the best example of these

explorations of male pathology that refuse to resort to misogyny or homophobia to explain male violence.

2   The representation of women who had poor partner selection skills occurred sometimes through anecdotes, a genre which the Gertz story imitates, but evades through the sheer force of its protagonist's intelligence and verve. The reader is sutured to a subject position that unequivocally delights in the pleasure of 'meeting' Gertz: if she couldn't tell that her partner might have had sex with men, then no one could. Previous stories indicted the protagonist's judgement before the fateful meeting with the heterosexual impersonator, or, most damning, showed pictures which coded him as 'gay', placing the reader in an adjudicatory position which implicitly reinforced the idea that women select partners based on a range of readings of the male body: when we decode the pictures of these 'bisexual' men, we think, 'I can tell, there must be something wrong with her that she can't see he's gay/bisexual.' This process of readings and critique of other women's readings of danger promotes partner select strategies over sexual repertoire strategies for risk reduction.

3   Many straight people and some gay men find it hard to imagine that there are many gay men who never or rarely engage in anal sex, since that practice has become over-associated with gay practice, at least in the 1970s and 1980s. I have attempted to trace recent changes among gay men about what constitutes 'real gay sex', and argued that these shifts may be importantly related to educational and media representations of the epidemic. In brief, I argue that increased discourse within gay male culture about condom use over-emphasized the centrality of intercourse, replacing a late 1970s view of gay sex as a veritable menu of possible delights, only one of which was 'butt fucking', with a hierarchy of acts assembled through varying interpretations of risk which simultaneously vilified anal intercourse and suggested it was the 'ultimate' gay-identity bestowing act. This shift, along with admonitions to pair bond monogamously attempted to bring gay sexual identity in line with that in the dominant culture, save the gender of the object choice. This 'heterosexualizing' of gay identity was schizophrenic, shifting focus away from 'safe practices' which had been widely accepted in gay culture ('mutual masturbation', fantasy play) and which heterosexuals largely still view as impractical 'substitutes' for intercourse; and demanding that gay men focus more on the sexual act alleged to be most dangerous, and pair bond in a society in which same-sex marriage is not sanctioned. It may also be that increased visibility of the diverse gay practices has made it more possible for heterosexuals to imagine a wider range of pleasures; see Patton (1990).

4   'Follow-up on Kaposi's sarcoma and *Pneumocystis* pneumonia' (Centers for Disease Control, 1990). This report lists one woman, race unstated. Women are listed again in 'Update on Kaposi's sarcoma and opportunistic infections in previously healthy persons – United States' (Centers for Disease Control, 1982), where eight women are described, including presumed 'risk factor' (four of seven for whom this information was available) and race (one white, four black, two Hispanic).

5   The next report to address women specifically is 'Antibody to human immunodeficiency virus in female prostitutes' (Centers for Disease Control, 1987).

6   'Queer-bashing' has shifted from being something like a national sport engaged in by anyone to a specific phenomenon in which individuals occupying one subject position commit violence against people occupying others. Only socially

sanctioned forms of 'hatred', which tend to correlate with socially accepted forms of identity, are counted. Crimes against gay people are not always included in statute-mandated collection of information on 'hate crimes' and, despite feminist argumentation, rape is not considered a 'hate' crime in most states, probably because it is considered a distortion of a 'normal' act, not a clash of social identities.

7 The notion of bisexuality has evolved twice since the 1960s notion of 'swingers' or hippies who were essentially heterosexual men who 'chose' both male and female partners. Next came a post-gay liberation idea which also included women and suggested that bisexuality was a sort of 'fence sitting' preparatory to actually 'coming out' as gay or lesbian. These 'bisexuals' were partly 'in the closet' and led a 'double life', an asexual, pretend heterosexual one and a true gay/lesbian one. In so far as men's sexuality was concerned, in the first instance, sleeping with women at all still marked the sexual actor as 'straight', while in the second, any sex with men marked him as 'gay'. The bisexual male who emerged after Rock Hudson's much publicized AIDS diagnosis in 1985 was represented as living in a netherworld *in between* two clearly marked identities. This post-AIDS construction of male bisexuality suggests that US culture has begrudgingly accepted and stabilized two positive sexual identities – gay and straight – based on gender of object choice plus a 'lifestyle' supported by two completely separate sexual economies. Once both homosexuality and heterosexuality have rigid cultural definitions, rather than one being the residual and unmarked category of the other, it becomes more difficult to situate a sexuality that apparently refuses to choose either distinguishing category. Indeed, it is not only straight culture that refuses this ambiguity: the past five years have seen important debates in gay communities about the status of 'bisexuality'. 'Bisexuals' who were once imagined as almost 'gay' are now not homosexual enough. In the US and Britain, a new definition of radical sexuality claims the name 'queer', a term which reverts to the idea of polymorphous perversity invoked in the early gay liberation movement: Under the sign 'queer' the new 'bisexuals' are people whose identity is less an issue of problematic sexual desire than one of gender non-preference.

8 See Alexander et al. (1990). In two reviews of completed and current studies of 'heterosexual' transmission, i.e. male-to-female or female-to-male transmission, the authors note that while data from developing countries (largely Africa) and US/Europe differ, the latter showed higher rates of male-to-female than female-to-male transmission. They list nine studies of female-to-male transmission, all with sample sizes of 30 and under, while the 13 studies of male-to-female transmission have samples of 56 to 164. By the end of 1988, epidemiological reports from the US suggested that male-to-female transmission cases represented some 20 per cent of all US AIDS cases, while female-to-male cases represented 6 per cent (1,757 versus 539 cases). Thus, examining epidemiological counts of cases reported by gender and by route transmission, and biological factors like alterations in vaginal flora during the menstrual cycle and response to decreasing function of the immune system, women are considered more consistently infectable than infectious.

9 For an account of these first data and their effects on AIDS discourse and policy, see Patton (1985b, ch. 3).

10 For more on Western discourse about AIDS in Africa, see Patton (1990, 1991).

11 Gay men are never considered each other's partners. If gay men had been

considered 'partners' rather than mysterious links in a vast sex network, it might have been clear that it is bilateral transmission and not 'promiscuity' which accounts for apparent differences in rates of transmission between male–female and male–male partners. It was evident from the earliest studies that the receptive partner in intercourse (regardless of gender) was always at much greater risk. However, interpretation was thwarted by homophobia and sexism. The fact is, women who engage in intercourse with men are by definition 'receptive' while men who engage in intercourse with other men may be either or both.

12   There is a third, confounding, category of women who trade sex for drugs. Generally, this image is invoked in stories about crack, in which the 'war on drugs' enlists the 'fight against AIDS'. There has been confusion among HIV educators about the specific risks of HIV infection in crack culture, since it seems autonomous of injection drug culture and since most of the 'sex' seems to be oral. Importantly, the media and educators overlook the reality that women are much more heavily involved in crack use than in either cocaine injection or heroin use. In addition, the sex for crack phenomenon seems largely a non-professional barter which professional sex workers eschew, preferring to sell sex for money, even if the money goes to buy crack. For an extensive ethnographic report on sex for crack which is extremely sensitive to gender and ethnic issues see Ratner (1991).

13   As I have argued elsewhere, this association of 'heterosexual transmission' with anal sex was fallacious, a way of associating the heterosexual individuals who had acquired HIV with the paradigmatic 'homosexual' practice. I have called this the 'queer paradigm', that is, the tendency within discussions of sexual practice related risk to maintain 'heterosexual' (that is, penile–vaginal) intercourse as safe, by nature by associating infected persons with some other, putatively deviant sexual practice, see Patton (1985a).

14   Especially important here are: ACTUP/NY Women and AIDS Book Group (1990); Patton and Kelly (1987); Richardson (1988); Rieder and Ruppelt (1988); Stevens (1988).

15   Although there are no data on needle-sharing risk by gender, research on drug injection in general suggests that men predominate in this form of drug use. In my own work, I have observed that male injectors have strong prejudices against female injectors (except those whose long-term relationships are with women they inject with). Women say that their male partners often insist on 'hitting' them, and will not always instruct them in how to prepare drugs and injection apparatus, even though most women who inject for a long time covertly learn how to 'hit' themselves. Female injectors view this as men's attempt to maintain power over their female partners. Thus, it seems probable that more women have shared predominantly with men than with women, and that this sharing bond involves a gendered power relation which disadvantages women.

16   Studies released as early as 1985 suggested that transfusion-related cases of HIV infection, specifically in women and children, have been underestimated due to statistical 'hiding' of this risk factor. In most African countries, malarial, malnutrition and pregnancy-related anaemia are commonly treated with whole blood transfusion. Because pregnancy, being sexually active and receiving transfusion all map on to each other, statistically, it is difficult to factor out transfusion. While this phenomenon has been noted, it is virtually never raised as an explanation of why there are so many more women, proportionately, with HIV in Africa.

17   Exact figures are complicated by the fact that women are in different stages of
      HIV infection. Few studies have controlled for stage of infection, and most
      studies are small cohorts. A French study which showed an overall 33 per cent
      transmission rate grouped mothers by clinical features of their HIV infection
      (CD4 count, positive antigenaemia p 24, and high replication rate of HIV in
      culture) to determine whether stage of infection affected perinatal transmission.
      Women with features suggestive of low infectivity gave birth to infected infants
      (determined by follow-up 15 months later) in about 20 per cent of cases. Women
      with features suggestive of high infectivity gave birth to infected infants in about
      60 per cent of cases; see Boue et al. (1990).
18   The following papers, presented at the 5th International AIDS Conference in
      Montreal, 1989, describe a consistent pattern of decisions to pursue pregnancy
      among infected women who are *in a variety of counselling programmes*.
      Sunderland et al. (1989): 'HIV infection does not have a clear impact, if any, on
      reproductive decisions in this population [New York City low-income women],
      psychosocial and economic variables may have a greater influence.' Wiznia et al.
      (1989): 'Neither the presence of an HIV infected older child nor HIV associated
      symptoms in HIV infected pregnant [New York low-income] women appear to
      influence decision making concerning termination of pregnancy.' Anderson et
      al. (1989): 'Knowledge of HIV infection was not associated with [Maryland
      women's] pregnancy termination or prevention of subsequent pregnancy.'
      Kaplan et al. (1989): Especially among women who were infected with HIV
      during sex with men, 'pregnancy continues to occur frequently.' Shneck et al.
      (1989): 'Despite counselling for risks associated with HIV, a high percent of
      HIV Ab+ women in this cohort became pregnant an average of 8 months after
      delivering an HIV Ab+ child.' Hassig et al. (1989): '71% wanted more
      children . . . (mean desired family size = 5.2). Counselling services for HIV +
      women in Kinshasa must be prepared to address the current low level of
      contraceptive usage and the definite pro-natalist sentiment in the population
      reflected by the high levels of desired and completed fertility.'
19   This phenomenon has been widely noted in the international development
      literature concerning the introduction of new technologies and new primary
      health care techniques. Although there have been many successful programmes
      with women's organizations in Africa and Asia, outside planners have generally
      had difficulty generating projects in a way that ensures female participation,
      except in a few programmes where women are already chiefly involved in the
      activity (for example, water sanitation); see Rifkin (1990) and Pizurki (1987).
20   Gallois et al. (1990). The same phenomenon seems to hold true for some gay
      men, see Stall et al. (1990).

References

ACTUP/NY Women and AIDS Book Group (1990) *Women, AIDS and Activism.*
    Boston: South End Press.
Alexander, Nancy J. et al. (1990) *Heterosexual Transmission of AIDS.* New York:
    Wiley-Liss.
Anderson, J. et al. (1989) Knowledge of HIV Serostatus and Pregnancy Decisions.
    Paper presented at the Fifth International AIDS Conference, Montreal.
Antonio, Gene (1986) *The AIDS Cover-Up? The Real and Alarming Facts about
    AIDS.* San Francisco: Ignatius Press.

Boue, F. et al. (1990) Risk for HIV 1 Perinatal Transmission Vary with the Mother's Stage of Infection. Paper presented at the Sixth International AIDS Conference, San Francisco.

Centers for Disease Control (1981) Follow-up on Kaposi's sarcoma and pneumocystic pneumonia. *Morbidity and Mortality Weekly Report* 30, 409–10.

Centers for Disease Control (1982) Update on Kaposi's sarcoma and opportunistic infections in previously healthy persons – United States. *Morbidity and Mortality Weekly Report* 31, 294–301.

Centers for Disease Control (1987) Antibody to human immunodeficiency virus in female prostitutes. *Morbidity and Mortality Weekly Report* 36, 157–61.

Centers for Disease Control (1990) Follow-up on Kaposi's sarcoma and pneumocystic pneumonia. *Morbidity and Mortality Weekly Report* 39, 409–10.

Gallois, Cynthia et al. (1990) Preferred Strategies for Safe Sex: Relation to Past and Actual Behaviour among Sexually Active Men and Women. Paper presented at the Sixth International AIDS Conference, San Francisco.

Hassig, Susan et al. (1989) Contraceptive Utilization and Reproductive Desires in a Group of HIV-Positive Women in Kinshasa. Paper presented at the Fifth International AIDS Conference, Montreal.

Kaplan, Mark et al. (1989) Pregnancy Arising in HIV Infected Women while being Repetitively Counselled about 'Safe Sex'. Paper presented at the Fifth International AIDS Conference, Montreal.

Masters, William H., Johnson, Virginia and Kolodny, Robert C. (1988) *Crisis: Heterosexual Behaviour in the Age of AIDS*. London: Weidenfeld and Nicolson.

Nelson, Alvin et al. (1990) Characteristics Associated with a Low Return Rate for HIV Post Test Counselling among Clients in a Community-Based STD Clinic in Los Angeles County. Paper presented at the Sixth International AIDS Conference, San Francisco.

Norris, Barbara et al. (1990) Evaluation of Compliance Rate in a Clinic Serving Minority and Low Income Communities [Brooklyn, NY]. Paper presented at the Sixth International AIDS Conference, San Francisco.

Patton, Cindy (1985a) Heterosexual AIDS panic: a queer paradigm. *Gay Community News*, 9 February.

Patton, Cindy (1985b) *Sex and Germs: The Politics of AIDS*. Boston: South End Press.

Patton, Cindy (1990) *Inventing AIDS*. New York: Routledge.

Patton, Cindy (1991) Containing safe sex. In Andrew Parker, Doris Somer, Mary Russo and Patricia Yaeger (eds), *Nationalisms/Sexualities*. New York/London: Routledge.

Patton, Cindy and Kelly, Janis (1987) *Making It: A Woman's Guide to Sex in the Age of AIDS*. Ithaca: Firebrand Press.

Pizurki, Helena et al. (1987) *Women as Providers of Health Care*. Geneva: World Health Organization.

Ratner, Michael et al. (1991) Crack Pipe as Pimp: An Eight-City Ethnographic Study of the Sex-for-Crack Phenomenon. NIDA Contract Number 271–88–8248.

Richardson, Diane (1988) *Women and AIDS*. New York: Methuen.

Rieder, Ines and Ruppelt, Patricia (eds) (1988) *AIDS: The Women*. Pittsburgh: Cleis Press.

Rifkin, Susan B. (1990) *Community Participation in Maternal and Child Health/ Family Planning Programmes*. Geneva: World Health Organization.

Schneck, Mary et al. (1989) Reproductive History of HIV Ab+ Women Followed in a Prospective Study in Newark, New Jersey, USA. Paper presented at the Fifth International AIDS Conference, Montreal.

Stall, Ron et al. (1990) Relapse from Safer Sex: The AIDS Behavioural Research Project. Paper presented at the Sixth International AIDS Conference, San Francisco.

Stevens, P. Clay (1988) US women and HIV infection. *New England Journal of Public Policy* 4 (1), 381–402.

Sunderland, Ann et al. (1989) Influence of HIV Infection on Pregnancy Decisions. Paper presented at the Fifth International AIDS Conference, Montreal.

Treichler, Paula (1988) AIDS, homophobia, and biomedical discourse: an epidemic of signification. In Douglas Crimp (ed.), *AIDS: Cultural Analysis/Cultural Activism*. Cambridge, Mass.: MIT Press.

Wilkinson, S. and Kitzinger, C. (1993) *Heterosexuality: A 'Feminism and Psychology' Reader*. London: Sage.

Wiznia, Andrew et al. (1989) Factors Influencing Maternal Decision-Making Regarding Pregnancy Outcome in HIV Infected Women. Paper presented at the Fifth International AIDS Conference, Montreal.

World Health Organization (1990) *The Work of WHO, 1988–1989, the Biennial Report of the Director-General*. Geneva: WHO.

Conclusion

The World Health Organization (1991) predicts that 40 million people will be HIV positive by the year 2000, and that 10 million people will be living with AIDS. At least a third of each group is likely to be women. At the beginning of the second decade of the HIV and AIDS epidemic, the increasing debate about the place of women in the epidemic offers some foundation for preventing such predictions from being fulfilled. Psychological aspects of women's relationship to HIV and AIDS have so far been only schematically and incompletely explored. But psychologists interested in these relationships cannot simply deploy 'good psychology', or even a pre-existing feminist psychology. Women's subjective engagements with the conditions demand a reconceptualization of the connections between psychology, its clients and research participants, and feminism. This may seem to be asking a lot of psychologists when simply providing AIDS-related services to people who need them is materially and personally so difficult. But if psychologists do not take this demand seriously, they run a substantial risk of doing irrelevant and ineffective work around women and AIDS.

Three significant shifts in the psychological address to women and AIDS are indicated by this book. First, it seems that a feminist perspective on the psychology of women and AIDS will have in some ways to sideline conventional psychology in order to deal with the subjective complexity of the condition. Such a perspective will have to put psychological research conventions into question: to call, as Lorraine Sherr and Jane Ussher do, for an abatement in the rush of repetitive studies currently appearing, for research planned more specifically around the demands of HIV and AIDS, and for more careful research analysis. This feminist perspective will also involve rethinking the centrality of psychological factors: questioning the assumptions that decision-making about seropositive pregnancies can be explained by a model of cognitive processes, and that there is a direct relationship between feeling better about yourself and acting safer, for instance, as Hortensia Amaro, and Sherry Deren and her co-writers do. This decentring of psychology also means conceiving of even the most intimate experiences as social: understanding, like Ussher, the social structuring of women professionals' pleasures and griefs in working with gay men with AIDS; or formulating anger as Alexandra Juhasz does as a political, activist force – which does not mean, of course, that pleasures, griefs and angers are not also personal emotions.

The second shift that the book indicates is towards a different understanding of the social 'context' of subjectivity. Psychology is always social (Rose, 1990). What happens in this volume is that the 'social' in psychology is rendered very explicit. Subjectivity is viewed as developing within social relations of gender, rather than as a basic material which social context genders, and attempts are made to extend our understanding of the social relations within which the psychology of women and AIDS exists. Sometimes such attempts are fashioned concretely, as in Deren and her co-authors' proposal for more detailed and meaningful demographic analyses in studies of particular communities of women, or Halina Maslanka's description of the conflicts of power and interest between changing groups of volunteers and clients in AIDS service organizations. Sometimes contributers demand wider initiatives: the integrated policy-making around women, AIDS and reproduction that Sherr and Hortensia Amaro call for; or E. Anne Lown and her colleagues' stipulation that efforts to rebuild economically and socially disen-franchised neighbourhoods, and not AIDS education programmes, must ground AIDS prevention strategy.

The third shift which the book signals is towards a critical engagement between feminism and the psychology of women and AIDS. Women's relationship to HIV and AIDS raises many long-standing feminist issues: threats to reproductive rights; dismis-sive, hostile or absent representations of women; women's lack of institutional power. At the same time the field resurrects long-term debates within feminism about the relationship of feminism to other forms of analysis and campaigning, and about differences between women. Within psychology, feminists often treat these issues somewhat abstractly, or as add-on extras to the real business of constructing a psychology for the undifferentiated category of 'women'. Looking at the impact of HIV and AIDS on women undoes this homogenization instantly, but establishes too some patterns of similarity in the epidemic and reactions to it that link women across social categories. How do we deal with this contradiction? Patton suggests that successful HIV education and treatment for women demands a reinvention of their identities. Her model is the 'queer' identity which has been produced in many lesbian and gay communities living with AIDS, an identity which includes a diversity of sexual practices and personal affiliations, held together by a common affirmation of different, abnormal sexuality. This queer identity can help support a consensus of resistance to discrimination around AIDS. In relation to the psychology of women and AIDS, such a reinvention of 'women' would involve a similar acknowledgement of sexual and identity possibilities, within the frame of a careful recognition of the different circumstances in which women live, work, form relationships and have children: an understanding of their difficulties, differences and achievements to set against the predominant discounting and pathologizing of their experiences with AIDS. This book begins such a reinvention.

References

Rose, N. (1990) Psychology as a 'social' science. In I. Parker and J. Shotter (eds), *Deconstructing Social Psychology*. London: Routledge.
World Health Organization (1991) *In Point of Fact*. Geneva: WHO.

Index